The first John Robert Seeley lectures, given by James Tully in 1994, address the six types of demands for cultural recognition that constitute the most intractable conflicts of the present age: supranational associations, nationalism and federalism, linguistic and ethnic minorities, feminism, multiculturalism and Aboriginal self government. Neither the prevailing schools of modern Western constitutionalism nor post-modern constitutionalism provide a just way of adjudicating such diverse claims to recognition because they rest on untenable assumptions inherited from the age of European imperialism. However, by means of a historical and critical survey of four hundred years of European and non-European constitutionalism, with special attention to the American Aboriginal peoples, Tully develops a post-imperial philosophy and practice of constitutionalism. This consists in the conciliation of claims for recognition over time through constitutional dialogues in which citizens reach agreements on appropriate forms of accommodation of their cultural differences, guided by common constitutional conventions. This form of constitutionalism has the capacity to mediate contemporary conflicts and bring peace to the twenty-first century.

D0896888

STRANGE MULTIPLICITY
Constitutionalism in an age of diversity

THE JOHN ROBERT SEELEY LECTURES

The John Robert Seeley lectures have been established by the University of Cambridge as a biennial lecture series in social and political studies, sponsored jointly by the Faculty of History and the University Press. The Seeley lectures will provide a unique forum for distinguished scholars of international reputation to address, in an accessible manner, themes of broad and topical interest in social and political studies. Subsequent to their public delivery in Cambridge the University Press will publish suitably modified versions of each set of lectures. Professor James Tully of McGill University delivered the inaugural series of Seeley lectures in 1994 on the theme of *Constitutionalism in an age of diversity*, and subsequent series will be delivered in 1996 by Professor Jeremy Waldron of the University of California and in 1998 by Professor Martha Nussbaum of Brown University.

STRANGE MULTIPLICITY

Constitutionalism in an age of diversity

JAMES TULLY

McGill University

CAMBRIDGE
UNIVERSITY PRESS

Published by the Press Syndicate of the University of Cambridge
The Pitt Building, Trumpington Street, Cambridge CB2 2RU
40 West 20th Street, New York, NY 10011–4211, USA
10 Stamford Road, Oakleigh, Melbourne 3166, Australia

© Cambridge University Press 1995

First published 1995

Printed in Great Britain at the University Press, Cambridge

A catalogue record for this book is available from the British Library

Library of Congress cataloguing in publication data
Tully, James, 1946–
Strange multiplicity: constitutionalism in an age of diversity /
James Tully.
p.   cm. – (The John Robert Seeley lectures)
Includes bibliographical references.
ISBN 0 521 47117 6 (hardback)   0 521 47691 2 (paperback)
1. Minorities – Politics and government. 2. Indigenous peoples –
Politics and government. 3. Ethnicity – Political aspects.
4. Federal government. 5. Nationalism. 6. Multiculturalism.
7. Pluralism (Social sciences) I. Title. II. Series.
JF1061.T85 1995
323.1′73–dc20   95–1378   CIP

ISBN 0 521 47117 6 hardback
ISBN 0 521 47694 1 paperback

WD

to Quentin

And yet we live in the era of progress don't we? I suppose progress is like a newly discovered land; a flourishing colonial system on the coast, the interior still wilderness, steppe, prairie. The thing about progress is that it appears much greater than it actually is.

Johann Nestroy, *Der Schützling* 4, 10.

Contents

Preface

These lectures were given as the John Robert Seeley lectures at the University of Cambridge, from 2 March to 11 March 1994, in the Little Hall, Sidgwick Avenue site. I rewrote them for publication over the summer of 1994. The theme is constitutionalism in circumstances of cultural diversity. It is discussed in the light of a single work of art, *The spirit of Haida Gwaii* by Bill Reid. In these dark and discordant times, I do not expect the lectures to move more than a few readers. Nevertheless, the only way to lessen the darkness and discord is to take up the responsibility to speak in the dialogue initiated by *The spirit of Haida Gwaii*. This is my response.

Acknowledgements

I would like to acknowledge the assistance of the many friends of *Strange multiplicity* a little more fully than is conventional so that readers may appreciate the conversation in which the lectures were composed. First, I wish to thank all the people associated with the John Robert Seeley lectureship who made it such a rewarding and enjoyable experience. My two hosts, Quentin Skinner of the Faculty of History and Jeremy Mynott of Cambridge University Press, have my deepest gratitude for their gracious hospitality. The master and fellows of Christ's College were exceptional hosts, providing me with commodious rooms, the most beautiful gardens to walk in and fellowship at meals. Here I must mention David Sedley in particular for making me feel at home.

Permit me also to express my gratitude to all the scholars and students who attended the lectures, discussed them with me over breakfast, lunch, dinner, a beer or two, opera and walks around the ancient maze of little streets and squares which Wittgenstein mentions in Lecture four. Cambridge is the best university in the world for the study of political philosophy and it is more than a little daunting to have seated in front of you such great scholars as Tom Baldwin, John Dunn, Mark Goldie, Ross Harrison, Geoffrey Hawthorn, Istvan Hont, Susan James, Onora O'Neill, Anthony Pagden, Quentin Skinner, Gareth Stedman Jones, Richard Tuck and Sylvana Tomaselli. However, they transformed lecturing into the most pleasurable of tasks by the co-operative spirit in which they listened, occasionally even nodding in agreement, and then went on to offer encouragement and constructive criticism in discussions and correspondence. I am especially indebted to Richard Tuck for thoughtful questions after every lecture and his outstanding scholarship on early modern constitutionalism.

My thanks also go out to all the students who attended and were equally forthcoming in their considered and helpful comments. I wish to mention especially Monique Deveaux, David Kahane (now a colleague), Patrick Miller and Norberto de Sousa, whose suggestions have assisted me in the process of revision.

I am honoured to acknowledge my gratitude to John Robert Seeley. It is ironical that I was elected as the first Seeley lecturer. He came to Cambridge from the centre of the British empire to praise imperialism in his great work, *The expansion of England* (1884). One hundred years later, I came from the furthest frontier of the empire, Vancouver Island, with all due respect, to bury it. Despite this conspicuous difference, however, we share an important similarity. We both believe that the study of politics and political philosophy should be historical. John Seeley is responsible for placing the study of political philosophy in the Faculty of History in the late nineteenth century. As a consequence, Cambridge has developed its unique and celebrated historical approach to the study of politics today. Since I am a graduate of Cambridge, the very approach I use to question the imperialism that John Seeley defended descends from his teaching and curriculum reform. Now, in the ethics of both Seneca the Roman stoic and the Aboriginal nation named after him, a few miles from where I write, the highest compliment a pupil can pay her or his teacher is to become a worthy opponent. This is the spirit in which I gratefully offer the lectures to the custodians of the John Robert Seeley lectureship.

The lectures also have many friends who have kindly commented on earlier sketches of sections at different presentations. I would like to thank all of them and to mention those who have been most influential: Stephen Munzer, John Simmons and Jeremy Waldron in San Francisco; Seyla Benhabib, Peter Berkowitz, Pratap Mehta, Uday Mehta and

Michael Sandel at Harvard; at a conference with Vaclav Havel in Prague, Jean Bethke Elshtain, Josef Moural, John Pocock and the scholars at the Centre for Theoretic Study, Charles University; Alan Cairns, Simone Chambers, Curtis Cook, Tim Fuller and Alain Noël in Colorado Springs; at a conference on the future of the nation state in Cambridge, Bhikhu Parekh, Geoffrey Hawthorn, Sudipta Kaviraj and especially (as always) John Dunn; in Vancouver, Stephen Davis, Avigail Eisenberg, Lysiane Gagnon, John Russell and especially Peter Russell; Dennis Patterson of Rutgers; and at McGill, Arlene Broadhurst, Gretta Chambers, David Davies, Elisabeth Elbourne, Mette Hjort, Rod MacDonald, Jim McGilvray, David Norton, Bruce Trigger and Jeremy Webber. In the discussions in Québec, Alain-G. Gagnon and Guy Laforest have shown me what is worthy of recognition in diverse nationalism, Daniel Weinstock in plural liberalism, Peta Tancred in feminism and Gerald Alfred and Dale Turner in Aboriginal nationalism.

One of my deepest debts is to the students who have come from Québec, Canada, Aboriginal America and around the world to make political philosophy at McGill an intercultural common ground. My gratitude goes to all the students who have listened and responded critically to my attempts to elucidate the themes of the lectures in seminars. Among these I am most thankful to Susan Drummond, Natalie Oman and Dale Turner for a reading course on the lectures; Peta Bowden, Natalie Brender and Cressida Heyes for showing me that the *Philosophical investigations* can be read as a dialogue in which feminine voices can be heard; and Ravindar Chimni, Murat Dagli, Eric Darier, Mary Foster, Glen Hughes, Duncan Ivison, Afra Jalabi, Dimitri Karmis, Rebecca Kingston, Guy Laforest, James MacInnis, Darius Rejali, Anne-Marie Sorrenti, Michael Temelini, Anoush Terjanian, Yasuo Tsuji and Ardith Walken for fruitful discussions and suggestions.

I am also most grateful to the many people associated with the Canadian Royal Commission on Aboriginal Peoples who have provided a unique forum for discussion throughout the composition of the lectures. I wish to thank all the participants and to mention the following in particular for their help: Marlene Brant Costellano, Paul Chartrand, René Dussault, Georges Erasmus, Louie Lamothe, Oren Lyons, Patricia Monture Okanee, Mary Ellen Turpel, Sharon Venne, Daisy Watts and Bertha Wilson. My greatest debt here is to the co-directors of research, David Hawkes and Fred Wien, who generously placed their vast erudition at my disposal and commented constructively on the papers which led to the lectures.

Within this intercultural dialogue in which the lectures have taken shape, two interlocutors deserve special recognition. I have been discussing the themes of the lectures with them for seventeen years and their solidarity and distinctive voices have made a profound difference to the way I think about constitutionalism and cultural diversity. My gratitude is beyond words. They are Quentin Skinner and Charles Taylor.

My aim is neither to take sides among the different and similar voices I have heard and read nor to try to reconcile them. Rather, it is to offer a philosophy and practice of their continuous *conciliation* in dialogue – an offer which just might bring peace. For this approach, I am indebted to Jenny, who came before the others and taught me the most important aboriginal lesson: the primary practical ability is not speaking well but, like Little Wing, listening well.

Finally, I wish to thank Bill Reid for his wonderful work of art. He has inspired me at every step in the making of the lectures. My greatest pleasure was to place a large picture of *The spirit of Haida Gwaii* beside me as I lectured in Cambridge and to point affectionately to the myth creatures from my childhood home who travelled so far with me. The lectures are a hopelessly inadequate gift to Bill Reid in return for the magnificent one he has given us.

As the lectures go to press, it is a pleasure to thank Richard Fisher of Cambridge University Press as well as Jeremy Mynott, whose companionship and faith in the journey have sustained me from beginning to end. Last, but definitely not least, I am most grateful to Hilary Scannell for her excellent and invaluable copy editing.

The poem on page 21, from *Poems of Rita Joe* (Halifax: Abernaki Press, 1978) is reprinted by permission of the author. The excerpt from 'Old Timers' in *Cornhuskers* by Carl Sandburg, copyright 1918 by Holt, Rinehart and Winston, Inc. and renewed 1946 by Carl Sandburg, is reprinted by permission of Harcourt Brace & Company.

The spirit of Haida Gwaii

CHAPTER I

Demands for constitutional recognition

The constitutional question raised by the politics of cultural recognition: six examples and three similarities

The question I wish to address in this book is the following. Can a modern constitution recognise and accommodate cultural diversity? This is one of the most difficult and pressing questions of the political era we are entering at the dawn of the twenty-first century. The question can even be said to characterise the coming era, for when it is not described in relation to the preceding period, as a post-imperial or post-modern age, it is often described in its own terms, as an age of cultural diversity. The question is not whether one should be for or against cultural diversity. Rather, it is the prior question of what is the critical attitude or *spirit* in which justice can be rendered to the demands for cultural recognition.

We can begin to gain an initial grasp of this elusive question by briefly surveying the range of political struggles which have rendered cultural diversity problematic, causing it to become a locus of political action and philosophical reflection. In contemporary political vocabulary, the various struggles for recognition of cultural diversity are classified as different in kind and studied by different specialists. There is no single term which covers them all. As a result, whatever similarities and differences in degree, rather than in kind, may exist among them are hidden from view by our ordinary forms of language. Accordingly, I will introduce the phrase 'the politics of cultural recognition' to gather together the broad and various political activities which jointly call cultural diversity into question as a characteristic constitutional problem of our time.

The most familiar form of the politics of cultural recognition is the claims of nationalist movements to be constitutionally recognised as either independent nation states or as autonomous political associations within various forms of multinational federations and confederations. As existing nation states and former empires are hard pressed by these cultural demands from within, they are also faced with pressures to recognise and accommodate larger, supranational associations with powerful cultural dimensions, such as the European Union and the North American Free Trade Agreement. Caught in the interstices of these large and volatile struggles, longstanding linguistic and ethnic minorities advance claims for constitutional recognition and protection.

Cutting across the complex terrain of these three forms of demand, and frequently conflicting with them, the multicultural or 'intercultural' voices of hundreds of millions of citizens, immigrants, exiles and refugees of the twentieth century compete for forms of recognition and protection of the cultures they bring with them to established nation states. These intercultural demands (as I shall call them) range anywhere from schools and social services in one's first language, publicly supported TV, film and radio, affirmative action, and changes in the dominant curricula and national histories, so that they respect and affirm other cultures, to the right to speak and act in culture-affirming ways in public institutions and spheres. In response, modern societies have begun to be called 'multicultural', yet with no agreement on what difference this makes to the prevailing understanding of a constitutional society.

Complicating further this bewildering landscape, the demands of feminist movements for recognition are raised within and across each of these struggles for national, supranational, minority and intercultural recognition. The claim of cultural feminists, broadly speaking, is not only that women should have an equal say within the constitutional institutions of contemporary societies and their authoritative traditions of interpretation. Because the constitutional institutions and traditions of interpretation were established long ago by men to the exclusion of women, it follows that they should be amended from the ground up, so to speak, in order to recognise and accommodate women's culturally distinctive ways of speaking and acting, so that substantive gender equality will be assured in the daily political struggles in the institutions the constitution founds. Making this task even more difficult, women's culture itself is not homogeneous, but multicultural and contested.

The last example of the politics of cultural recognition, yet the first in time and history, is the demands of the 250 million Aboriginal or Indigenous peoples of the world for the recognition and accommodation of their twelve thousand diverse cultures, governments and environmental practices. Throughout the world, they are fighting to be recognised as First Nations in international law and in the constitutions of modern societies that have been imposed over them during the last five hundred years of European expansion and imperialism. Their struggles for constitutional recognition intersect and clash with the other examples of cultural recognition in many different ways.

The struggles of the Aboriginal peoples of the world, and especially those of the Americas, for cultural survival and recognition are a special example of the phenomenon of the politics of cultural recognition. By my lights, they are exemplary of the 'strange multiplicity' of cultural voices that have come forward in the uncertain dawn of the twenty-first century to demand a hearing and a place, in their own cultural forms and ways, in the constitution of modern political associations. By 'exemplary', I do not mean that their challenge is an instance of a general rule or an ideal type of the politics of cultural recognition, but that it is a particularly enlightening example.

There is abundant scholarship on constitutionalism from the perspective of nationalism, supranationalism, linguistic and ethnic minorities, interculturalism and feminism. There is also considerable specialised scholarship on Aboriginal peoples and international law and the constitutional law of specific countries. However, there is little on the Aboriginal peoples and the historical formation of contemporary constitutionalism. One of the central arguments of this book is that if constitutionalism is approached from the perspective of the struggles of Aboriginal peoples, unnoticed aspects of its historical formation and current limitations can be brought to light. I believe that the vision of constitutionalism that this unique perspective affords, in conjunction with the perspective of the other, more familiar, demands, is capable of transforming the way we think about constitutionalism.

If sharp boundaries are drawn around each of these six types of cultural recognition on the basis of their dissimilarities and they are studied separately, as is usually the case, then the similarities among them are overlooked. Their separation in theory is reinforced by the fact that they clash, often violently, in practice. It is thus often assumed that they are incompatible and incommensurable. However, when they are rearranged and grouped together as examples of the politics of cultural recognition, and we look and see, their disregarded resemblances come to light and disclose the landscape of contemporary political conflict which raises the question of constitutionalism and cultural diversity.

Among the many similar aspects, three are important for the purposes of this book. First, demands for cultural recognition are aspirations for appropriate forms of self government. The forms of self rule appropriate to the recognition of any culture vary. Some, such as nationalist movements and Aboriginal peoples, strive for their own political institutions. Others, such as linguistic minorities, multicultural groups and women, seek to participate in the existing institutions of the dominant society, but in ways that recognise and affirm, rather than exclude, assimilate and denigrate, their culturally diverse ways of thinking, speaking and acting. What they share is a longing for self rule: to rule themselves in accord with their customs and ways.

The call for forms of self rule, the oldest political good in the world, has been obscured by the redescription and adjudication of the various claims in terms of nationalism, self determination, the rights of individuals, minorities and majorities, liberalism versus communitarianism, localism versus globalism, the politics of identity and the like. Although these dominant and exhaustively analysed categories catch aspects of the phenomenon, they mis-identify the shared aspiration and segment it into a cacophony of heterogeneous claims. The resemblance is further obscured by the sheer diversity of forms of self rule they long for and, as we shall see, by the restricted conception of self government available in the prevailing language of constitutionalism.

The second similarity is the complementary claim that the basic laws and institutions of modern societies, and their authoritative traditions of interpretation, are *unjust* in so far as they thwart the forms of self government appropriate to the recognition of cultural diversity. The sovereignty of the people is in some way denied and suppressed, rather than affirmed and expressed, in the existing constitutional forms, thereby rendering unfair the daily politics that the constitution enframes. The constitution, which should be the expression of popular sovereignty, is an imperial yoke, galling the necks of the culturally diverse citizenry, causing them to dissent and resist, and requiring constitutional amendment before they can consent. Again, the similarity of the injustice claimed in each of the six examples is obscured by the wide variety of forms it takes.

The final similarity I wish to draw to your attention is the ground of both the aspiration to culturally appropriate forms of self rule and the claim of injustice. It is the assumption that culture is an irreducible and constitutive aspect of politics. The diverse ways in which citizens think about, speak, act and relate to others in participating in a constitutional association (both the abilities they exercise and the practices in which they exercise them), whether they are making, following or going against the rules and conventions in any instance, are always to some extent the expression of their different cultures. A constitution can seek to impose one cultural practice, one way of rule following, or it can recognise a diversity of cultural ways of being a citizen, but it cannot eliminate, overcome or transcend this cultural dimension of politics.

Hence, the argument is that if the cultural ways of the citizens were recognised and taken into account in reaching an agreement on a form of constitutional association, the constitutional order, and the world of everyday politics it constitutes, would be just with respect to this dimension of politics. Since the diverse cultural ways of the citizens are excluded or assimilated, it is, to that extent, unjust. Moreover, a certain priority is claimed for justice with respect to cultural recognition in comparison with the many other questions of justice that a constitution must address. Since other questions of justice must be discussed and agreements reached by the citizens, the first step is to establish a just form of constitutional discussion in which each speaker is given her or his due, and this is exactly the initial question raised by the politics of cultural recognition.

So, despite their variety and apparent novelty, the examples of the politics of cultural recognition, in virtue of their three family resemblances, share a traditional political *motif*: the injustice of an alien form of rule and the aspiration to self rule in accord with one's own customs and ways. Seen in this light, they are struggles for 'liberty' in the remarkably enduring sense of this term. From the struggles of the Italian city states for *libertas* against imperial rule during the Renaissance, to the European and American revolutions for liberty in the early modern period, and to the national liberation movements of the twentieth century, 'liberty' has meant freedom from domination and of self rule. What is distinctive of our age is a multiplicity of demands for recognition at the same time; the demands are for a variety of forms of self rule; and the demands conflict violently in practice.

The mutual recognition of cultural diversity: three features of the
common ground and three historical movements
Consequently, the question of our age is not whether one or
other claim can be recognised. Rather, the question is whether
a constitution can give recognition to the legitimate demands
of the members of diverse cultures in a manner that renders
everyone their due, so that all would freely consent to this
form of constitutional association. Let us call this first step
towards a solution 'mutual recognition' and ask what it
entails.

In the first instance, it cannot be the traditional nationalist
recognition of one culture at the expense of excluding or
assimilating all others. This widespread constitutional
nationalism comes in a variety of types and has been recommended by writers as different as the authors of *The federalist
papers* in the 1780s, Johann Gottlieb Fichte in the *Addresses to the
German nation* in 1807–8 and Sir John Seeley, in *The expansion of
England* in the 1880s. I also believe the solution cannot be to
presume that a constitution can avoid recognising any culture.
As we shall see, such Esperanto constitutionalism, recently
defended by a number of liberal theorists, is an illusion
which hides from view the imperial culture embodied in
most liberal constitutions, as the classic liberal theorists
realised. A recent example of presumed, culture-blind liberal
constitutionalism is the Canadian Charter of Rights and
Freedoms of 1981. Rather than uniting the citizens on a
constitution that transcends cultural diversity, it has fostered
disunity. The province of Québec, the Aboriginal peoples,
women and the provinces resisted it at various times as
the imperial imposition of a pan-Canadian culture over
their distinct cultural ways. Many other countries, such as the
United Kingdom and New Zealand, have experienced
similar public debates over charters of rights and cultural
diversity.

The consequence of national and liberal constitutions,
which have been the dominant forms over the last three
hundred years, is precisely the contemporary resistance and
demands for recognition of the members whose cultures have

been excluded, assimilated or exterminated. A just form of constitution must begin with the full mutual recognition of the different cultures of its citizens.

Second, mutual recognition cannot be simply the recognition of each culture in the same constitutional form. There is a tendency to imagine this is possible because 'cultures' are conceived as analogous to the more familiar constitutional concept of 'nations'. Hence, the age of 'multiculturalism' is seen as a kind of extension of the last three centuries of multi-nationalism with no fundamental change in constitutional thinking required.

When the revolutions of central and eastern Europe over-threw the old imperial constitutions after 1989, the peoples who demanded recognition redescribed their cultures as 'nations' (the most prestigious form of cultural recognition). They then inferred that the only form of constitutional recognition of a nation must be an independent nation state. Under the logic of this inference, they tended to pass rapidly through multinational constitutional federations and to disintegrate into nationally defined states. These revolutions thus continued one of the oldest conventions of modern consti-tutionalism: every culture worthy of recognition is a nation, and every nation should be recognised as an independent nation state. Although this has been the dominant form of constitutional recognition since the seventeenth century, it cannot be simply extended to the demands for cultural recognition today.

As writers as different as Ernest Gellner and David Maybury-Lewis have argued, the consequence is impractical. There are over fifteen thousand cultures whose members demand recognition, yet a world system of fifteen thousand independent states on this tiny and interdependent planet would be unworkable. It does not follow that the present system of nation states is unalterable, as conservatives have concluded. Change and impermanence have been features of the system since 1648. The international system would still be workable if, say, East Timor separated from Indonesia, Scotland from the United Kingdom, Catalonia from Spain,

Québec from Canada or the predominantly Spanish-speaking states from the United States.

The system would be unworkable only if the norm that every nation should be a state were applied universally as the solution to demands for cultural recognition. The established nation states have constrained the proliferation of states in the past by restricting the application of the term 'nation' in international law. The reason why continuing in this manner is now in question is the sheer number of demands for recognition as nations, coupled with the exposure of the manipulation of the criteria of nationhood in the past to preserve the powers that be.

It is clear that the dominant constitutional norm that every nation should be recognised as an independent state needs to be supplemented by the idea that nations can achieve just recognition in multinational federations of various kinds, such as Germany, Israel–Palestine, India, the United Kingdom, the Russian federation and the European Union. However, even though the *practice* of multinational and multiregional federation is as old as modern constitutionalism, the norm of independent nation states is so predominant that the basic concepts of contemporary constitutionalism are defined in agreement with it. The concepts of the people, popular sovereignty, citizenship, unity, equality, recognition and democracy all tend to presuppose the uniformity of a nation state with a centralised and unitary system of legal and political institutions. Accordingly, when forms of multinational federalism are advanced as solutions to some of the demands for cultural recognition, they appear *ad hoc*, even as a threat to democracy, equality and liberty, rather than as forms of recognition that can be explained and justified in accordance with the principles of constitutionalism.

The more important reason why the two assumptions that cultures worthy of recognition should be nations and nations should be recognised as states need to be revised is that they mis-identify the phenomenon of cultural diversity we are trying to understand. According to the concept of a culture (or nation) that developed with the formation of modern constitutionalism from the seventeenth to the twentieth century, a culture is separate, bounded and internally uniform. Over the last forty years this billiard-ball conception of cultures, nations and societies has undergone a long and difficult criticism in the discipline of anthropology. As Michael Carrithers summarises in *Why humans have cultures*, it has gradually been replaced by the view of cultures as overlapping, interactive and internally negotiated. Let us look at each of these three features of cultural diversity, for we cannot grasp the politics of cultural recognition without them and the way they transform our understanding of being with others in the world.

The way the inherited normative vocabulary misrepresents the cultural diversity of our time was tragically exposed in the early 1990s across the Ukraine, the Baltic states, the Caucasus, central Asia, Russia and the former Yugoslavia. As new nation states were formed and recognised, overlapping minority cultures within, as well as nationals left without the new boundaries, in turn immediately demanded recognition as nations. Cultural minorities in these minorities in turn demanded recognition and protection. There is no end or exception to this criss-crossing and overlapping of cultures in the world. The tragedy of Bosnia–Herzegovina, or of the Hutu, Twa and Tutsi of Rwanda, Burundi, Zaire and Tanzania in East Africa, is only a recent example of the policies and wars of repression, assimilation, exile, extermination and genocide that compose the long and abhorrent history of attempts to bring the overlapping cultural diversity of contemporary societies in line with the norm of one nation, one state. Aboriginal peoples of America, for example, have suffered similar ethnic cleansing for five hundred years. Far from silencing demands for cultural recognition, these wars in the name of the unity of the nation have been met with unconquerable resistance, as the suppressed cultures snap back like so many bent yet unbreakable twigs, as Sir Isaiah Berlin aptly puts it.[1]

Constitutionalism in an age of diversity is yet more difficult than this. Not only do cultures overlap geographically and come in a variety of types. Cultures are also densely inter-dependent in their formation and identity. They exist in complex historical processes of interaction with other cultures. The modern age is intercultural rather than multi-cultural. The interaction and entanglement of cultures has been further heightened by the massive migrations of this century. Cultural diversity is not a phenomenon of exotic and incommensurable others in distant lands and at different stages of historical development, as the old concept of culture made it appear. No. It is here and now in every society. Citizens are members of more than one dynamic culture and the experience of 'crossing' cultures is normal activity. In *Europe and the people without history* (1982), Eric Wolf showed that the interaction and interdependency of cultures is not a recent phenomenon; the cultures of the world have been shaped and formed by interaction for a millennium.

Finally, cultures are not internally homogeneous. They are continuously contested, imagined and reimagined, trans-formed and negotiated, both by their members and through their interaction with others. The identity, and so the meaning, of any culture is thus aspectival rather than essen-tial: like many complex human phenomena, such as language and games, cultural identity changes as it is approached from different paths and a variety of aspects come into view. Cultural diversity is a tangled labyrinth of intertwining cultural differences *and* similarities, not a panopticon of fixed, independent and incommensurable worldviews in which we are either prisoners or cosmopolitan spectators in the central tower.

Let me illustrate these three features of cultural diversity with an example from Canada. When the former prime minister of Canada, Pierre Trudeau, sought to recognise and affirm an unifying Canadian constitutional identity in the Canadian Charter of Rights and Freedoms, the ten provinces immediately claimed that it failed to recognise the legal and political cultures of the provinces and demanded a consti-tutional amendment. The government of Québec further argued that the Charter constituted an imperial yoke over

Québec's distinctive French-language and civil-law culture, forged through centuries of interaction with English-language Canada, and that it needed to be amended to recognise Québec's cultural distinctiveness. The 633 Aboriginal First Nations of Canada protested that the Charter oppressed and failed to recognise their Aboriginal cultures: that is, their forms of self government, legal systems, languages and so on.

The way in which Aboriginal cultures were to be constitutionally recognised was then immediately contested by Aboriginal people who live on reserves as opposed to those who live off the reserves. The French-speaking minorities in the English-speaking provinces protested that the provinces had failed to recognise and protect their distinctive minority status, and the English-speaking minority within Québec did the same with respect to Québec's claim to cultural recognition.

Moreover, women protested that the entire exercise was being carried on in a male voice and that the Charter would have to be amended to recognise the substantive equality of women in the basic institutions and traditions of interpretation of the constitution. Women in Québec and women in the rest of Canada, as you will be by now not surprised to learn, formulated their demands for constitutional recognition in slightly different ways, challenging the presumed unity of the nationalisms in Québec and the rest of Canada on the one hand, and of women's cultures on the other. Aboriginal women also protested against the way in which Aboriginal men articulated the identity of Aboriginal cultures. Then, Aboriginal women themselves divided along lines that are familiar around the world today. Some sought to have their voices heard within Aboriginal governments as they were identified by traditional male leaders, while others sought to protect themselves by having the Charter applied directly to Aboriginal governments. Finally, the multicultural groups and visible minorities of Canada demanded recognition of their cultural distinctiveness across each of these constitutional claims.

This Canadian example of cultural diversity is not exceptional. The constitutional negotiations from 1990 to 1994 in South Africa, the velvet revolution and the break up of Czechoslovakia, the Waitangi Tribunal in Aotearoa–New Zealand, the public debates of language and gender in the United States, Faustin Twagiramungu's negotiations towards multicultural rule in Rwanda, the negotiations towards Palestinian self rule or the conflict over minorities in the European Union illustrate the points just as well. Of course, the way the politics of cultural recognition is expressed varies in accord with the constitutional traditions of different societies. In many cases, it remains in the political realm, barely questioning the background constitution, especially if the constitution is flexible. In many other cases constitutional negotiations are unavoidable. When these fail, recourse is made to armed conflict. Often a struggle for recognition ranges across all three strategies, as in the cases of Northern Ireland, the Chukchi of Russia, the Basques, the Maya of the Chiapas region of Mexico, the Sioux nation of the United States, or countless other examples. A tangled labyrinth of cultural voices constitutes the popular sovereignty of contemporary societies.

As a consequence of the overlap, interaction and negotiation of cultures, the experience of cultural difference is *internal* to a culture. This is the most difficult aspect of the new concept of culture to grasp. On the older, essentialist view, the 'other' and the experience of otherness were by definition associated with another culture. One's own culture provided an identity in the form of a seamless background or horizon against which one determined where one stood on fundamental questions (whether this identity was 'British', 'modern', 'woman' or whatever). Having an identity consisted in being oriented in this essential space, whereas the loss of such a fixed horizon was equated with an 'identity crisis'; with the loss of all horizons. On the aspectival view, cultural horizons change as one moves about, just like natural horizons. The experience of otherness is internal to one's own identity, which consists in being oriented in an aspectival intercultural space constituted by the three features mentioned above.

Jacques Derrida, in his brief reflection on European unity, puts it this way:[2]

What is proper to a culture is to not be identical to itself. Not to not have an identity, but not to be able to identify itself, to be able to say 'me' or 'we'; to be able to take the form of a subject only in the non-identity with itself or, if you prefer, only in the difference *with itself* [*avec soi*]. There is no culture or cultural identity without this difference *with itself.*

Consequently, from the outset citizens are to some extent on a negotiated, intercultural and aspectival 'middle' or 'common' ground with some degree of experience of cross-cultural conversation and understanding; of encountering and being with diverse others who exhibit both cultural similarities and dissimilarities. The politics of cultural recognition takes place on this intercultural 'common' ground, as I shall call the labyrinth composed of the overlap, interaction and negotiation of cultures over time. Of course, mutual recognition is not rendered unproblematic by the reconceptualisation and clarification of the ground on which we stand, for encounters on the common ground are shot through with inequality, misrecognition, domination and strife. However, the problem of mutual recognition is put in a new light and rendered possible by the disclosure of a common ground. Any serious reflection on the problems of constitutionalism in the age of cultural diversity should begin, therefore, with the three features of the common ground as its initial conditions. Yet, despite this transformation in the understanding of cultures, as Clifford Geertz remarks, theorists tend to continue to uphold variations of the old view, inherited from the age of European imperialism, of humans situated in independent, closed and homogeneous cultures and societies, and so to generate the familiar dilemmas of relativism and universalism that accompanied it.[3]

No one reasonably doubts that these claims for cultural recognition constitute one of the most dangerous and pressing problems of the present age. The racial, linguistic, national, ethnic and gender tensions of these struggles are a dimension of almost every social relation of modern societies. It is not as if cultural relations could be separated from other social relations and treated in isolation. Culture is a way of relating to others in any interaction, a way of following or challenging a social rule, and so a dimension of any social relation, from a cultural slur in the workplace to the relations among nations. As Hobbes put it at the beginning of modern constitutionalism, the third cause of political conflict is 'a word, a smile, a different opinion, and any other signe of undervalue, either direct in their persons, or by reflexion in their Kindred, their Friends, their Nation, their Profession, or their Name'.[4] What we need to understand today is the extent to which the solutions advanced by Hobbes and the other modern theorists of constitutionalism are now part of the problem

There is no sign that these struggles will dissipate in the future. Quite the opposite. All the signs indicate that the massive dislocation, movement and interaction of peoples caused by decolonisation and globalisation will increase cultural diversification and conflict. One may greet the coming age with despair, as Sir Isaiah Berlin has done, or with hope, as Carlos Fuentes and Edward Said have recommended. Either way, the question of whether a constitution can recognise and accommodate cultural diversity will be, so to speak, a political centre of gravity of the age, held firmly and irrepressibly in place by the conflicting struggles for recognition that lie around it.

The situation I believe we face can now be brought into focus with a broad and rough sketch. I will fill in the details and nuances in later chapters. Modern constitutionalism developed over the last four centuries around two main forms of recognition: the equality of independent, self-governing nation states and the equality of individual citizens. It also developed in opposition to imperialism. First, in Europe, constitutional nation states defined themselves in opposition to the *imperium* of the papacy and the Holy Roman Empire without, and to the feudal and absolutist society of ranks within. European nations in turn constructed their own imperial systems over the non-European world, thus adding an imperial dimension to modern constitutionalism.

Second, constitutionalism came into prominence throughout the world as former colonies freed themselves from European imperialism, built equal and independent constitutional nation states, and grappled with their older customs and traditions, while citizens struggled for equal recognition within and the new states created their own empires over Indigenous peoples. The global movement of anti-imperialism, modern constitutionalism and neo-imperialism began with the thirteen colonies in 1776 and continued through the monumental wars of liberation and decolonisation in the nineteenth and twentieth centuries, down to the overthrow of the Soviet imperial system after 1989 and South Africa today. No doubt it will continue.

The politics of cultural recognition constitutes a third movement of anti-imperialism and constitutionalism, this time by the peoples and cultures who have been excluded and suppressed by the first two movements of decolonisation and constitutional state building. Aboriginal peoples, women, linguistic and ethnic minorities, intercultural groups, suppressed nations and supranational associations experience the constitution of modern nation states as an imperial yoke imposed over their cultures, in a manner analogous to the way in which the proponents of the first two movements of constitutionalism experienced the old imperial systems they overthrew. This continuity among the three movements explains why the older language of imperial oppression and liberation has reappeared in the newer struggles and why they are often called struggles against cultural imperialism.

The second continuity is, as I mentioned above, that the people wish to govern themselves constitutionally by their own cultural ways. The difference from the first two movements is that, for the most part, they do not seek to build independent nation states in order to gain independence and self government. Rather, they seek forms of cultural recognition and degrees of self rule on the culturally various common ground within and across existing nation states. Seen in this light, the politics of cultural recognition is a continuation of the anti-imperialism of modern constitutionalism, and thus the expression of a genuinely post-imperial age.

It is not a radical break, heralding the beginning of post-modern constitutionalism. Yet it is a continuation that cannot be merely assimilated into the conventional forms of recognition available in modern constitutionalism for, as I have indicated, it is these stultifying forms of constitutional recognition that suppress and thwart the cultural identities of those who demand recognition. The task of this book is to investigate how much of the inherited forms of modern constitutionalism needs to be amended to do justice to these tangled demands for cultural recognition. Paraphrasing a famous Cambridge political theorist, this book might be called *Western constitutional theory in the face of a culturally diverse future.*

'The spirit of Haida Gwaii' as a symbol of the age of cultural diversity
I would now like to introduce a symbol of the spirit of a post-imperial age of cultural diversity. It is the wonderful sculpture by Bill Reid, the renowned artist of Haida and Scottish ancestry from the Haida nation of *Haida Gwaii* (the Queen Charlotte Islands) off the northwest coast of Great Turtle Island (North America). The sculpture is a black bronze canoe, over nineteen feet in length, eleven feet wide, and twelve feet high, containing thirteen passengers, *sghaana* (spirits or myth creatures) from Haida mythology. (Please refer to the illustration at the front of the book.) *Xuuwaji*, the bear mother, who is part human, and bear father sit facing each other at the bow with their two cubs between them. *Ttsaang*, the beaver, is paddling menacingly amidships, *qqaaxhadajaat*, the mysterious, intercultural dogfish woman, paddles just behind him and *Qaganjaat*, the shy but beautiful mouse woman is tucked in the stern. *Ghuuts*, the ferociously playful wolf, sinks his fangs in the eagle's wing and *ghuut*, the eagle, seems to be attacking the bear's paw in retaliation. *Hlkkyaan qqusttaan*, the frog, who symbolises the ability to cross boundaries (*xhaaidla*) between worlds, is, appropriately enough, partially in and out of the boat. Further down in the

canoe, the ancient reluctant conscript, brought on board from Carl Sandburg's poem, 'Old Timers', paddles stoically (up to a point). *Xuuya*, the legendary raven – the master of tricks, transformations and multiple identities – steers the canoe as her or his whim dictates. Finally, in the centre of this motley crew, holding the speaker's staff in his right hand, stands *Kilstlaai*, the chief or exemplar, whose identity, due to his kinship to the raven (often called *Nangkilstlas*, the One who gives orders), is uncertain. Bill Reid asks of the chief, 'Who is he? That's the big question.' So the chief has come to be called 'Who is he?' or 'Who is he going to be?'[5]

The name of this amazing work of art is *The spirit of Haida Gwaii*. Since *Haida Gwaii* means 'the island home (or place) of the Haida', and 'Haida', like many Aboriginal national names, means simply 'the people', including all the animal and spiritual people who live in *Haida Gwaii*, the sculpture is 'the spirit of the home of the people'.

The spirit of Haida Gwaii came into being in Bill Reid's hands between 1984 and 1991. The passengers had to be rearranged several times and work had to be interrupted to protest against logging on *Haida Gwaii* and support the struggle for recognition of Haida sovereignty. The sculpture was transported to Washington DC and placed in the courtyard of the Canadian Chancery on 19 November 1991. Sitting directly across the street from the National Gallery, it is destined to become one of the major artistic landmarks of the Americas. A second bronze canoe in jade green patina was cast in 1994 and placed in the Vancouver Museum. *The spirit of Haida Gwaii* thus now sits on both shores of its Great Turtle Island home as a symbol of the 'strange multiplicity' of cultural diversity that existed millennia ago and wants to be again.

Claude Lévi-Strauss has said that, 'thanks to Bill Reid, the art of the Indians of the Pacific coast enters into the world scene: into a dialogue with the whole of mankind'.[6] The question is, what kind of dialogue does Bill Reid's artwork invite humankind to engage in? How is a non-Aboriginal person to approach *The spirit of Haida Gwaii* in the right spirit, in, so to speak, the spirit of *Haida Gwaii*, in order to try to answer this question? How can a non-Aboriginal person, after centuries of appropriation and destruction of Indigenous civilisations, free himself or herself from deeply ingrained, imperious habits of thought and behaviour and approach this symbol in the appropriate way? Exploring this question will introduce many of the themes of cultural recognition that will concern us in later chapters.

When James Cook landed on *Haida Gwaii* in 1778 and super-imposed the name of a queen who bore no relation to it, there were ten thousand Haida flourishing on the islands and main-land. They maintained a delicate balance with the sea and forest and sustained a civilisation that had evolved over the previous twelve thousand years. Within 138 years of contact with Europeans their population was reduced over 90 per cent by the spread of European diseases, such as measles and smallpox, cultural dislocation and killing. Only 558 Haida remained alive in 1915. Forty villages were reduced to four.

The near extermination of the Haida by European imperial expansion is entirely typical of how Aboriginal peoples have fared throughout the Americas and wherever Europeans settled. The population of the Americas at the time of contact and invasion is estimated by historical demographers to be 80 to 100 million people. (The population of Europe was 60 to 70 million people.) They lived in a wide variety of complex and interrelated societies, some over thirty thousand years old. Ninety to ninety-five per cent of the Indigenous population was destroyed by European diseases, war, starvation and cultural destruction. For many nations, such as the Beothuk, Taino and Massachusetts, only the names remain. The Aboriginal popu-lation of what is now commonly called the United States and Canada was reduced from 8 to 12 million in 1600 to half a million by 1900, when the genocide subsided.

Bill Reid writes:[7]

Sometimes they [the European invaders] found great cities, the homes of people with cultures as advanced as their own, and some-times so beautiful they thought they had stumbled into fairyland, so they promptly destroyed them. Sometimes they found beautiful, gentle, generous people, so they made slaves of them and killed them.

Sometimes they found people who weren't so nice, so beautiful, or gentle and generous, but were almost as avaricious and acquisitive as they were themselves. These they dealt with as allies or trading partners until they'd relieved them of the goods they coveted; then they destroyed them and their cultures.

Like many other Aboriginal nations in the nineteenth and twentieth centuries, Haida government, constitution, religion, language, trade, family structures and burial practices were classified as a primitive stage of historical development, out-lawed and uprooted. Haida land and fishing areas were taken and forests cut. Plant and animal species were reduced to a shadow of their former abundance and diversity. A modern constitutional regime was superimposed over ancient Haida customs and ways without Haida consent. Haida people were assimilated to this so-called superior state of development by being taken from their families at a young age and forced into residential schools where they learned European languages and ways, and suffered physical and sexual abuse. When these techniques of assimilation failed, they were returned to tiny areas of logged out and polluted land, called reserves, classified as obstacles to progress and left to gradually disappear because they were judged unfit for modern consti-tutional society.

Looking back on the wreckage of this long injustice in 1933, the Lakota Sioux Elder, Luther Standing Bear, asked the question that is now posed by the politics of cultural recog-nition to the constitutionalism that accompanied and legitimated it:[8]

Did a kind, wise, helpful and benevolent conqueror bring this situation about? Can a real, true, genuinely superior social order work such havoc? Did not the native American possess human qualities of worth had the Caucasian but been able to discern and accept them; and did not an overweening sense of superiority bring about this blindness?

During each period of this 'American holocaust', as the historian David Stannard argues it should be called, the

Aboriginal peoples have resisted and refused to submit as best they could, from silent forms of refusal and tactical compliance in residential schools and prisons to armed battle, confrontation, negotiation, accommodation, agreement and co-operation on the land and in the courts. The result has been, as we shall see, the complex, historical interaction on a vastly unequal common ground between the relentless domination of an overpowering imperial order and the indomitable liberty of ancient peoples.

Since the early twentieth century, and especially since World War II, the Haida and other Aboriginal nations, in the face of appalling social and economic conditions, have sought not only to resist and interact, but to rebuild and reimagine their cultures; to 'celebrate their survival'. *The spirit of Haida Gwaii* is both a symbol and an inspiration of this revival and 'world reversal', as the Aboriginal peoples call it: to refuse to regard Aboriginal cultures as passive objects in an Eurocentric story of historical progress and to regard them from Aboriginal viewpoints, in interaction with European and other cultures. Although this monumental work of art cannot but be grounded in, and a celebration of, Bill Reid's own cultures, it is as well an ecumenical symbol for the mutual recognition and affirmation of all cultures that respect other cultures and the earth. The difficult reversal of worldview enjoined by *The spirit of Haida Gwaii* and required for mutual recognition is described by the Mi'kmaq poet Rita Joe, from her perspective, in the following way:[9]

> Your buildings tall, alien,
> Cover the land;
> Unfeeling concrete smothers,
>   windows glint
> Like water to the sun.
> No breezes blow
> Through standing trees;
> No scent of pine lightens my burden.
>
> I see your buildings rising skyward,
>   majestic,
> Over the trails, where men once walked,

Significant rulers of this land
Who still hold the aboriginal title
In their hearts
By traditions known
Through eons of time.

Relearning our culture is not difficult,
Because those trails I remember
And their meaning I understand.

While skyscrapers hide the heavens,
They can fall.

The spirit of Haida Gwaii evokes a boundless sense of wonder. It is the mystical. I want to walk in silence around its overflowing spirits, letting their endless perspectives and interrelations awaken the play of my imagination from its dogmatic slumber. I know its meaning is unfathomable and my words are unworthy. Mine is a crude voice over a multiplicity of cultural voices who, if one could only learn to look and listen, speak for themselves. The sheer, manifest presence of the myth creatures confronts and calls into question the overweening sense of superiority which, since first contact, has rendered us deaf and blind to the multiplicity of spirits who constitute this place and its ways and led us to impose alien constitutions and interpretations over them.

Here, Aboriginal and European myths cross, for the oldest European constitutional story is that of Oedipus who, led by his own sense of superiority, transgresses the customs and ways of Thebes and imposes an alien constitutional culture, which then blinds him to the injustice that lies at the foundation of his rule. Oedipus and the citizens of Thebes are so accustomed to their constitutional order that it takes an outsider, the blind Tiresias, to see the underlying fault. This tragedy of misrecognition and usurpation is finally revealed to him in *Oedipus at Colonus*, but it is fully grasped only by Antigone, daughter of Oedipus and Jocasta, the child of the crossing of native and newcomer cultures. Antigone courageously tries to bring this most fundamental of political lessons to the attention of Creon, king of Thebes, by upholding the customary ways of burial against the prevailing law. Creon, like Oedipus, is blinded by the imposed constitutional order and its immanent, yet seemingly universal, standards of justice. This terrifying stance of cultural hybris and blindness he portrays is graphically depicted by the chorus in the 'Ode to man'. As a result, he fails to recognise either the justice of Antigone's demand or the means of accommodating it offered by the conciliatory Haemon, his son and Antigone's lover, and exemplary citizen of the intercultural common ground. And so the tragedy continues.

First and foremost, it is surely safe to infer, the spirit in which *The spirit of Haida Gwaii* should be approached is a willingness to listen to its culturally diverse spirits. Let us listen to the voice of Bill Reid:[10]

Here we are at last, a long way from *Haida Gwaii*, not too sure where we are or where we're going, still squabbling and vying for position in the boat, but somehow managing to appear to be heading in some direction. At least the paddles are together, and the man in the middle seems to have some vision of what's to come.

Bill Reid seems to interpret *The spirit of Haida Gwaii* as if he were not the creator but witness, fellow traveller and mediator. He is reluctant to say anything definitive about its meaning. Tentatively and with respectful circumspection, he describes how it seems and appears to him, as if he too were trying to find or to hear the appropriate words to recognise this strange multiplicity that has come into being, somewhat inadvertently, before him. Although this collection of Indigenous beings has been here for millennia, it is as if we are being asked to see and hear them for the first time, and so to learn the art of mutual recognition.

Approaching *The spirit of Haida Gwaii* in the right spirit does not consist in recognising it as something already familiar to us and in terms drawn from our own traditions and forms of thought. This imperial attitude is to be abjured. Rather, recognition involves acknowledging it in its own terms and traditions, as it wants to be and as it speaks to us. No matter from which direction you approach the canoe, the crew members manifestly seem to say that, after centuries of suppression, they are here to stay, in their own cultural forms and ways. Hence, if there is to be a post-imperial dialogue on the just constitution of culturally diverse societies, the dialogue must be one in which the participants are recognised and speak in their own languages and customary ways. They do not wish either to be silenced or to be recognised and constrained to speak within the institutions and traditions of interpretation of the imperial constitutions that have been imposed over them. This world reversal, from a habitual imperial stance, where one's own customary forms of reflection set the terms of the discussion, to a genuinely inter-cultural popular sovereignty, where each listens to the voices of the others in their own terms, is the most important and difficult first step in contemporary constitutionalism.

A constitutional dialogue in 'The spirit of Haida Gwaii'

The spirit of Haida Gwaii, I would now like you to imagine, can be seen as just such a constitutional dialogue, or multilogue, of mutual recognition. The passengers are squabbling and vying for recognition and position each in their culturally distinct way. They are exchanging their diverse stories and claims as the chief appears to listen attentively to each, hoping to guide them to reach an agreement, without imposing a meta-language or allowing any speaker to set the terms of the discussion. The chief's subjection to the rule of mutual recognition is symbolised by the crests of the crew's nations and families carved in the speaker's staff. Bill Reid has spent decades preparing to portray such a dialogue by recreating the cultural distinctiveness and interrelations of each of the spirit creatures, first by mastering the great Haida artistic traditions of formline sculpture in which they appear and then by learning the myth stories they are telling each other.

The conversation also seems to be 'diverse' in the three respects of overlap, interaction and negotiation mentioned above. The narratives of the thirteen *voyageurs* tell of how their identities have been shaped and formed through millennia of overlapping interaction together. They exist as they are, in all their distinctiveness, not in spite of, but in virtue of, their interdependency over time and history. These aspects are embodied in the endless ways in which they overlap and criss-cross without losing their identities in their astonishing arrangement in the canoe. The intercultural dimension of the sculpture is further heightened by the presence of non-Haida travellers: the mainland beaver and wolf, and the ancient reluctant conscript from European–American mythology.

The questioning, contestation and renegotiation of their cultural identities seem plain for all to see. Is this not the constitutional game they are playing as they vie and squabble for position, both in the canoe and in Haida mythology? The chief signals this Derridean feature because, although a Haida chief is usually a man, he is called *laana augha*, village mother, so he must act like a mother in caring for the common good if s/he is to secure respect and authority. All the passengers are Métis, exhibiting the non-identity of cultural identities: the dogfish and mouse women, the bear mother, who is part human, the wolf with his human forepaws and the others, for they are other-than-human persons who take off their furs and feathers at home and converse like human persons.

The theme is crystallised in *Xuuya*, the raven steering the canoe, who is forever changing his or her identity and so illustrating that things are not always as they appear – that our habitual forms of recognition are often stultifying forms of misrecognition which need to be upset and reversed from time to time. Members of the black canoe thus have the civic ability to see their association from multiple viewpoints. Jamake Highwater, a Blackfoot–American philosopher, explains that this ability of reflective disequilibrium, which is common to Aboriginal cultures, has been learned by twentieth-century European artists and writers through their interaction with 'primitive art' and slowly introduced into European cultures under the name 'post-modern'.

Now, the ability to change perspectives – to see and under-stand aspectivally – is acquired through participation in the intercultural dialogue itself. By listening to the different stories others tell, and giving their own in exchange, the participants come to see their common and interwoven histories together from a multiplicity of paths. Nurturing a reflective awareness of the diversity of cultural perspectives is a major function of Aboriginal storytelling at public festivals and constitutional negotiations. *The spirit of Haida Gwaii* is designed to awaken and stimulate this dialogical capacity for diversity awareness. As you walk around the canoe you soon realise that it is impossible to take it in from one comprehensive viewpoint. It defies this form of representation. Rather, you are drawn to see it from the perspective of one passenger after another, and their complicated interrelations guide you to see the whole now under one aspect, now under another.

Since recognition is never definitive, the particular constitutional arrangement of the members of the canoe is presumably not meant to be fixed once and for all. Constitutional recognition and association change over time, as the canoe progresses and the members change in various ways. A constitution is more like an endless series of contracts and agreements, reached by periodical intercultural dialogues, rather than an original contract in the distant past, an ideal speech-situation today, or a mythic unity of the community in liberal and nationalist constitutionalism.

The spirit of Haida Gwaii also depicts in a striking manner a specific concept of equality as equity. All members are equally recognised and accommodated, as far as possible, in terms of their own cultural identity. The result is that the constitutional arrangement of the canoe is far from uniform. The members make up an association more akin to the irregular arrangement of an ancient, custom-based constitution than to a modern, uniform constitutional association. The overall cultural diversity is a thing of justice and beauty, analogous to ecological diversity and just as important for living and living well on this planet. However, as we shall see, it offends against a powerful norm of uniformity in modern constitutionalism and provides one of the major objections to the politics of cultural recognition.

How do the citizens tell if the constitutional arrangement they have reached at this point in their journey is equitable and just? There is no transcendental standard beyond the discussion in the canoe from which it can be measured. This Platonic viewpoint is, as we have seen, unavailable. The answer would seem to be that they practise the spirit they embody. They are always willing to listen to the voices of doubt and dissent within and reconsider their present arrangement, just as *The spirit of Haida Gwaii* asks us to listen to the voices of cultural dissent around the world. This foundation of the constitutional association in the sovereignty of the people, rather than the sovereignty of the existing constitution, is symbolised by the ancient reluctant conscript, the unobtrusive paddler Bill Reid brought fondly aboard from European and European–American history:[11]

> I am an ancient reluctant conscript.
>
> On the soup wagons of Xerxes I was a cleaner of pans.
> On the march of Miltiades' phalanx I had a haft and head;
> I had a bristling gleaming spear-handle.
> Red-headed Caesar picked me for a teamster.
> He said, 'Go to work, you Tuscan bastard,
> Rome calls for a man who can drive horses.'
> . . .
> Lincoln said, 'Get into the game; your nation takes you.'
> And I drove a wagon and team and I had my arm shot off
> At Spotsylvania Court House.
> I am an ancient reluctant conscript.

Like Antigone, this ancient citizen reminds us of stoical survival and endurance, but also of the limit to reluctant conscription and submission. Bill Reid speaks of the conscript in a voice perhaps close to his own:[12]

A culture will be remembered for its warriors, philosophers, artists, heroes and heroines of all callings, but in order to survive it needs survivors. And here is our professional survivor, the Ancient Reluctant Conscript, present if seldom noticed in all the turbulent histories of men on earth. When our latter day kings and captains have joined their forebears he will still be carrying on, stoically obeying orders and performing tasks allotted him. But only up to a point; it is he who finally says, 'Enough', and after the rulers have disappeared into the morass of their own excesses, it is he who builds on the rubble and once more gets the whole thing going.

If the strange cultural multiplicity of *The spirit of Haida Gwaii* is not recognised and accommodated after all the oppression over all the years, then the mute inglorious conscript says 'enough' and refuses to bear the burden any longer. This is neither the revolt of the glorious nation nor the revolution to end the agony of politics and usher in the universal constitution of the kingdom of ends. No, the conscript is more humble and lower down in the boat, carrying the constitutional association on his shoulders. She is you and me. His 'enough' is the irruption of popular sovereignty, as old and endless as politics itself, against the suppression of difference. She is the true *laana augha*, the mother of the disappeared and the child of Antigone and Haemon. Because of his dissent, politics is not a series of necessary stages of historical development, the progression of a universal rule or the evolution or homogeneous nations, but the unpredictable voyage we call history. Over the centuries, and perhaps forever, she has breathed the spirit of both endurance and liberty into politics and, in so doing, preserved the wonderful multiplicity against all the power piled up to silence it.

The spirit of Haida Gwaii evokes one final and immensely optimistic vision of cultural diversity. For all the celebration of diversity and the vying for recognition, the paddles are somehow in unison and they appear to be heading in some direction. The ship of state glides harmoniously into the dawn of the twenty-first century. This seems to imply that the kind of constitutional change required to meet the just demands for recognition can be carried out without capsizing a society. Instead, it seems to suggest that a society can amend its constitution in the course of engaging harmoniously in its daily, subconstitutional politics.

This is a difficult, *Xuuya*-like image to grasp because the tendency since the seventeenth century has been to think of a modern constitution as an unsurpassable form established long ago by founding fathers, standing behind and providing the foundation for democratic politics. The constitution is thus one area of modern politics that has not been democratised over the last three hundred years. Constitutional change can occur in one of two ways: either by amendment within the forms of recognition laid down in the constitution and its traditions of interpretation or by overthrow of the constitution through war and revolution. Yet if the demands for cultural recognition are taken up and translated into the given forms of constitutional recognition, then the sovereignty of the people, which the constitution is presumed to express, will be thwarted, for this is the injustice of the prevailing language of constitutionalism according to the politics of cultural recognition. Popular sovereignty in culturally diverse societies appears to require that the people reach agreement on a constitution by means of an intercultural dialogue in which their culturally distinct ways of speaking and acting are mutually recognised.

Perhaps the great constitutional struggles and failures around the world today are groping towards a third way of constitutional change, symbolised in the ability of the members of the canoe to discuss and reform their constitutional arrangements in response to the demands for recognition as they paddle. On this *Haida Gwaii* an view, a constitution can be both the foundation of democracy and, at the same time, subject to democratic discussion and change in practice. The chapters that follow are an exploration of this possibility.

CHAPTER 2

Diversity and
contemporary constitutionalism

Answering the constitutional question: an outline
The first chapter laid out the difficult issues raised by the
question of the constitutional recognition of cultural diversity
in a post-imperial age. In the following chapters I propose an
answer to the question. A contemporary constitution can
recognise cultural diversity if it is reconceived as what might
be called a 'form of accommodation' of cultural diversity. A
constitution should be seen as a form of activity, an intercultural dialogue in which the culturally diverse sovereign
citizens of contemporary societies negotiate agreements on
their forms of association over time in accordance with the
three conventions of mutual recognition, consent and cultural
continuity.

To see the justice of this simple and somewhat obvious
answer, however, it is necessary to question and amend a
number of assumptions of contemporary constitutionalism. I
carry out this task of critical reflection in the following steps.
In this chapter I lay out the main conventions of the language
of contemporary constitutionalism and discuss the ways in
which contemporary legal and political theorists have
employed them to respond to the politics of cultural recognition. Just as Bill Reid turned to Haida artistic traditions to
do justice to the spirit of *Haida Gwaii*, I then turn to the
traditions of constitutionalism over the last four centuries to
do justice to the demands of cultural recognition.

The argument of the next three chapters is that, from the
perspective of the problem of cultural recognition, the con-

temporary European and European–American language of constitutionalism (which I call the 'contemporary' language) is a composite of two dissimilar languages: a dominant, 'modern' language and a subordinate, 'common-law' or simply 'common' language. The common language is in turn connected to other, non-European languages of constitutionalism. Chapter 3 is a critical survey of the various ways in which the modern language has been developed by leading theorists since the seventeenth century to exclude and assimilate cultural diversity in the name of uniformity.

Despite the dominant trend to uniformity, subordinate areas of constitutional theory and practice have been open to the recognition and accommodation of different cultures, for example when Europeans trained in the common law have encountered vibrant and powerful non-European peoples. Chapters 4 and 5 are a critical survey of the 'common' language of constitutionalism employed in the course of these cultural encounters on the common ground in order to recover and reconstruct three constitutional conventions which evolved to guide intercultural negotiations on just forms of constitutional association.

The sixth chapter returns to the present. On the basis of the historical surveys of the two constitutionalisms, modern and common, I argue that the composite, contemporary language of constitutional thought and practice need not be either blindly defended against any claim to cultural recognition or blindly rejected for its male, imperial and Eurocentric bias. Rather, it can be amended and reconceived to do justice to demands for cultural recognition. I seek to explain what the just constitutional recognition and accommodation of cultural diversity entails and to show that it enhances, rather than threatens, the primary goods of individual liberty and equality, which are correctly associated with modern constitutionalism, but in a manner appropriate to an age of cultural diversity. In the penultimate section I argue that the larger purpose of constitutionalism so reconceived, in addition to the recognition and accommodation of cultural diversity, is to mediate the two goods whose alleged irreconcilability is often seen as the source of current constitutional conflict: freedom and belonging.

The conciliation of freedom and belonging should dawn slowly over the course of the book. Nevertheless, it will be helpful to provide a preliminary sketch as a guide. The conflict of the six examples of the politics of cultural recognition is said by many to derive from clashes between the aspiration to be free from the ways of one's culture and place, to free oneself from oneself (*se déprendre de soi-même*, in Michel Foucault's memorable phrase),[1] and the equally human aspiration to belong to a culture and place, to be at home in the world. The tension between these two goods cannot be resolved or transcended, and it cannot be overcome by a rootless cosmopolitanism on one side or purified nationalism on the other. The twentieth century is a graveyard of failed attempts. Yet there is a form of constitutionalism and a spirit of citizenship in which these two human-all-too-human longings can be voiced and conciliated over time, and so help to bring negotiated peace to a troubled world.

Although Bill Reid is characteristically circumspect about the purpose of *The spirit of Haida Gwaii*, I believe it is not far from this spirit of conciliation. He asks:[2]

So there is certainly no lack of activity in our little boat, but is there any purpose? Is the tall figure who may or may not be the spirit of *Haida Gwaii*, leading us, for we are all in the same boat, to a sheltered beach beyond the rim of the world as he seems to be or is he lost in a dream of his own dreamings?

We should not take his refusal to draw an explicit purpose from the story of *The spirit of Haida Gwaii* as a licence to ignore the lessons this magnificent gift teaches. We are all, as he reminds us, in the same boat and so we have to find our appropriate place and attitude.

Like all great Aboriginal storytellers Bill Reid refuses to provide answers to the questions raised by his story. This would defeat the didactic purpose of storytelling, which is not to set out categorical imperatives but to develop the listeners' ability to think for themselves. Elders tell stories in a manner that encourages and guides listeners to reflect independently on the great problems of life that the story presents to them through myths. The test of understanding a story is not the answer listeners might give in an exam, but how it affects their attitude and how they go on in various circumstances to conduct their life in light of what they have learned from reflection on the story. Their grasp of the wisdom of the allegory guides them in their conduct, empowering them to carry on with the wisdom (*manitou*) of the Elder present to mind. Because there is not one right answer or one truth to an allegory, it is possible to go on in a variety of ways and still be acting in accord with the story. There are a multitude of ways of being guided.

To this end, Aboriginal stories usually finish with an easily memorised epigram of the story's central dilemma. The epigram functions as a mnemonic, enabling listeners always to recall and reflect on the difficult issues the story brings to their attention. To draw an analogy with European ethics, the epigram which evokes the purpose of the story becomes an ethical touchstone. True to form, Bill Reid leaves us with an epigram: 'The boat goes on forever anchored in the same place.'[3]

I believe that this well-made epigram distils the enigmatic purpose of *The spirit of Haida Gwaii* with Sophoclean clarity. The goods of freedom ('the boat goes on') and belonging ('anchored in the same place') are conciliated in miraculous equipoise on the common word they share ('forever'). This in turn brings to mind the equipoise of these two goods in all the aspects of the canoe: the raven, for example, at the stern exercising the freedom to be other than we are and the bear at the bow looking back to his family and traditional dwelling place. From the perspective of the passengers, the chief appears to be cautiously looking forward to see what lies on the changing horizon *and* carefully looking over the tangled customs and ways of the passengers. The canoe, like the word 'forever', points in both directions at once; the common place where the vying and squabbling endlessly goes on.

The big question Bill Reid leaves unanswered is, *how* do

these ambassadors from *Haida Gwaii* conciliate the goods which appear irreconcilable to us? To discover the answer, and learn our way around on this strange common ground, we need to travel through the last four centuries of constitutional history and return to where we are from their direction.

Two languages of contemporary constitutionalism and three schools of modern constitutionalism

The first and often overlooked step in any enquiry into justice is to investigate if the language in which the enquiry proceeds is itself just: that is, capable of rendering the speakers their due. To respond justly to the strange multiplicity of culturally diverse voices that have come forward like so many Antigones to demand a hearing in the gathering dusk of the imperial age it is necessary to call into question and amend a number of unexamined conventions, inherited from the imperial age, that continue to inform the language of constitutionalism in which the demands are taken up and adjudicated. These amendments add up to a fairly substantial renovation of the prevailing assumptions of modern legal and political theory. Perhaps it is not too much to speak of a 'conceptual revolution'; a significant change in the way of thinking about constitutions.

This first step is of paramount importance in the politics of cultural recognition because one of the central contentions is that persons or a people are not recognised in their own cultural language or voice. The language in which they are constrained to present their claims is the language of the master: masculine, European or imperial. So the injustice of cultural imperialism occurs at the beginning, in the authoritative language used to discuss the claims in question. Hence, the ethical watchword of the post-imperial age is always 'to listen to the voices of others' and to abide by the principle of 'self identification' in international law and elsewhere. Both express this new aspect of 'civic dignity', of speaking in one's own cultural voice, and the corresponding 'civic indignity' of speaking *for* others or of being compelled to speak in the dominant language and traditions of discourse.

If this first step of clarifying mutual recognition, or *audi alteram partem*, had already been taken, this book would be much shorter. But it has not. It functions as a kind of promissory note or ceremonial display before constitutional negotiations begin in both theory and practice. The language employed in assessing claims to recognition continues to stifle cultural differences and impose a dominant culture, while masquerading as culturally neutral, comprehensive or unavoidably ethnocentric.

To carry out the investigation, I adapt the form of historical critique developed in Cambridge over the last three decades by Quentin Skinner, John Dunn and their many students. It consists in the historical application of Wittgenstein's method of dissolving philosophical problems, not by presenting yet another solution, but by a survey which brings to critical light the unexamined conventions that govern the language games in which both the problem and the range of solutions arise. In this case, it consists in a survey of the language employed in the current debate over recognition in order to identify the shared conventions (the distinctions, concepts, assumptions, inferences and assertability warrants that are taken for granted in the course of the debate) which render recognition problematic and give rise to the range of conflicting solutions. To free ourselves from the hold of these conventions of the age, so that we do not remain blinded by them like Oedipus, a historical survey of the philosophical debates and practical contexts in which they were forged and they acquired the role of undoubted conventions is then carried out in the following chapters. This *Xuuya* exercise, which functions like Wittgenstein's 'objects of comparison' (discussed in chapter 4) and is partly indebted to Foucault's later method, then provides the critical distance to ascertain which conventions unjustly thwart cultural recognition and so require revision and, conversely, which claims to recognition can be shown to be unjust by the conventions which survive the critique.

The language in which claims to cultural recognition are taken up and adjudicated is the language of contemporary constitutionalism. It is the terms and the uses of those terms that have come to be accepted as the authoritative vocabulary for the description, reflection, criticism, amendment and overthrow of constitutions and their characteristic institutions over the last three hundred years of building modern constitutional societies. To adapt Wittgenstein's metaphor, it is the language that has been woven into the activity of acting in accordance with and going against modern constitutions. It consists in the uses of the term 'constitution', its cognates, and the other terms associated with it, such as popular sovereignty, people, self government, citizen, agreement, rule of law, rights, equality, recognition and nation.

This is an extremely complex language. It is a vast network of conventions, of ways of employing these terms over three hundred years. It is far more complicated than anyone who can use these terms imagines. The actual use of the vocabulary in ordinary circumstances is extremely familiar to us. Yet, the various ways any one term is employed, and thus its part in the life of contemporary constitutional societies, are extremely difficult to describe on reflection, even in rough outline. A person could easily spend a lifetime trying to describe the uses of just one of these terms over a small stretch of time – say, for example, the term 'property'.

The complexity of the language of constitutionalism is important to bear in mind. What has happened is that a relatively narrow range of familiar uses of these terms has come to be accepted as the authoritative political traditions of interpretation of modern constitutional societies. For the purposes of this book, the three most important authoritative traditions of interpretation are liberalism, nationalism and communitarianism. Often, when a demand for constitutional recognition is judged to contradict the norms of constitutionalism by the proponents of these three schools, what they mean is that it is incompatible with the range of normal usage of the terms of contemporary constitutionalism that is constitutive of their traditions of interpretation. The narrow range of normal usage these three traditions share comprises the 'modern' language of constitutionalism.

In the cases where a claim for constitutional recognition is rejected because it is incompatible with the narrow range of normal uses the three traditions share, the apparent incompatibility can often be dissolved simply by pointing to distinctions and uses in the language of contemporary constitutionalism that the forms of expression in liberalism, nationalism and communitarianism cause us to overlook, yet which are perfectly justifiable. This is in fact one of my strategies in the later chapters. I show that the prevailing language of the three schools of modern political theory has elbowed aside entire areas of the broader language of constitutionalism – such as the common law, earlier varieties of whiggism and civic humanism – which provide the means of recognising and accommodating cultural diversity. (I am sure this technique will be familiar to many, for it is an approach pioneered by Quentin Skinner, John Pocock and Richard Tuck.)

Not only is the broader language of contemporary constitutionalism more complex than the three dominant schools allow, it is also neither exclusively imperial nor exclusively European. The modern features of it were developed during the age of European imperialism, and served to legitimate it, as we shall see. Notwithstanding, it is also the language in which the anti-imperial struggles have been fought, both within and against Europe, during the same period. Moreover, the great struggles of women and others for constitutional recognition have been waged and justified in these terms. As we have seen, the reason why the politics of cultural recognition today can be described as a type of anti-imperial movement is that the proponents are able to use the language of constitutionalism in analogous ways to earlier anti-imperial theorists and practitioners.

Therefore, it is a misrepresentation to regard the language of contemporary constitutionalism as a monolithic masculine, European and imperial structure that must be swept away if the first step of recognition is to be just. Rather, it is more akin to an assemblage of languages, somewhat like European languages around the world, composed of complex sites of interaction and struggle, both within Europe and with non-European peoples and cultures. In the course of the contests for recognition, the language of constitutionalism has been shaped and formed by other cultures in ways that the European imperial writers would find unrecognisable. Indeed, to decry the language of contemporary constitutionalism as solely an European, imperial monolith, imposed from the centre on to the periphery without any change or interaction is, ironically, uncritically to accept the very self image the most chauvinistic imperial theorists of modern constitutionalism sought to uphold, and which Eric Wolf decisively exposed in *Europe and the people without history*.

As Edward Said puts it in *Culture and imperialism*, it is necessary to approach the European texts of the modern period with 'an acute and embarrassed awareness of the all-pervasive, unavoidable imperial setting'. Notwithstanding, it is equally important to see the political language that developed not as solely the independent creation of imperial apologists, but as what he calls 'contrapuntal ensembles', formed through cultural interaction and conflict, however unequal it may have been.[4]

Having pointed to the flexibility and adaptability of the language of constitutionalism, it is necessary to say something about its stability: its power to exclude and assimilate. There is a regular or customary agreement in judgements manifested in the actual use of the terms of constitutionalism in public discussion of the constitution of contemporary societies. That there is such a public discussion is part of what is meant by a contemporary constitutional society. The agreement in judgements is 'customary' or 'conventional' in the sense that the discussants do not explicitly agree to use these terms in such and such a way but, rather, that their explicit and reflexive agreements and disagreements rest on this implicit agreement in usage. This customary or conventional agreement is a necessary condition of there being a discussion. As Wittgenstein elucidates, such a customary agreement in use is not an agreement in 'opinions' (that is, explicit agreements reached by discussion), but a background agreement in 'language' or 'forms of life'.[5]

When a demand for constitutional recognition is advanced, the customary uses of the terms of modern constitutionalism function as a normative foundation for the discussion in two ways. In the first step, as you will recall, the demand is redescribed as a claim in the prevailing language of constitutionalism. This is a condition of it being recognised as a constitutional demand at all. When, for example, Aboriginal peoples strive for recognition, they are constrained to present their demands in the normative vocabulary available to them. That is, they seek recognition as 'peoples' and 'nations', with 'sovereignty' or a 'right of self determination', even though these terms may distort or misdescribe the claim they would wish to make if it were expressed in their own languages.

Second, the claim for recognition is then critically adjudicated. For example, the conventional criteria for the application and criticism of the terms 'people', 'nation', 'right of self determination', and 'sovereignty' function as the normative and intersubjective grounds for testing the claim to recognition. The ways in which the claim is interpreted and critically adjudicated are different in the liberal, nationalist, and communitarian traditions, for each has its own customary forms of critical reflection, and each is aware of the others.

This is not to suggest that the criteria for applying and criticising the terms of modern constitutionalism remain the fixed and unquestioned norms around which the discussion proceeds, although, of course, each of the three schools seeks to hold its set firmly in place. In any given circumstances of a claim for recognition some, but never all, of the customary uses and criteria of testing are called into question. When Aboriginal people at the United Nations, for example, demand recognition as 'nations' with 'the right of self determination', they are arguing that the prevailing criteria and reference of these terms ought to be revised to include them, rather than to exclude them, as they have done for the last five hundred years. When women argue for an equal rights amendment, the logic of the claim is analogous. Despite the efforts of the three schools to lay down unalterable rules for critical discussion, it is safe to say that we would not recognise public discussions of the constitution of contemporary societies as *critical* discussions unless they had this second-order reflective dimension: that is, the norms of rational acceptability of constitutional recognition are themselves questioned, in a piecemeal fashion, in the course of the discussion.

Contemporary constitutionalism is thus a game in which the participants alter the conventions as they go along. For example, landless labourers, slaves, corporations, religious and linguistic minorities, non-Europeans, women, prisoners and a host of other legitimate constitutional actors would never have gained constitutional recognition over the last three hundred years if this were not a feature of constitutionalism. However, to come back to the first point, the piecemeal alteration of the rules in the course of the discussion takes place against, and is justified with reference to, the broad and relatively stable background of customary agreements in judgement that are not questioned in any given critical discussion.

Constitutional language, as Harold Berman has argued, is also held in place by its use in the habitual and characteristic activities of a modern constitutional society. Parliament, voting, the courts, bureaucracy, police, dissent, protest, international war and even revolutions are all activities in which the terms of constitutionalism are used in fairly conventional ways. The regular activities in which the vocabulary is used are, with the exception of revolutions, also institutionalised in fairly durable relations of power which make up the legal and political structures of constitutional states. So, adapting the work of Foucault, we can say that the language of constitutionalism is held in place in spite of, and even as a result of, the continual challenges to aspects of it, by customary linguistic usage, normal activity and institutionalisation.

Accordingly, the public discussion of constitutionalism is not an ideal speech-situation, but a critical discussion firmly within the authoritative traditions of interpretation of the institutions of modern constitutional societies. Hence, the discussion is distorted not only by the instrumental use of power. For example, when Aboriginal peoples seek recognition as 'people' with the 'right of self determination', established nation states with Aboriginal peoples within their borders use their considerable instrumental power to keep the claim out of public discussion. They seek to discredit their claims or, if all else fails, to silence the claimants. At a deeper level, the very activity of using the language of modern constitutionalism in the normal activities and central institutions of modern societies holds the system of conventional uses in place. It is not only the force of habits of thought but also this interrelation between the language of constitutionalism and the public institutions of modern societies that makes it extremely difficult in practice to challenge the prevailing forms of constitutional recognition.

Now, the language of modern constitutionalism – the range of customary and well-institutionalised uses of constitutional terms that defines the three authoritative traditions of political theory – holds in place a picture of a modern constitution consisting of seven main features. The seven features will be discussed in detail in the third chapter. A rough sketch will suffice for the present purpose of illustration. The picture is of a culturally homogeneous and sovereign people establishing a constitution by a form of critical negotiation. The sovereign people are culturally homogeneous in one of the three ways: as a society of undifferentiated individuals, a community held together by the common good or a culturally defined nation. The constitution founds an independent and self-governing nation state with a set of uniform legal and representative political institutions in which all citizens are treated equally, whether their association is considered to be a society of individuals, a nation or a community.

A constitution of this modern type first came into being in the seventeenth and eighteenth centuries in Europe, in opposition to the 'ancient constitution' based on custom, tradition and irregularity on one side, and to pre-constitutional societies, associated with a state of nature or a lower stage of development on the other. It was given theoretical expression in the writings of the modern European political theorists from John Locke to John Stuart Mill. Contemporary liberals, nationalists and communitarians interpret each of these constitutional features differently, present competing narratives of the rise and maintenance of modern constitutions, and interpret the modern theories of constitutionalism in competing ways. Yet no one can fail to see on reflection the shared horizon against which their disagreements take place.

To a remarkable extent, this is the same picture sketched by Charles Howard McIlwain, the Eaton Professor of the Science of Government at Harvard, in his classic study, *Constitutionalism: ancient and modern* (1940). McIlwain claimed that Thomas Paine provided the authoritative expression of this vision of a modern constitution. This seems fitting, since Paine's theory was very much a European theory, yet it was used to justify a war of colonial independence against European imperialism and to establish an independent constitutional nation state in America with sovereignty over the Aboriginal peoples; just the roles the language of modern constitutionalism has played ever since. If the founding fathers of modern constitutional theory are extended to include Paine's contemporaries, especially Jean-Jacques Rousseau, Adam Smith, Immanuel Kant, Benjamin Constant and Georg Wilhelm Friedrich Hegel, as well as several of his predecessors, such as John Locke and Thomas Hobbes, then I think McIlwain's characterisation remains fairly accurate. (I will note my disagreements in the next chapter.)

This picture remained unquestioned as long as the political struggles the theorists chose to discuss could be seen to be driven by demands to be included in these forms of constitutional recognition: to become independent nation states or to become citizens with equal rights and dignity. As we have seen, the contemporary demands for cultural recognition are not of this inclusive type. They involve the claim that the forms of recognition in this picture fail to take into account cultural diversity from the first step: that is, in the three initial accounts of popular sovereignty. As a result, the forms of constitutional recognition on which the sovereign people reach agreement overlook and exclude or assimilate cultural differences. This is the residual imperialism of the modern theorists' picture. It begs the question of its own impartiality and sovereignty as the authoritative language of description and adjudication of claims to recognition.

Each of the six examples of the politics of cultural recognition I mentioned in the first chapter pose this question to different features of the shared language of modern constitutionalism. In this sense, the politics of cultural recognition is as fundamental a challenge to modern constitutionalism as Paine's theory was to the vision of the ancient constitution. It is not a challenge within the picture, as I shall now illustrate, but to the basic assumptions of modern constitutionalism.

The challenge of post-modernism and cultural feminism

Let us now briefly review how contemporary theorists from the three modern traditions have responded to the challenge posed by the politics of cultural recognition. These responses will be treated in more detail in later chapters. Their responses illustrate precisely the dichotomy that a more historically informed response can avoid: that is, either the demands are assimilated to the prevailing forms of recognition or they are judged to be unwarranted.

Among the three authoritative schools, the response has been to argue that if the demands for recognition are to be considered legitimate, then they must be redescribed and adjudicated within the prevailing norms of constitutional recognition. This response has taken two general forms. First, liberal, communitarian and nationalist theorists of a conservative bent have argued that the demands for the recognition of cultural diversity are incompatible with, and a direct threat to, the respective norms of their understanding of modern constitutionalism. They fly in the face of cultural neutrality for liberals, the integrity of the nation for

nationalists and the shared conception of a community
for communitarians. In each case, the demands are seen to be
a threat to the unity of a constitutional association and the
solution is to assimilate, integrate or transcend, rather than
recognise and affirm, cultural diversity. If these strategies are
impossible, then the only alternative is for the cultural group
demanding recognition to secede. Some of the better known
proponents of this view are liberals such as John Rawls, Allen
Buchanan and Jürgen Habermas, communitarians such as
Michael Sandel, and a host of nationalist writers.

A second and more tolerant response has been to argue that
many of the demands can be comprehended to some extent
within the prevailing norms because the recognition and
protection of cultures is a necessary condition of some of the
primary goods that liberals, nationalists and communitarians
seek to realise. Liberals such as Will Kymlicka, Daniel
Weinstock and Seyla Benhabib, communitarians such as
Charles Taylor and Michael Walzer, and nationalists such as
Yael Tamir, Guy Laforest and Isaiah Berlin have argued in
different ways that a fair degree of recognition and accommodation of cultural diversity is justifiable within the respective
constitutional traditions of modern societies.

However, a number of writers have replied that no manipulation of the norms of the three authoritative traditions can
ever do justice to the diverse demands for cultural recognition
because, as we have seen, the demands are a challenge to the
hegemony of these three traditions and their shared language
of constitutional recognition. For the purposes of illustration,
let me mention three counter, or non-authoritative, schools of
interpretation of constitutional societies that have arisen:
post-modernism, cultural feminism and interculturalism.
These three new schools are non-authoritative in the sense
that they did not develop along with the formation of contemporary constitutional societies and their language of self
understanding, as the other three schools did. The texts and
authors they refer to, the interpretations of the modern
theorists they advance, the narratives of constitutionalism
they employ and the forms of recognition they champion

have been marginal to, if not suppressed by, the dominant language of modern constitutionalism shared by liberals, nationalists and communitarians.

Their argument is that the three authoritative traditions of interpretation have been formed by European men in an age of imperialism, and thus their shared language of modern constitutionalism has a European, male and imperial cultural bias. As a result it is impossible to do impartial justice to the demands for cultural recognition within the vocabulary of these three traditions. Post-modern writers have turned especially to the concepts of identity, sovereignty and recognition to show how these are used to co-opt, rather than to recognise, the cultural demands of women, non-Europeans and others who have previously been excluded from the public sphere of modern societies. From their perspective, the rise of post-modernism is connected to the dismantling of European imperialism. The language of modern constitutionalism is seen as an imperial meta-narrative which needs to be thoroughly deconstructed. 'One can say with total security', Jacques Derrida wrote in the early 1960s, 'that there is nothing fortuitous about the fact that the critique of [European] ethnocentrism . . . should be systematically and historically contemporaneous with the destruction of the history of metaphysics.'[6]

The criticism of the prevailing concept of identity is both the strength and weakness of post-modern constitutionalism. Post-modern writers have shown that liberal, national and communitarian theorists customarily use a shared concept of identity when they identify their main concepts, such as culture, citizen, society, community, association, nation or people. This concept of identity, as we saw in the first chapter, is unable to account for a crucial feature of contemporary identity: that it is always different from itself, as well as from others. They have then shown how this compromises the theories constructed with these concepts. Unfortunately, many post-modern writers have gone on to draw the unwarranted conclusion that any concept of identity is self deconstructing and contingent, thereby heralding the end of sovereignty and constitutionalism in an unidentifiable fragmentation.

Perhaps the best overview of this consequence of post-modern legal and political theory is not in the works of the political theorists themselves, but in the writings of the anthropologist James Clifford. In *The predicament of culture* he sets out to explore the consequences of the new concept of culture as overlapping, open and negotiated, with the aim of freeing his readers from the earlier, separate, closed and homogeneous conception. However, in the description of 'the condition of uncertainty' from which he writes, instead of attending and giving appropriate recognition to the different types of overlapping cultural differences and similarities that come into view (as he does in the insightful chapter on the Mashpee Aboriginal nation on Cape Cod), he reduces post-modern societies to a homogeneous culture of contingent and dissolving differences. He writes,[7]

> I think we are seeing signs that the privilege given to natural languages and, as it were, natural cultures, is dissolving. These objects and epistemological grounds are now appearing as constructs, achieved fictions, containing and domesticating hetero-glossia. In a world with too many voices speaking all at once, a world where syncretism and parodic invention are the rule, not the exception, an urban, multinational world of institutional transience – where American clothes made in Korea are worn by young people in Russia, where everyone's 'roots' are in some degree cut – in such a world it becomes increasingly difficult to attach human identity and meaning to a coherent 'culture' or 'language'.

Of course, it is increasingly difficult to attach human identity and meaning to a coherent culture or language on the common ground, given the forces of globalisation and mobility mentioned in the first chapter. This is why there is a politics of cultural recognition at the end of the twentieth century, and why it will intensify in the twenty-first. However, dissolving this difficulty, and the demands it has engendered, into a homogeneous 'post-cultural situation' is to finesse rather than face the problem post-modernism sets out to address. The end result is strikingly similar to that put forward by conservative critics of cultural diversity. The conservative political theorist Peter Emberley, for example, writes,[8]

> It [the current pluralism] is . . . a mere multiplicity or hetero-geneity of deracinated voices (or 'discourses'), constituted in great part through the communications media, and distanced from any reality commonly attested to, other than that which is the product of subjective grievance or private fantasy. This radical heterogeneity and fragmentation is the context in which contemporary efforts to reappraise and renew constitutions is taking place, and it is placing burdens upon courts and legislators which the 'metaphysic' of modern constitutionalism cannot bear.

Let us recall the more cautious conclusion that Derrida recently drew from the insight that a culture is not identical to itself. He writes that this is 'not to not have an identity' at all, but rather, 'to be able to take the form of a subject only in the non-identity with itself or, if you prefer, only in the difference with itself'.

The second school, which stands in an agonic relationship with the three authoritative schools, is cultural feminism. The claim of its members is that it is not a sufficient condition of justice that women participate within the public institutions and traditions of interpretation of contemporary societies, as women have struggled to do in this century. Since the institutions and traditions have been established and sustained by men to the exclusion of women until recently, it is not unreasonable to question if they have a masculine partiality which discriminates in some ways against feminine ways of speaking, thinking and acting.

As women have gained access to the political and consti-tutional domains of societies in the twentieth century, they have, for the most part, acted within the dominant institutions and spoken within the three authoritative traditions, albeit in different ways in different countries, as Gisela Bock and Susan James illustrate in their international collection of feminist articles. Many women and men have defined themselves as liberal, nationalist and communitarian feminists, and engaged in politics in these terms. The general trend I mentioned above has appeared in this specific case: conservative members of the three schools argue that the admission of women requires no change in the institutions and traditions, while the progressive members submit that changes are necessary to comprehend the demands of feminists, but that the changes amend rather than challenge the prevailing traditions.

Cultural feminists welcome the ensuing plurality of feminist approaches, especially in daily political struggles where interests and alliances shift and intersect among different groups in society. Nevertheless, they question if what I am calling the 'first step' has not been bypassed at the constitutional level in this understandable rush to participate in politics within the horizons of the dominant modern language of constitutionalism. Allow me to illustrate the residual question that cultural feminists continue to raise to their sisters and brothers in the three leading schools with a North American example; the debate over care and justice initiated by the publication of Carol Gilligan's aptly titled *In a different voice* in 1982.

In the debate, which shows no signs of abating, one response has been to reject care as a political issue because it is incompatible with the domain of public justice in modern constitutionalism. The progressive response has been to argue that it is a political issue, but whatever aspects of political association it brings to light (such as relatedness) can be adequately articulated and comprehended within the conceptual resources of the three reigning traditions. Several feminists, such as Susan Moller Okin, Seyla Benhabib and Jean Bethke Elshtain, have brilliantly reworked the authoritative traditions to this end. Still, cultural feminists ask if this is not a subtle yet familiar form of cultural imperialism in which feminine voices are given a distorted hearing within traditions that remain masculine in several respects. Like Antigone, Carol Gilligan continues to insist that the ways in which humans are seen by many women to be in constitutive relations of care with each other are covered over and disregarded by the different initial conditions laid down in the conventions of the three traditions. This precludes, Peta Bowden persuasively argues, the kind of dialogue of mutual recognition in which different articulations of care, each in their own language of articulation, could be fairly compared and contrasted to determine, rather than presuppose, their similarities and differences.

A similar kind of question begging occurs when cultural feminists seek to present a diversity-sensitive conception of gender-related cultural differences, and to work out how rights and other constitutional devices could be interpreted and applied in a manner sensitive to forms of cultural differences. Again the response has been to turn to the resources of the mainstream traditions and argue that culture differences can be either transcended or, in so far as they are inelimin-able, articulated with the theories of difference available in the dominant traditions or, as feminists such as Julia Kristeva suggest, accounted for in the terms given in post-modern theories of difference. Despite the comprehensive and plural conceptions of identity and difference that the defenders of the three traditions are able to find by rereading their canonical European, male authors, cultural feminists remain sceptical. Maria Lugones and Elizabeth Spelman, for example, plead that the general conceptions of difference in these traditions, even after they have been amended by feminist members, can scarcely do justice to the criss-crossing and overlapping cultural differences they are trying to articulate *within* the feminist movement, such as the multiple identifications women have with their nation, communities, class, race, linguistic group, family, age group and rights, as well as gender. This differentiated concept of cultural differences, Linda Alcoff further submits, is not identical to the disintegrative concept of difference advanced by post-modern theorists. Moreover, if these insights into cultural differences in diverse societies are to be integrated into constitutional theory and practice, then, Martha Minow's work illustrates, one has to reach beyond the narrow language of modern constitutionalism to the broader or 'common' language of constitutionalism to do so (as we shall see in chapter 5).

Consequently, cultural feminists claim that the first step of cultural recognition has not been, and cannot be, addressed within the terms and traditions of the three schools. To do so in theory would be to investigate if there is an unexamined masculine bias in the language they share which occludes what remains to be said in women's other voices and traditions. The reason why cultural feminists believe that there may be such a bias is not simply because the language has been forged by men. Rather, the central concepts of the language of modern constitutionalism are defined authoritatively by the classic modern theorists in explicit contrast to what the theorists took to be characteristically feminine concepts.

Genevieve Lloyd and many others have shown that, in the canonical texts, the allegedly universal man of public politics, with his forms of reasoning, rights, virtues, interests and constitutional associations, is defined in contrast to the private woman, with her contrasting qualities and associations. These now conventional uses of the central terms of modern constitutionalism were advanced by the majority of classic male theorists from the seventeenth to nineteenth centuries to justify the exclusion of women from politics. When women and men now write, speak and act in the conventions of this language, merely changing 'man' to 'man and woman', they cannot help but do so in what the classic theorists took to be a masculine way.

To ascertain if the language of modern constitutionalism is itself a just language for enquiring into constitutional justice, therefore, it is necessary to carry out the same sort of critique of its potential masculine bias as I laid out above for other aspects of constitutional language. First, as Adrienne Rich puts the general point, it involves a constant critique of language:[9]

It is not easy to think like a woman in a man's world. To think like a woman in a man's world means thinking critically, refusing to accept the givens, making connections between facts and ideas which men leave unmentioned. It means remembering that every mind resides in a body; remaining accountable to the female bodies in which we live; constantly testing given hypotheses against lived experience. It means a constant critique of language, for as Wittgenstein – no feminist – observed, the limits of my language are the limits of my world.

Much of this work has been done, some of it by self-critical writers in the three conditions. However, it is insufficient for, like Oedipus, it remains within the conventions of the prevailing constitutional order.

To bring Antigone's perspective to bear, as Rich also recommends, the critique involves the recovery of counter-traditions of interpretation by women who have written and acted both within and outside the authoritative traditions of modern constitutionalism:[10]

What does a woman need to know? Does she not, as a self-conscious, self-defining human being need a knowledge of her history, her much politicised biology, an awareness of the creative work of women in the past, the skills and crafts and techniques and powers exercised by women in different times and cultures, a knowledge of women's rebellions and organised movements against our oppression and how they have been routed or diminished?

Without such knowledge women live and have lived without context, vulnerable to the projections of male fantasy, male prescriptions for us, estranged from our own experience because our education has not reflected or echoed it. I would suggest that not biology, but ignorance of ourselves, has been the key to our power-lessness.

The question not to ask is if, say, Mary Wollstonecraft and Mary Shelley are liberal and romantic, rationalist and expressivist. Before their voices are drowned out in this conventional way, one should ask what is it in what they are saying, and in the way they say it, that is not said, and perhaps cannot be said, in these male-dominated traditions. What are the differences left over after all the similarities are enumerated? The mental asylum in which Maria is confined is not a footnote to Bentham's panopticon. It is a woman's different interpretation of the institutions of modern societies. *Frankenstein* is not a romantic or communitarian criticism of atomism, but a woman's criticism of the inhumanity of romanticism. If the complex genealogy of contemporary constitutionalism is to be understood, these courageous texts should be read not as supplements to the deafening constitutional traditions founded by Locke, Rousseau, Paine and Herder, but in real historical confrontation and entanglement with them.

Enough historical scholarship has been done by cultural feminists to suggest that patriarchy, despite Locke, has yet to be 'unmonarched' in modern constitutionalism, and so to support their claim to a fair hearing for recognition. The question remains of how cultural feminists can engage in critical dialogues in which their traditions are recognised on equal footing with the authoritative traditions, the aim being to discover and constitutionally protect what cultural similarities and differences remain after a fair exchange. Then, when the mouse woman and the dogfish woman engage in politics and share institutions with the bear and the wolf, they will not have to speak and act exactly like them but, rather, their culturally dissimilar ways of being citizens will be respected.

However, when the topic of such a dialogue is raised, the progressive feminist members of the three traditions take it up in their conventional ways, proposing that it take the suitably amended form of the original position in contractarianism, discourse ethics in critical theory, the overlapping consensus of the three authoritative traditions in pragmatic liberalism, the dialogue of virtuous citizens on the common good in communitarianism and the sovereign nation in conversation with itself in nationalism. Cultural feminists such as Iris Young reply as they have done in all the earlier examples: none of these can do full justice to women's culturally different ways of engaging in a dialogue. More generally, no one of these forms of dialogue can do justice to all the speakers, for each fails to recognise the three features of the culturally diverse common ground on which the dialogue takes place. The presumption that there must be one comprehensive form of dialogue, which underlies the current debate on the just form of constitutional dialogue among the competing schools, is an unexamined convention left over from the imperial age. A moment's reflection on or participation in any recent constitutional negotiations will make one realise that there are many more legitimate, culturally different ways of giving reasons and defending a claim than are dreamed of in the current theories of a just dialogue. Only a dialogue in which different ways of participating in the dialogue are mutually recognised would be just (even if the first piece of business is to agree on which forms of dialogue are admissible). Consequently, the question of how women can enter into a dialogue on equal footing with members from the authoritative traditions without being marginalised or assimilated remains unanswered.

The challenge of interculturalism

The third challenge has come from intercultural citizens: Aboriginal peoples, members of suppressed and divided nationalities, linguistic and visible minorities, and citizens who seek constitutional recognition of international cultural relations among peoples. From their perspectives, as Rita Joe illuminated in chapter 1, the cultural imperialism of modern constitutionalism is obvious and glaring. They seek liberation by means of the constitutional recognition of suppressed Indigenous and non-European traditions of interpretation and corresponding degrees of self rule. Their response to progressive attempts to stretch the dominant traditions and institutions to comprehend their demands, such as the impressive work of Will Kymlicka in liberalism, Michael Walzer in communitarianism and Philip Resnick in nationalism, is, as I am sure you will anticipate, sceptical. While this is a welcome movement in theory and practice, it skips over the first step of questioning the sovereignty of the authoritative traditions and institutions they serve to legitimate.

For example, the claims of the Aboriginal peoples of the world for recognition of the equality of their constitutions and traditions, many of which precede modern constitutionalism by thousands of years, are taken up, when they are noticed, within, and subordinate to, the European-derived traditions and institutions. Yet it is precisely the prior question of their presumed sovereignty and impartiality that Aboriginal people claim, with good reason, deserves a fair hearing. Even in the many cases where interculturalists advance their claims within the prevailing institutions, the available language cannot help but distort their voices. As we noted in the first chapter, the customary ways of speaking and acting in the public institutions of modern societies have for centuries sustained dominant cultures which served to enslave, exclude, denigrate, dispossess and assimilate peoples of non-European cultures or of oppressed European cultures. Critical works of intercultural historical scholarship, such as Ronald Takaki's *A different mirror: a history of multicultural America*, expose the bias of the dominant traditions of interpretation and the unlikelihood of a fair hearing within their conventions.

Interculturalism challenges modern constitutionalism by starting from the three features of cultural diversity: citizens are in cultural relations that overlap, interact and are negotiated and reimagined. The experiences of crossing and living in more than one culture, such as Arab–Western, Indian–British, Scottish–UK, Hispanic–American, Aboriginal–Canadian, Maori–New Zealand and Asian–Canadian, have been central to their claims to recognition. Although interculturalists are understandably critical of the homogeneous concepts of identity and association constitutive of liberalism, communitarianism and nationalism, they none the less reject the deconstructive conclusions of post-modernism. Intercultural writers such as Paula Gunn Allen, Carlos Fuentes, bell hooks, Bhikhu Parekh, Edward Said, Mary Ellen Turpel and Iris Marion Young, as well as the thousands who are just beginning to be heard in the dialogue of humankind, have given a certain, obstinate stability to cultural identities with their distinctive vocabulary of voice, narrative, recovery and struggle.

Interculturalism presents a further challenge to modern

constitutionalism than the constitutional right to speak and act politically in intercultural ways in the prevailing institutions (as 'multiculturalism' is often taken to mean). Many interculturalists also come to constitutional dialogues with the claim that they should be recognised as already constituted not only by their cultures, but also by thwarted or usurped constitutional associations of various kinds: nations, communities and minorities. Two conventions of modern constitutionalism block a fair representation of this claim, as *québécois-canadiens* Alain Gagnon and Guy Laforest disclose. The premise of the authoritative traditions is that the people who come together to deliberate on a constitution are in a pre-constitutional situation of some kind, such as the three types of original positions mentioned earlier. The increasingly common situation of a constitutional dialogue of people who are already constituted in various ways (such as Israel–Palestine, the four nations of the United Kingdom, Bosnia–Herzegovina, the European Union, Canada, New Zealand, India, Spain, the circumpolar Inuit and Mexico) cannot be entertained. Indeed, as we shall see in the next chapter, modern constitutionalism was designed to efface such 'ancient' constitutional situations. The premises of the authoritative traditions, like the certitudes taken for granted by Creon in silencing Antigone, serve to dispossess the citizens of the constitutional identities they seek to discuss.

Second, the aim of such constitutional discussions is a 'diverse' federation which recognises and accommodates appropriate forms and degrees of self rule for the claims that survive a fair hearing. Yet a firm convention of modern constitutionalism is that the aim of constitutional dialogue is a uniform and comprehensive legal and political association. The question of a federation capable of accommodating the diverse ways citizens are already culturally constituted by means of a variety of legal and political institutions is either beyond the pale of Rawls' 'reasonable pluralism',[11] which must converge on a uniform legal and political order, or an unfortunate deviation from the norm of uniformity. In either case, the norm of uniformity remains unexamined, whereas its presumed impartiality is exactly what interculturalists are attempting to call into question.

In conclusion, the confrontation between the politics of recognition and modern constitutionalism faces an impasse. How can the proponents of recognition bring forth their claims in a public forum in which their cultures have been excluded or demeaned for centuries? They can accept the authoritative language and institutions, in which case their claims are rejected by conservatives or comprehended by progressives within the very languages and institutions whose sovereignty and impartiality they question. Or they can refuse to play the game, in which case they become marginal and reluctant conscripts or they take up arms. No one wants this tragic impasse that covers the common ground of so many contemporary societies with the scars of battle.

Of course there are many reasons for the impasse. The one which concerns me in this book is the way a just dialogue is precluded by the conventions of modern constitutionalism. The unexamined imperial convention I hope this chapter has brought to your attention is the constant conjunction of two senses of the verb 'to comprehend': 'to understand' and 'to include within'. When the defenders of modern constitutionalism take up claims for recognition, they assume that to comprehend (understand) what the claimants are saying consists in comprehending it within an inclusive language or conceptual framework in which it can then be adjudicated. The conservatives exclude the claims, because they are incompatible with the conventions, and the progressives amend the conventions to try to include the claims. This practice of running together the two senses of 'to comprehend' is one of the most deep-seated conventions of modern constitutionalism.

As the black canoe illustrates, one of the important discoveries of the twentieth century is that such a comprehensive language or point of view is an illusion. There is no view from no where. No matter how comprehensive such a language may appear to be, and some recent candidates in the philosophy of cross-cultural understanding have a very comprehensive appearance, it will always bring to light some aspects of the phenomenon it is employed to comprehend at the expense of disregarding others, as a result of the aspectival character of most social phenomena. It will not be a meta-language of recognition and adjudication but, rather, one language among others.

If one such language or tradition gained ascendancy in a constitutional negotiation, it would cease to be a dialogue at all. It would be a (liberal, nationalist or communitarian) monologue. Therefore, the post-imperial injunction to listen to the voices of others must involve listening not only to what they say, but also to the way or language in which it is said, if the imperial habit of imposing our traditions and institutions on others in both theory and practice is to be abjured. The way to break with convention is to discover a post-imperial dialogue, like the black canoe, in which the interlocutors participate in their diverse cultural forms, and a form of intercultural understanding which does not presuppose a comprehensive language.

By tracing the historical formation of the language of modern constitutionalism in the following three chapters, I seek to show that the current impasse is an illusion which is caused by the restricted vision held in place by the conventions shared by the authoritative schools. A broader survey of the history of contemporary constitutionalism reveals that in many interactions with other cultures which, like the killing of Laius, are forgotten, ignored or misinterpreted by the members of the authoritative traditions, a 'common' intercultural language of conventions evolved to facilitate the mutual recognition of culturally diverse constitutional negotiators. This hidden constitutional language can be reconstructed to change our vision of a constitution and dissolve the impasse.

CHAPTER 3

The historical formation of modern constitutionalism: the empire of uniformity

Constitutions ancient and modern

This chapter is a survey of the tendency to cultural uniformity in the formation of the language of modern constitutionalism. It answers the question of why it is so difficult to recognise and affirm cultural diversity in the schools of modern constitutionalism discussed in the last chapter. Or, put differently, why does the black canoe appear to us as a 'strange multiplicity', rather than as a normal negotiation among members of a culturally diverse society over how they are going to recognise and accommodate their differences and similarities over time as they paddle the ship of state? The answer is that the language of modern constitutionalism which has come to be authoritative was designed to exclude or assimilate cultural diversity and justify uniformity.

The design is difficult to see because this 'modern' language has become the customary way of thinking about, reflecting on and envisioning a just constitutional order. Since all three schools share it, disagreeing only over the interpretation and application of some of its terms, forms of critical reflection and narratives, the debates over the legitimacy of cultural diversity reinforce the shared vision. As Wittgenstein described this sort of philosophical problem: 'A *picture* held us captive. And we could not get outside it, for it lay in our language and language seemed to repeat it to us inexorably.'[1]

Hence, the tendency is not to notice the philosophical and ideological debates over the last three hundred years between the successful modern theorists and the defenders of diversity who struggled against them in theory and practice. Only the result of these debates is seen – the victorious modern language of constitutional uniformity – and claims for recognition are viewed through its framework as if it were impartial and universal. Hence, to overcome the partiality of the inherited language of modern constitutionalism we need to retrace our steps, recover the arguments the modern theorists used to set this imposing edifice in place and re-examine the justifications they advanced for silencing the cultures which have returned to demand a hearing.

The main features of the vision of a modern constitution which are shared by the authoritative traditions of constitutionalism can be found in the writings of contemporary political and constitutional theorists. For an initial synopsis, let us start from the formulation by McIlwain in *Constitutionalism: ancient and modern*, mentioned in chapter 2, which recent work on the history of constitutionalism continues to endorse. McIlwain argues that Thomas Paine articulated a distinctively modern picture of a constitution in the era of the American and French Revolutions. At the centre of the picture are the sovereign people who exist prior to the constitution of a political association. By a self-conscious act of reflective reason and agreement, the people give rise to a constitution which 'constitutes' the political association. The constitution lays down the fundamental laws which establish the form of government, the rights and duties of citizens, the representative and institutional relation between government and governed, and an amending formula.

This modern constitution, which has its roots in the contractarian tradition, and especially in the development from Hobbes to Paine, is defined by its proponents in contrast to an 'ancient' constitution. An ancient constitution, McIlwain writes, 'was probably never better indicated than by Bolingbroke, when he said in 1733':[2]

By 'constitution' we mean, whenever we speak with propriety and exactness, that assemblage of laws, institutions and customs, derived from certain fixed principles of reason, directed to certain fixed objects of the public good, that compose the general system, according to which the community hath agreed to be governed.

The defining contrast could scarcely be sharper. A modern constitution is an act whereby a people frees itself (or themselves) from custom and imposes a new form of association on itself by an act of will, reason and agreement. An ancient constitution, in contrast, is the recognition of how the people are already constituted by their assemblage of fundamental laws, institutions and customs.

Recent historical scholarship has confirmed that some such contrast between imposition and recognition is one defining aspect of modern constitutionalism in European and European–American political thought. The people are said to be sovereign and free in so far as they are not tied to custom, but are constitutionally self determining, whether the 'people' are thought of as individuals, in the theories of Hobbes, Pufendorf, Locke and Kant, a community, in Rousseau's *Social contract*, or as a nation, in *The declaration of the rights of man and citizen* and in the writings of Johann Herder and Johann Fichte. However, the contrast is only one aspect and it is not unique to modern constitutionalism. The contrasting aspects under which a constitution can be seen – as a form of association brought into being by imposition or as an existing form of association brought to awareness by recognition – have been present throughout the history of constitutional thought.

The Greek term for constitutional law, *nomos*, means both what is agreed to by the people and what is customary. When Cicero translated *politeia* as *constitutio* he used it to mean both the fundamental laws that are established or laid down by the mythical lawgiver and the fitting or appropriate arrangement in accord with the preceding customary ways of the people.[3] As I suggested in the first chapter, Sophocles' *Antigone* is a tragic dramatisation of the ambiguity of the term 'constitution'. Creon defends the constitutional laws of Thebes as they have been deliberately imposed by men, whereas Antigone protests that the constitution fails to recognise the underlying assemblage of customs of family, hearth and burial, to which the people are subject, and Haemon tries unsuccessfully to persuade Creon that both aspects of a constitution must be conciliated if justice is to be served. The concept of a constitution and its associated terminology have remained Janus faced ever since: looking back to an already constituted order under one aspect and looking forward to an imposed order under the other.

The ambiguity of 'constitution' appears to be resolved in favour of the imposition conception in modern constitutionalism by the tendency, noticeable in the theories of Paine and his followers, to assume that a modern constitution is based on 'agreement', while an ancient constitution is based on *de facto* habit or custom. This is a false contrast because, as the quotation from Bolingbroke summarises, the reason why the customary ways of the people have the authority of constitutional law, and so are worthy of recognition by the ruler, is that they are the expression of the 'agreement of the people'. This is not the same sense of 'agreement' as the modern concept of an 'explicit agreement' on a written constitution which a people reach by deliberation, as in Paine's definition, but it is not reducible to *de facto* habit either.

Rather, the 'long use and practice' of a custom reflects and manifests the deliberate judgement of reason, and so the consent, of a free people. The consent of a free people expressed by their 'agreement in' their customary ways counts more than the authority of the ruler. (This sense of agreement is similar to 'agreement in judgements' discussed in chapter 2.) Hence, in Thomas Aquinas' influential formulation, the customary ways of a people have the authority of law because they manifest the agreement of a free people and they cannot be changed by the ruler without their explicit agreement.[4] One of the major themes of McIlwain's study, amplified recently by Donald Kelley, is the immense importance of this conception of authoritative customary agreement in the development of ancient constitutionalism up to Bolingbroke. Therefore, paradoxically, the ancient constitution, by recognising custom, and the modern constitution, by overriding custom, both claim to rest on the agreement of the people.

If the entire scope of modern constitutionalism could be defined in terms of an unambiguous contrast between self-determining imposition and custom-based recognition, as it

appears in the contrast between Paine and Bolingbroke, then
the task of cultural recognition would not be too difficult. One
could point out that the demands for the recognition of
cultures are demands that people's agreement in customary
ways of speaking and acting be recognised and accommodated
to some extent. Since the irreducible role of culture is now
widely acknowledged, the error in modern constitutionalism
in disregarding it can be exposed, as the progressive liberals,
nationalists and communitarians have begun to do.

However, the task is more difficult because, as we have
seen, the contrast between ancient recognition and modern
imposition is drawn within the comprehensive language of
modern constitutionalism. Despite the wide acceptance of
McIlwain's account, the theorists of modern constitutionalism
did not disregard the role of custom altogether. Rather, they
developed sophisticated accounts of customs, cultures and
history as part of their theories of a modern constitution. To
grasp the full vision of modern constitutionalism, it is
necessary to understand how the 'ancient' recognition of
custom was incorporated and transformed in the classic
theories of modern constitutions, for the current attempts
to recognise cultural diversity remain entangled in these sophisticated modern conceptions of customs, cultures and history.

Seven features of modern constitutionalism
Seven features of the language of modern constitutionalism
serve to exclude or to assimilate cultural diversity. This
language is properly called 'modern' because most of the
theorists who forged it claimed to present theories of a
'modern' constitution, which they defined in opposition to
what they called the 'ancient' constitution of their critics. By
this linguistic sleight of hand, they made it appear that the
only legitimate constitution in the modern age is a 'modern'
one. Their opponents, in upholding an 'ancient' constitution,
appear anachronistic and nostalgic, inappropriate to modern
times. *The liberty of the ancients compared with that of the moderns*
(1819) by Benjamin Constant is perhaps the most successful
exemplar of this genre. As we saw in the previous chapter, this

strategy of comprehension has been so successful that even recent critics have been taken in by it. Post-modern writers criticise the conventions of modern constitutionalism as if they were the contours of the modernity itself.

The first feature of modern constitutionalism comprises three concepts of popular sovereignty which eliminate cultural diversity as a constitutive aspect of politics. The people are sovereign and culturally homogeneous in the sense that culture is irrelevant, capable of being transcended, or uniform. They reach agreement on a form of constitutional association by a hypothetical or historical process of deliberation in one of three ways.

First, the people are taken to be a society of equal individuals in a state of nature, behind a veil of ignorance or in a quasi-transcendental speech-situation prior to the constitution, and with the aim of constituting one uniform political association. This is the way of thinking about constitutionalism most closely associated with Paine and recent liberalism.

The second concept of popular sovereignty is that the people are taken to be a society of equal individuals who exist at a 'modern' level of historical development and recognise as authoritative a set of threshold, European institutions, manners and traditions of interpretation within which they deliberate and reach agreement on a constitution. The institutions and traditions are authoritative, not authoritarian: they are open to reflection and amendment in the course of deliberation towards agreement on the constitution, as the deliberators seek to articulate the principles that underlie their overlapping consensus on these institutions and traditions. This historical way of conceptualising popular sovereignty, which has been brought back into prominence by John Rawls and Richard Rorty, looks at first blush like a return to the ancient constitution of Bolingbroke. However, it is characteristic of many of the classic theorists of modern constitutionalism, such as David Hume, Smith, Sieyès, Paine, Kant and Constant. As recent scholars such as Biancamaria Fontana and Knud Haakonssen have highlighted, they took as their starting point the premise that a modern constitution must recognise the institutional and sociological conditions of a modern society and the type of liberty and equality that corresponds to them.

The third form of popular sovereignty is the communitarian version of the historical conception. The people are seen as a community bound together by an implicit and substantive common good and a shared set of authoritative European institutions, manners and traditions of interpretation. Within the horizons of these institutions and traditions, they interpret and articulate the common good through public deliberation and give it expression in a constitution.

The second feature of a modern constitution is that it is defined in contrast to an ancient or historically earlier constitution. An 'ancient constitution' refers to pre-modern European constitutions, as McIlwain notes, and, secondly, to the customs of non-European societies at 'earlier' and 'lower' stages of historical development. These two contrasts ground the imperial character of modern constitutionalism. The contrast is made in reference to two aspects of pre-modern European and non-European constitutions: their stage of development and their irregularity.

First, the ancient constitution of pre-modern and non-European societies is closely tied, or even identical, to the customs of those societies, which are defined as 'traditional'. The contrast is not that a modern constitution is completely independent of custom, but that it is appropriate to, and the result of a self-conscious critical reflection on, the customs, manners and civilisation of modern societies (as in the second and third concepts of popular sovereignty). This aspect of modern constitutionalism rests on the 'stages' or 'progressive' view of human history which the classic theorists produced in order to map, rank and thereby comprehend the great cultural diversity encountered by Europeans in the imperial age.

In the stages view of human history, all cultures and peoples are mapped hierarchically in accordance with their location on a historical process of progressive development. European constitutional nation states, with their distinctive institutions and cultures of manners and civility, are at the highest and most developed or improved stage. Modern constitutions only come into being as a result of this development, 'amongst', as Locke puts it, 'those who are counted the Civiliz'd part of Mankind'.[5] As the processes of colonisation and modernisation spread around the world from Europe, the colonies and lower peoples will become objects of the causal process of improvement, gradually shedding their primitive customs and ways, appropriate to their lower level of development. They will be assimilated into modern nations within a European imperial structure or into independent modern constitutional nation states, as European states have done, or they will be pushed to the wayside by the march of progress.

This feature of modern constitutionalism contains the concept of cultures that anthropologists and historians have challenged in our era. Cultures are seen as separate, closed, internally uniform and relative to a stage of socio-economic development. Humans reason within the bounds of the cultures of which they are members, from the primitive and 'child-like' Aboriginal to the universal European. Locke illustrates this thesis of cultural relativity in a conventional manner:[6]

Had you or I been born at the Bay of Soldania, possibly our Thoughts, and Notions, had not exceeded those brutish ones of the *Hotentots* that inhabit there: and had the *Virginia* King *Apochancana*, been educated in *England*, he had, perhaps, been as knowing a Divine, and as good a Mathematician, as any in it. The difference between him, and a more *improved English*-Man, lying barely in this, That the exercise of his faculties was bounded within the Ways, Modes, and Notions of his own Country, and never directed to any other, or farther Enquiries.

Consequently, the modern constitution and its associated concepts are defined in contrast to what Michel-Rolph Trouillot calls 'the savage slot', which is filled by the non-European 'other' who is defined as lower in development and earlier in time: in a state of nature, primitive, rude, savage, traditional or underdeveloped, depending on the theorist. The various theories of progress, from Locke to the latest theories about the triumph of the West or the end of history, make up a comprehensive map of mankind, drawn, like a Mercator projection, entirely from a European and masculine point of view, but with the pretension of universality. As Edmund Burke wrote to William Robertson, the Aboriginal-hating author of the *History of America* in 1777:[7]

I have always thought with you that we possess at this time very great advantages towards the knowledge of human Nature ... But now the Great Map of Mankind is unrolld at once; and there is no state or Gradation of barbarism, and no mode of refinement which we have not at the same instance under our View.

The third feature of modern constitutionalism is the contrast with the irregularity of an ancient constitution. An ancient constitution is multiform, an 'assemblage' as Bolingbroke puts it, whereas a modern constitution is uniform. Because it is the incorporation of varied local customs, an ancient constitution is a motley of overlapping legal and political jurisdictions, a kind of *jus gentium* 'common' to many customary jurisdictions, as in the Roman republic or the common law of England. The assemblages of laws, customs and institutions of Europe prior to the Peace of Westphalia in 1648 were seen as the paradigm of ancient constitutions by the modern theorists.

The sovereign people in modern societies, in contrast, establish a constitution that is legally and politically uniform: a constitution of equal citizens who are treated identically rather than equitably, of one national system of institution-alised legal and political authority rather than many, and a constitutional nation equal in status to all the others. This feature of legal and political monism is perfectly understand-able. It emerged out of the one hundred years of wars in Europe which ended with the Thirty Years' War of 1618–48. These wars were seen by the modern theorists as conflicts over the locus of sovereignty. As Locke put it:[8]

the great Question which in all Ages has disturbed Mankind, and brought on them the greatest part of those Mischiefs which have ruined cities, depopulated countries, and disordered the Peace of the World, has been, Not whether there be Power in the World, nor whence it came, but who should have it.

The diagnosis of the modern theorists was that the conflicting jurisdictions and authorities of the ancient constitutions were the cause of wars. Accordingly, their response was that authority had to be organised and centralised by the constitution in some sovereign body: in a single person or assembly, a system of mixed or balanced institutions, or in the undifferentiated people. Such an authority could recognise custom from time to time, as even Hobbes concedes, but custom has its authority only in virtue of its recognition by the sovereign, not vice versa. In the modern theories of the sovereignty of the people, the plurality of existing ancient authorities is eliminated by construing the people as the single locus of authority and their aim as the constitution of a uniform system of government.

The fourth feature is the recognition of custom within the theory of progress. The reason why the people establish a uniform constitutional system of government is not that they disregard the plurality of ancient customs in the process of consolidation and centralisation of modern constitutional states, as the crude contrast between recognition and imposition suggests. Rather, as Smith, Sieyès and Constant argue, the unintended historical progress of economic and social conditions gradually undermines the ancient constitution of customs and ranks and creates a society of one 'estate' or 'state' of equal and legally undifferentiated individuals with similar 'manners'. This is what Sieyès meant when he famously wrote, 'What is the third estate? Everything.'[9] A modern constitution thus merely recognises the transformed character of modern societies. Modern constitutional governments help this process along, but their policies of discipline and rationalisation are understood within the background vision of the historical progression through various stages towards uniform manners and institutions.

Fifth, a modern constitution is identified with a specific set of European institutions; what Kant calls a 'republican constitution'. Since the social and economic conditions of modern European societies are converging, modern constitutions will establish a uniform type of legal and political institution appropriate to these conditions to represent the sovereignty of the people. The people alienate or delegate political power to governments in these institutional forms. Institutions of representative government, separation of powers, the rule of law, individual liberty, standing armies and a public sphere are definitive of a modern or republican constitution, for it is only at the modern level of historical development that they are necessary. These definitive constitutional institutions in turn compose a modern sovereign state, as Quentin Skinner has shown, marking it off from lower, stateless, irregular and ancient societies.[10]

Since the French and American revolutions, the sixth convention has been that a constitutional state possesses an individual identity as a 'nation', an imaginary community to which all nationals belong and in which they enjoy equal dignity as citizens. Although the nation is interpreted differently in each society, as Anthony Smith and Benedict Anderson have shown, it engenders a sense of belonging and allegiance by means of the nation's individual name, national historical narrative and public symbols. By naming the constitutional association and giving it a historical narrative, the nation and its citizens, who take on its name when they become members, possess a corporate identity or personality. From Pufendorf onward, this corporate identity of nation and nationals in a state is seen as necessary to the unity of a modern constitutional association.

The constitutional nation contains two complementary concepts of equality. The citizens are formally equal under the law and thus the differential treatment of the ancient constitution is experienced as an intolerable indignity. Second, each constitutional nation is equal in authority to any other, and thus the inequality of imperialism is seen as an intolerable indignity. This feature justified the building of independent nation states in Europe against the claims of papal and Roman imperialism. As a result of the stages view of historical development, only European political associations were initially considered to be modern constitutional nation states worthy of being recognised as independent and equal.

Colonies were considered to be at an earlier stage of development and so not yet meeting the criteria of nationhood. From the American revolution on, the identification of nationhood with an independent and equal state served to justify anti-imperial wars of independence against Europe and to stigmatise any other form of constitutional relationship as degrading and intolerable. Since the 'primitive' peoples were much lower down the developmental ladder, it would of course be a category mistake to identify them as equal nations. In most cases, as we shall see, they were seen to be in a state of nature without a constitution.

Finally, a modern constitution comes into being at some founding moment and stands behind – and provides the rules for – democratic politics. This feature is reinforced by the popular images of the American and French revolutions as great founding acts performed by founding fathers at the threshold of modernity. It is further entrenched by the assumption that a modern constitution is universal, something that the people agreed on at some time, but for all time. This image is enhanced by the myths of the single lawgiver in the republican tradition, the original consensus of the community or nation in the nationalist tradition and the original or hypothetical contract, to which all citizens today would consent if they were rational, in the liberal tradition.

A modern constitution thus appears as the precondition of democracy, rather than a part of democracy. This antidemocratic feature is mitigated by the assumption that the people gave rise to it at some time, and by the elaborate theories of modern constitutionalism from Hobbes to the present which serve to persuade us that we would consent today if we were reasonable. In this respect, the ancient constitution appears more democratic. It was changed and adjusted by the government, as the customs and circumstances changed, in accordance with nothing more, or less, than the conventions of the constitution: that is, the present interpretation of customary ways of changing the constitution in the past. But, as Paine acidly notes, this changing and impermanent constitution, founded in nothing but custom and convention, is no constitution at all from a modern point of view:[11]

the continual use of the word 'constitution' in the English parliament shows there is none; and that the whole is merely a form of government without a constitution, and constituting itself with what power it pleases. The act by which the English Parliament empowered itself to sit for seven years, shews there is no constitution in England. It might, by the same authority have sat any number of years, or for life.

Examples of forging the seven features: Locke and Aboriginal peoples
These seven features have been woven into the fabric of constitutionalism over the last three centuries, providing the dominant conventions in which the cultural diversity of the world has been misrecognised and suppressed. Not all modern theorists adopted the seven features. In some cases, one part of a 'modern' text, such as Locke's chapter 'On conquest' in the *Two treatises*, contains a passage which serves to recognise cultural diversity. Conversely, several of the defenders of cultural diversity, such as Gottfried Leibniz, Charles-Louis de Secondat Montesquieu, Baron de Lahontan, Wollstonecraft or John Marshall, share some of these conventions. For example, Herder broke with the second convention of ranking cultures relative to a European norm, undermining the prevailing justification of European imperialism, but he retained, and gave an expressive interpretation to, the conventional view of cultures as separate and homogeneous, thereby deepening the sixth feature of a constitutional nation.

Let us now survey a few examples of how these seven ways of thinking about constitutionalism were forged and used to justify the extinction or assimilation of different cultures. The first example illustrates one way the features were employed, and continue to be employed, to dispossess the Aboriginal nations of their sovereignty and territory and to subject them to European constitutional nation states and their traditions of interpretation. As Richard Tuck and Anthony Pagden have shown, the 'discovery' and 'settlement' of the 'Americas' was regarded as a defining event of the modern age. Its justification, against the resistance of Aboriginal peoples and their defenders from Bartolomé de Las Casas to John Marshall, was accordingly seen as a leading task of European political philosophy. A central figure was John Locke, who administered and invested in the imperial system in practice and justified it in theory. Although his justification in the *Two treatises* of 1690 is only one of many, it is exemplary because it gathers together many of the arguments of earlier theorists and sets out many conventions that later theorists accepted, even though they disagreed with him in other respects.

The problem facing Locke and his like-minded contemporaries was that the Aboriginal peoples recognised themselves as organised into sovereign nations with jurisdiction over their territories when the Europeans arrived. In the next chapter we shall see that many Europeans came to accept this form of recognition because it rested on three of the oldest conventions of constitutionalism. They concluded that the only legitimate way for Europeans to settle in America was to gain the consent of the Aboriginal nations by means of nation to nation negotiations, as a Royal Commission concluded in 1665, fifteen years before Locke wrote the *Two treatises*. Since the Aboriginal peoples were unwilling to cede all the land the settlers desired to take, a justification was required for taking land and establishing European sovereignty without requiring the consent of the native peoples. Locke reworked the arguments that had been advanced to this end in the 1630s and 1640s, against Roger Williams' defence of the Aboriginal nations, into a consistent answer to this 'very great difficulty' of justifying appropriation 'without any express Compact of all the commoners'.[12]

First, Locke sets the stages theory of world history in place and identifies Aboriginal peoples within it as the earliest and most primitive members of the human race. 'In the beginning', he proclaims, 'all the world was *America*.' America is 'still a Pattern of the first Ages in *Asia* and *Europe*'. European societies, by contrast, are in the most 'improved' or 'civilized' age. This premise provides the stage setting for his account of world-historical development and, as Ronald Meek has shown, for the grand theories that followed in the eighteenth century.[13]

In Locke's classic formulation of the concept of individual popular sovereignty, the first age represented by America is a 'state of nature'. There is neither nationhood nor territorial jurisdiction at this early stage. Rather, American Indians govern themselves on an individual and *ad hoc* basis by applying the law of nature and punishing offenders as cases arise; 'each being, where there is no other, Judge for himself, and Executioner; which is' to say 'the perfect *state of Nature*'. By contrast, Europeans live in sovereign nations or 'political societies' appropriate to their civilised level of development. They have left the state of nature by delegating their powers of self government to representative governments and set up modern constitutional institutions: 'a common establish'd Law and Judicature to appeal to, with Authority to decide Controversies between them, and punish Offenders'.[14]

The state of nature is also the first economic stage, that of hunters and gatherers. They have individual property rights in the labour of their body and the work of their hands and, consequently, in whatever they mix their labour with. Thus, Locke illustrates, the 'Indians' have property in the fruit and nuts they gather, the wild corn they pick, the fish they catch and the deer they hunt, but not in the land on which they hunt. Moreover, they are free to appropriate things in this way without consent as long as 'there is enough, and as good left in common for others', a condition which is met by their low population density. As a result, they are 'commonly without any *fixed property in the ground*'. By contrast, 'those who are counted the Civiliz'd part of Mankind' 'have multiplied positive laws to determine Property', for 'in Governments the Laws regulate the right of property, and the possession of land is determined by positive constitutions'.[15]

Two immensely influential conclusions follow, according to Locke, from these two features. No one doubts that Europeans who settle in America and the West Indies have the right to wage war 'against the *Indians*, [and] to seek Reparation upon

any injury received from them', without recourse to a constituted political authority. The reason is that, being in the state
of nature, all encounters, such as 'between a *Swiss* and an
Indian, in the Woods of *America*', are dealt with under the law
of nature. Since the Amerindians have no governments to deal
with and no rights in their hunting and gathering territories,
they violate the law of nature when they try to stop Europeans
from settling and planting in America and Europeans, or their
governments, may punish them as 'wild Savage Beasts' who
'may be destroyed as a *Lyon*'. This violent doctrine provided
a major justification for the imperial wars against the
Aboriginal peoples of North America.[16]

Second, Europeans may appropriate land in America
without the consent of the peoples who have lived there for
thousands of years. Since they are in a state of nature, any
person may appropriate uncultivated land without consent as
long as there is enough and as good left in common for others.
Illustrating this famous theory of original appropriation
without consent with examples drawn from America, Locke
concludes:[17]

let him [a European] plant in some in-land, vacant places of *America*,
we shall find that the *Possessions* he could make himself upon the
measures we have given, would not be very large, nor, even to this day,
prejudice the rest of Mankind, or give them reason to complain, or
think themselves injured by this Man's Incroachment.

It might appear from the phrase 'vacant lands' that Locke
means Europeans may cultivate and settle without consent
only in those parts of North America that are not the hunting
and gathering territories of Aboriginal peoples. On this
reading, the 'long use and occupation' of hunting and
gathering territories would give the Aboriginal peoples rights
in, and jurisdiction over their territories, as their defenders
argued. The text does not support this interpretation. It is
designed to subvert it and make Aboriginal rights unrecognisable. Locke stipulates that 'vacant land' is any land that is
'uncultivated' or 'unimproved'. The title to property in land
is solely individual labour, defined in terms specific to

European agriculture: cultivating, tilling, improving and subduing. Hence, land used for hunting and gathering is considered vacant and, as John Cotton concluded fifty years earlier, 'in a vacant soil [*terra nullius*], he that taketh possession of it, and bestoweth culture and husbandry upon it, his right it is'. Consequently, hunters and gatherers possess no rights in lands they have used and occupied for centuries and so have 'no reason to complain or think themselves injured' by European 'incroachment'.[18]

Although these two features of modern constitutionalism vacate America for settlement without consent by removing the sovereignty and property of Aboriginal peoples, Locke must still show that settlement leaves enough and as good in common for others. The reason for this proviso is that if appropriation adversely affects the Aboriginal peoples, their consent would be required, by the oldest convention of constitutionalism: *quod omnes tangit ab omnibus comprobetur* (what touches all should be agreed to by all). Just as Locke bypasses the convention of long use and occupation by invoking a criterion of labour partial to European agriculturalists, he bypasses the convention of *q.o.t.* by an equally biased argument that the Aboriginal people are better off as a result of European settlement. Specifically, they will benefit from assimilation to the more advanced European state of constitutionally protected private property in land and commercial agriculture.

Locke claims that a system of European commerce is superior to the native American Indian system of hunting and gathering and non-sedentary agriculture in three crucial respects. The system of private property and commercial agriculture uses the land more productively, produces more commodities and provides greater opportunities to work by expanding the division of labour. The standard of comparison he uses is the 'Conveniences of life', including both commodities and opportunities to labour, which each system produces. The advanced system of European agriculture, he reckons, uses one-hundredth the amount of land as hunting and gathering to produce the same quantity of goods:[19]

For I aske whether in the wild woods and uncultivated wast of America left to Nature, without any improvement, tillage or husbandry, a thousand acres will yield the needy and wretched inhabitants as many conveniences of life as ten acres of equally fertile land doe in Devonshire where they are well cultivated?

'*Americans*', he explains, 'are rich in Land, and poor in all the Comforts of Life.' Due to the 'want of improving' their land by 'labour', they 'have not one hundredth part of the Conveniences we enjoy'. In fact, a 'King of a large and fruitful Territory there [America], feeds, lodges, and is clad worse than a day Labourer in *England*'. Consequently, the Aboriginal peoples are better off as a result of assimilation to the commercial system for they too share in its greater abundance of commodities and jobs.[20]

It is difficult to overestimate the influence of this economic argument in the justification of planting European constitutional systems of private property and commerce around the world and in justifying the coercive assimilation of Aboriginal and other peoples. Even theorists who believe that Aboriginal peoples have some rights in their territories, contrary to Locke, often argue that they are nevertheless more than compensated for their loss of land by the material abundance and greater productivity of the commercial societies which have displaced theirs. Locke's standard of comparison, 'greater conveniences', in its many reformulations, such as the gross domestic product, is taken for granted as an impartial standard in judging different cultures. Yet it is partial. It measures all systems in terms of the commodities the commercial system delivers, without considering the goods of a steady-state system of replacement production, such as the hunting, gathering and non-commercial agriculture of many Aboriginal peoples of the world. If a dialogue of mutual recognition and fair comparison of the two systems from European and Aboriginal points of view were attempted, then the outcome might well be different, as the Baron de Lahontan suggested in his *Curious dialogues between the author and a savage [Huron] of good sense who has travelled* in 1703, or as

William Cronon and Carolyn Merchant have submitted more recently.

In the *New English Canaan* (1632), Thomas Morton observed first hand that American Indians had few needs, which they were able to satisfy with a minimum of work, leaving them with more leisure time than the colonists. When the colonists claimed that the Indians were poorly clothed, needy and lazy, Morton replied that they should be seen as rich and the colonists poor: 'Now since it is but foode and rayment that we that live needeth . . . why should not the Natives of New England be said to live richly, having no want of either?' Pierre Biard, an early Jesuit in New France, compared Aboriginals and Europeans even more bluntly:[21]

> their [Aboriginals'] days are all nothing but pastime. They are never in a hurry. Quite different from us, who can never do anything without hurry and worry; worry, I say, because our desire tyrannizes over us and banishes peace from our actions.

Locke agrees with these critics that the 'equality of a simple poor way of liveing confine[d] their desires within the narrow bounds of each mans smal propertie' in hunting and gathering societies. This reflects his thesis of cultural relativity that modes of life conform to the stage of historical development. He asks, why 'would a Man value Ten Thousand or an Hundred Thousand Acres of excellent *Land*, ready cultivated, and well stocked to with Cattle, in the middle of in-land Parts of *America*, where he had no hopes of Commerce with other Parts of the World, to draw *Money* to him by the Sale of the Product?' He answers, 'it would not be worth the inclosing'. However, once commerce is introduced, the same person inevitably begins to desire more. 'Find out something that hath the *Use and Value of Money* amongst his Neighbours, you shall see the same Man will begin presently to *enlarge* his *Possessions*.'[22]

This claim that human motivation is transformed by the introduction of a market system of private property so that any person will desire the goods it produces was repeated and established as conventional wisdom a century later by Adam

Smith. However, there is little evidence that the world commercial system causally homogenises the cultural diversity of lower societies that come into its orbit. Aboriginal peoples have interacted with and adapted to commercial trade with Europeans for hundreds of years without desiring to abandon their cultural ways or to identify with the Europeans' uniform institutions of private property and commodity production. The additional coercion of armies, missionaries and governments has not caused them to accept this feature of modern constitutionalism as their own.

The assimilation argument is part of a broader account of the historical development of forms of production and government in chapter 8 of the *Second treatise*. As we have seen, peoples at the earliest stage have limited desires which they satisfy with subsistence hunting and gathering. As a result, they have 'no Temptation to enlarge their Possessions of Land, or contest for wider extend of Ground', and 'so no need of many laws to decide' the 'few controversies' which arise. The *ad hoc* form of individual self government is appropriate to this level of development and there is no need for the institutions of a modern political society. Europeans, by contrast, have gone through the following stages of progress.[23]

The development of money and trade spurs the growth of population and the applied arts. An elastic desire for more than one needs arises, uprooting the pre-monetary economy of limited desires and needs. People seek to enlarge their possessions in order to sell the surplus on the market for a profit. The dynamic productivity of market-oriented labour causes land scarcity and property disputes which cannot be handled by the *ad hoc* system of self government in the state of nature. At this threshold people come together and agree to set up modern constitutional societies, 'uniting into Commonwealths and putting themselves under Government' for the sake of '*the Preservation of their Property*'.[24] Therefore, a constitutional nation state and its defining institutions arise only at the European level of historical development. Given this Eurocentric narrative of modern constitutionalism, it is obvious that Aboriginal peoples do not constitute independent and sovereign nations equal in status to European nations, as they and their defenders contend, but are, as Locke posits at the outset, in a pre-constitutional state of nature.

When Locke directly confronts the claim of Aboriginal sovereignty, he does so within this comprehensive narrative, just as the members of the three schools of modern constitutionalism do today. He acknowledges that some Aboriginal peoples are organised into nations and possess forms of government. Roger Williams had concluded earlier in the century that, since 'the wildest Indians in America agree upon some forms of Government', it follows that 'their civil and earthly governments be as lawfull and true as any government in the World'.[25]

However, as we have seen, the customs by which Aboriginal peoples govern themselves do not count as 'established laws' and cannot be cited as evidence of a constitution. More importantly, Locke argues that their 'kings' are 'little more than *Generals of their armies*' who, although 'they command absolutely in War', in peace time 'they exercise very little dominion, and have but a very moderate Sovereignty, the Resolution of Peace and War, being ordinarily either in the People, or in a Council'. Because Aboriginal governments are an ancient form of direct democracy in which the people do not delegate their powers of war and peace to an institutionalised legislature and executive, as Europeans have done, they are not sovereign. The founding of a modern European constitution and the existence of modern European political institutions are used to define sovereignty and so to dispossess the Aboriginal nations of their equal status.[26]

In summary, Locke's account covers over the real history of the interaction of European imperialism and Aboriginal resistance. The invasion of America, usurpation of Aboriginal nations, theft of the continent, imposition of European economic and political systems, and the steadfast resistance of the Aboriginal peoples are replaced with the captivating picture of the inevitable and benign progress of modern constitutionalism.

Vattel, Kant and their followers

The arguments presented by Locke were widely disseminated throughout the eighteenth and nineteenth centuries to legitimate European imperialism. For example, John Bulkley of Connecticut published 'An inquiry into the right of the aboriginal natives to the land in America' in 1725 to refute the claim advanced by the Mohegan nation that they constitute a sovereign nation under international law. The *Inquiry* is based entirely on Locke's *Two treatises*. In 1758, Emeric de Vattel, in *The law of nations, or the principles of natural law*, one of the most widely cited legal texts in America and now an authoritative text in international law, echoed Locke in his justification of French and British imperialism:[27]

> The cultivation of the soil is an obligation imposed upon man by nature. Every nation is therefore bound by the law of nature to cultivate that land which has fallen to its share. There are others who, in order to avoid labour, seek to live upon their flocks and the fruits of the chase. Now that the human race has multiplied so greatly, it could not subsist if every people wished to live after that fashion. Those who still pursue this idle mode of life occupy more land than they would have need of under a system of honest labour, and they may not complain if other, more industrious nations, too confined at home, should come and occupy parts of their lands. [W]hen the nations of Europe come upon lands which the savages have no special need of, and are making no present and continuous use of, they may lawfully take possession of them and establish colonies in them.

As the details of Locke's arguments were taken up, debated and altered by the modern theorists of the Scottish and French Enlightenments, the comprehensive vision the arguments uphold came to be the unquestioned framework of the debate. The legitimacy of European settlement and dispossession was assured. When theorists of what John Pocock calls the competing traditions of rights, virtues and manners debated the nature of modern constitutional societies in terms of Locke's rights-bearing and industrious labourers, James Harrington's virtuous republicans and Adam Smith's polished commercialists, they gave the implantation of European

institutions and traditions of interpretation the impression of
historical inevitability, for all three conceptions of modern
constitutionalism are defined in contrast to, and in super-
cession of, the Aboriginal peoples they displaced in practice –
the propertyless and wasteful hunter gatherer, the vicious
savage and the rude native respectively. Even if one looks on
Aboriginal peoples with admiration in this framework, as
Rousseau and Samuel Johnson did, the only available attitude
is nostalgia and regret for their inevitable passing.

The features of modern constitutionalism were also
accepted by Immanuel Kant, who is often seen as founding an
independent tradition of liberal political theory. In *An idea for
a universal history with a cosmopolitan intent* (1784) and *Towards
perpetual peace* (1795), Kant argues that humanity can achieve
full moral progress and freedom only after commerce and
republican constitutions are spread around the world.
Although there are important differences between Kant's
concept of a republican constitution and Locke's concept of a
modern political society, they are both defined by characteristically European features: the institutionalised rule of law
and representative government. Once these threshold institutions of civilisation are established, Kant explains, progress
towards moral freedom occurs by means of the mechanism of
'unsocial sociability'. Markets and republican constitutions
constrain self-interested individuals to co-operate with others
in order to satisfy their desires for more than they need for
bare subsistence.[28]

A republican constitution is defined in contrast to the
customs of Aboriginal peoples. The uncivilised hunting and
gathering peoples of America, Kant argues, lack a constitution, government and property because they have not
made the transition to a life of agriculture. In their pre-
constitutional state of nature they have a 'lawless freedom of
hunting, fishing and herding', which, 'of all forms of life is
without doubt most contrary to a civilised constitution'. Agriculture, commerce and finally republican constitutions are
brought to these uncivilised people by European wars and
commercial expansion. Kant condemns the excesses of

European imperial wars, especially outright conquest, and prefers expansion by trade, economic sanctions and diplomacy. Yet he none the less commends the spread of European markets and constitutions because they provide the threshold for moral progress, stating that is is 'our duty to work towards bringing about this goal'.[29]

Kant's justification of constitutional imperialism is quite similar to Locke's natural right to punish the Aboriginal people who violate natural law by resisting the Europeans who take their land. His third definitive article of perpetual peace, which he proposed for international law, is 'the right of hospitality'. It gives Europeans the right to engage in commerce with Aboriginal peoples and European nations the right to defend their traders if the Aboriginal peoples are so inhospitable as to deny the right. 'In this way', Kant concludes, 'distant parts of the world can establish with one another peaceful relations that will eventually become matters of public law, and the human race can gradually be brought closer and closer to a cosmopolitan constitution.' The non-European peoples of the world will be recognised as equals only once they have abandoned their lawless ways and submitted to European markets and republican constitutions.[30]

Many more examples could be given. In 'Superior people: the narrowness of liberalism from Mill to Rawls', Bhikhu Parekh elucidates how these conventions inform Mill's political theory and his justification of British rule and cultural assimilation in India and Québec. Whereas Locke, Kant and Mill at least presented arguments to answer the claims of non-European peoples to constitutional recognition, contemporary theorists of modern constitutionalism tend to take their conclusions for granted as authoritative premises and traditions of interpretation, without even asking if they might misrecognise the claims of others. For example, original contract theories simply overlook the presence of Aboriginal constitutions. This is obvious in theories which start from a Lockean state of nature or individual self-ownership, such as Robert Nozick's *Anarchy, state and utopia*. But it is no less true in theories which start from a more Kantian premise, such as John Rawls' *A theory of justice*, as Vernon Van Dyke has pointed out.

In the last decade, Rawls has suggested that his theory can be seen in a slightly different way, as a theory within an authoritative set of institutions and traditions of interpretation in North America. The institutions and traditions derive from post-Reformation European constitutional democracy: toleration, the rule of law, representative government, markets and individual rights. The role of the theorist is to articulate 'the basic intuitive ideas that are embedded in the political institutions of a constitutional democratic regime and the public traditions of their interpretation'.[31] This move posits Kant's modern, threshold institutions and their traditions of interpretation, which comprise the conventions of modern constitutionalism, as the authoritative framework for constitutional theory and practice. The independent institutions and traditions of the Aboriginal nations, which pre-exist Rawls' authoritative institutions and traditions by hundreds of years, are either ignored or, at best, imperiously discussed within the very uncosmopolitan institutions and conventions that have been forged to assimilate them.

To presuppose that the initial conditions of popular sovereignty are a state of nature, a veil of ignorance, a set of European traditions and institutions, or an already existing national community is to beg the question of the politics of recognition. It dispossesses Aboriginal peoples of their constitutions and authoritative traditions without so much as a hearing and inscribes them within the Eurocentric conventions of modern constitutionalism.

The reform of diversity in Europe and the colonies

The seven features of modern constitutionalism have also served to undermine cultural diversity within European societies. The vision of modern constitutionalism legitimates the modernising processes of discipline, rationalisation and state building that are designed to create in practice the cultural and institutional uniformity identified as modern in theory. These processes include the construction of centralised and uniform constitutional systems over the legal and political pluralism of early modern Europe, the implantation of similar systems by European colonisation, the extension of these by post-colonial states over Indigenous populations and customary law, the imposition of linguistic and cultural uniformity, and countless programmes of naturalisation, assimilation and eugenics to construct modern states and subjects.

The first way the empire of uniformity is established in theory is the premise that the sovereign people who establish the constitution are already culturally indifferent members of one society who aim to set up a regular constitutional association with a single locus of sovereignty. This was a fiction of the early modern theorists, as Hugo Grotius exposed in his survey of the diversity of existing constitutions, designed to ensure in theory the consolidation of early modern states that they wished to promote in practice. Leibniz replied to Hobbes and Pufendorf in 1677 that no known political society exhibited the cultural and institutional uniformity that they took for granted. Matthew Hale in England and Montesquieu in France upheld the authority of the diverse customs of their irregular realms. But these voices, barely heard today, were drowned out by the ascendancy of uniformity.

Consequently, within the dominant language of modern constitutionalism it is difficult to conceptualise the sovereign people as already constituted in customary ways by the authority of their different cultures because culture is conceived as relative to a stage of historical development, not as various within a society. It is even more difficult to conceptualise the people as agreeing to establish a constitutional association that recognises and accommodates cultural diversity by arrangements of legal and political pluralism so that citizens can relate to government in culturally different ways or participate in different political institutions. It is taken for granted that the unity of constitutional association consists in a centralised and uniform system of legal and political authority, or clear subordination of authorities, to which all citizens are subject in the same way, and from which all authority derives.

A federation or an association that has grown up over time with a variety of customary authorities and no single locus of ultimate authority was seen as weak, incoherent and prone to civil war and dissolution, as Hobbes classically argued in *Leviathan* in 1651. In 1673 Pufendorf labelled such ancient constitutional associations, which included almost all the early modern nations of Europe, 'irregular' and 'monstrous' deviations from the modern norm of uniformity:

An irregular form of government [*respublica irregularis*] is one in which we do not find that unity which is the essence of a state so completely established, not because of a disease or fault in the administration of the country, but because the irregularity of its form has been as it were legitimated by public law and custom.

After his influential attack, it is rare to find a major theorist who does not subscribe to the view that 'the unity which is the essence' of a modern constitutional state consists in a single and clearly ordered system of institutions and laws, emanating from a supreme legislature or executive, which is '*anhupeunthunos* or unaccountable'.[32]

In presenting the definitive case for uniformity, Pufendorf gave the following, remarkably generous definition of the irregular ancient constitutions of existing societies he sought to discredit and to encourage state builders to reform:

the parts of supreme sovereignty are dividedly and independently in the hands of different persons and bodies of the same common-wealth, in such a way that each of them holds that part which they possess in their own right and administer it according to their own judgement, but in respect of the other parts of sovereignty, [they] are like subjects.

His point was to show that this kind of multiformity was incompatible with the modern, unified conception of a sovereign state that he and Hobbes aimed to vindicate, and therefore a thing of the past. 'The essentials of a perfect and regular state require', he asserted, 'that in it there be such a union as makes everything which works to its administration appear to come, as it were, from one soul.' Although other modern theorists of constitutionalism such as Locke and

Rousseau disagreed with Pufendorf in many respects, they agreed on the unity of the soul of modern constitutional states. In the legislature, Locke writes, 'the Members of a Commonwealth are united, and combined together into one coherent living body. This *is the Soul that gives Form, Life, and Unity* to the Commonwealth.'[33]

In *The declaration of the rights of man and citizen* of 1789, the seven features of modern constitutionalism are gathered together in an exemplary form, providing the classic image of modern constitution for the constitutional movements of the nineteenth and twentieth centuries. A constitution is presented as a written document which creates the foundations of government *de novo* by an act of the sovereign will and reason of the people, without any reference to the customs and ways in which the people are constituted. The first two articles of *The declaration* declare that society is composed solely of free and equal male citizens with rights. The only noteworthy political difference among them is their usefulness to the public. Article 3 states that 'sovereignty resides essentially in the nation'. This has been interpreted in two ways since 1789: either as a nation of sovereign individuals with rights, as in article 1, or as the collective nation of the nationalist and communitarian traditions. Citizens set up and govern themselves by representative institutions which are, as article 6 states, 'the same for all'. A society which lacks these modern features, article 16 declares, 'has no constitution at all'.[34]

The declaration is the result of debates in the National Assembly over the summer of 1789 in which the proposals of Sieyès won out over those of Jean-Joseph Mounier. Sieyès' critics agreed that the ancient constitution of the three estates of France (clergy, nobility and third estate) had been eroded by the processes of modernisation over the previous century and formally abolished on 17 June 1789 when the third estate declared itself the 'National Assembly': that is, the representative body of the nation as a whole. Notwithstanding, they argued that France continued to be constituted by laws and customs into a confederation of regions. Any written constitution had to recognise and accommodate itself to this ancient constitutional diversity. This way of thinking about constitutionalism extends back to Claude de Seyssel, Louis le Roy and Michel de Montaigne. The proponents in the National Assembly drew their inspiration from the most famous theory in the tradition, the constitutional 'associationalism', as Rebecca Kingston aptly calls it, of Montesquieu's *The spirit of the laws* (1748).

The defenders of the ancient constitution claimed that the members of the National Assembly were not representatives of some abstract and hypothetical society of individuals, but *mandataires* from the various regions, bound to bring forward the regional grievances and visions of the confederation of their constituents as expressed in the *cahiers de doléances* (notebooks of grievances) of their regions, as had been done at every constitutional assembly since the fifteenth century. Sieyès and his followers overcame this confederal view of the people by arguing that, although the members of a constitutional assembly are elected by districts, each member represents all districts and must subordinate the particular will of his constituents to the general will of the nation, or no unity will emerge. The members are 'representatives of the people' as a whole.

Moreover, the very idea of an 'ancient' constitution of the existing customs and ways of the people, which the written constitution must recognise, was effaced in *The declaration* by the modern concept of a constitution brought into being by the will of the homogeneous people in accord with abstract principles. This concept was enunciated in the article on constitutions in the second edition of the *Encyclopedia* (1780). An entire chapter of Vattel's *On the laws of nations* is reprinted and 'constitution' is defined as the 'fundamental regulation that determines the manner in which public authority is exercised'.[35] This Roman or 'imposition' concept of a constitution, similar to Paine's, was also available in the influential editions of Pufendorf's *On the law of nature and nations* edited by Jean Barbeyrac. Jean-Nicholas Démeunier, in his article on constitutions in the *Methodical encyclopedia* of 1784, also repeated Vattel's definition and illustrated it with examples of the constitutions of the American colonies. Once Sieyès and his followers established this concept as authoritative, the existing constitution of the followers of Montesquieu disappeared from view.

Finally, the most powerful argument advanced by Sieyès was that the diverse regional customs and ways of France were being swept away in practice as the unintended consequence of progressive historical development. Modern European societies were becoming a clean state of individuals with universal rights, manners and interests, and with uniform representative institutions as the sole legitimate form of government. Each modern theorist had a slightly different theory of how progress unintentionally grinds moderns politically uniform, but the key causal factors, as we have already seen in Locke's theory, are commerce and the division of labour. Where Le Roy and his followers had seen 'the diversity or variety of things in the universe', Sieyès, following Smith, saw a one-dimensional order:[36]

Modern European peoples bear scarcely any resemblance to ancient ones. Amongst us it is a question solely of commerce, agriculture, manufacture, etc. The desire for wealth seems to make all the states of Europe into nothing other than immense workshops . . . Political systems too are today founded exclusively on work; the productive faculties of man are everything . . . We are thus compelled to regard the greater part of humanity as nothing other than work machines.

Most of the modern theorists did not believe that cultural diversity would disappear solely by the unintended consequences of progress. They also held that it is the duty of a modern constitutional government to assist the process with an unhidden hand and ensure in practice the consequences they predicted in theory. They put forward policies to break down the anachronistic customs of backward citizens and immigrants and reform them so that they acquired the manners and policy of a civilised and enlightened age. This aspect of constitutionalism was discussed in terms of 'sociability', the concept Pufendorf introduced to describe the habits and dispositions which render a person a 'fit member' of a modern society. The innumerable policies they recommended were designed to forge citizens who not only possessed the 'cosmopolitan' identity common to any 'republican constitution', but also the distinct national identity of their particular 'nation'.

The policies of making modern subjects fit members of nations, classically studied by Max Weber, Gerhard Oestreich and Michel Foucault, rely on a distinctly modern concept of custom. As Richard Tuck has shown in his magisterial study of European political thought from 1550 to 1650, the 'reason of state' writers first turned to the problem of reforming the customs of the 'masses' to make them productive and disciplined members of modern European states which, in turn, were regarded as locked in an international competition over the control and exploitation of the non-European world. The concept of custom that came to be widely accepted by the late seventeenth century was formulated by Locke in *An essay concerning human understanding* (1690), *Thoughts concerning education* (1694) and his proposal for the reform of the English poor law and workhouse system (1697). Custom is conceived as the habitual ways of thinking, speaking and behaving that are implanted in a person by the constant repetition of any way of thinking, speaking and behaving one wishes to instil. An individual, Locke writes, is 'only as white paper or wax, to be moulded and fashioned as one pleases' by 'use and practice'. 'Custom', he concludes, 'settles habits of Thinking in the Understanding, as well as Determining in the Will, and of Motions in the Body; all which seems to be but Trains of Motion in the Animal Spirits, which once set a going continue on the same steps they have been used to, which by often treading are worn into a smooth path, and the Motion in it becomes easy and as it were Natural.'[37]

Custom or culture is not, henceforth, the authoritative expression of the agreement of the people, whose consent is required for its amendment, but the *de facto* habits acquired by engaging in the practices and institutions of one's society, from the most primitive and least reflective to the most civilised and enlightened (as we saw in an earlier quotation from Locke). As Pierre Nicole wrote and Locke translated from the French:[38]

> If one takes a general Survey of the World, one shall find the Bulk of Mankind buried in a Stupidity so gross, that if it does not wholly dispossess them of their Reason, yet it leaves them so little Use of it, that one cannot but wonder how the Soul can be depressed into so low a Degree of Brutality. What does a *Canibal, Iroquoi, Brasilian, Negro, Cafer, Groenlander, or Laplander* think on during his whole life? The ordinary wants of the Body, and some dull ways of supplying them, Fishing and Hunting, Dancing, and Revenge on his Enemies, is the whole Compass of his Contemplations.

Accordingly, to prepare people for the superior life of a modern constitutional nation it is necessary and beneficial to break down their ancient cultural ways and instil modern ones through repetitive drills and exercises in schools, factories, prisons and armies. The Dutch army reforms of the mid-sixteenth century provided an important model for later reforms. The complex tasks of soldiering were broken down into a succession of minute and detailed behavioural movements. A raw recruit was put through repetitive exercises and drills of these movements until he became an habitual soldier. Techniques like these were applied in workhouses and schools to reform the children of the poor and immigrants throughout Europe. By the repetition and discipline of simple tasks from an early age, children can be 'inured to labour, which', Locke continues, 'is of no small consequence to the making of them sober and industrious all their lives'.[39]

Historians such as Linda Colley, in her study of Britishness, *Britons: the forging of a nation, 1707–83*, have shown how these techniques of reform have been integrated into broader policies by every modern nation to manufacture a homogeneous national identity. They were also employed throughout the colonies to reduce the primitive customs of lower peoples and gradually civilise them in the superior ways of the imperial societies. The model for these colonial policies was often the violent conquest and reduction of Ireland and the later clearance of the Scottish Highlands in the eighteenth century. The experience gained in hunting and subduing these 'wild beasts' was then applied in the colonies to Aboriginal and African Americans, as ethnohistorians James Axtell and Francis Jennings have traced in detail. Daniel N. Paul, a Mi'kmaq historian, sums up this research in the title of his recent study, *We were not the savages*. Theodore Allen and Ronald Takaki have reconstructed how the dominant white culture was moulded and passed off as universal and superior in colonial America at the same time as African American, Hispanic American and Aboriginal national identities were broken down and degraded. The vote was withheld from Aboriginal peoples and non-European immigrants in Canada and the United States until this century, when they were considered fit and the empire of the dominant institutions and traditions was beyond question. In *Torture and modernity*, Darius Rejali has studied how the imperial techniques of discipline and reform were applied in Iran and Arturo Escobar has discussed their dissemination, and resistance to them, throughout the Third World.

The experience of Aboriginal peoples in Canada at the hands of administrators, missionaries and educators is typical of reform movements throughout the British empire in the nineteenth and twentieth centuries. In 1857 the Act for the Gradual Civilization of the Indians Tribes of the Canadas was enacted to destroy their ways and to assimilate them completely to European ways by inculcating habits of speech, labour, private property and religion. For, as Hobbes had explained, although the colonists have the right to make war on the Indigenous peoples, because they live in a state of war of all against all, 'they are not to exterminate those they find there; but constrain them to inhabit closer together, and not range a great deal of ground, to snatch what they find; but to court each little Plot with art and labour, to give them their sustenance in due season'.[40] When these reforms failed, they were succeeded by a more comprehensive policy, The Indian Act of 1876. The act, which has survived a century of reforms, is a vast administrative dictatorship which governs every detail of Aboriginal life. The entire regime was imposed without the consent of Aboriginal peoples.

Although these coercive techniques met with resistance and failure, the administrators and theorists persisted. From within the parameters of modern constitutionalism, they saw themselves as enlightened guardians who were preparing lower, childlike and pre-consensual peoples for a superior, modern life; in this way they could regard the destruction of other cultures with moral approval. This kind of cultural imperialism continues, as we shall see, in the current view that assimilation to the dominant culture serves to provide a superior cultural context in which members of 'minorities' can better exercise their freedom of choice in modern societies.

The American revolution and the guardians of empire today

Many more examples could be given of the different ways European women and non-European women and men were first excluded from, and then later assimilated to, modern constitutionalism. However, to round off this chapter, allow me to return to Thomas Paine. In *Common sense* (1776) and *The rights of man* (1790–2), he set out a classic theory of the modern constitution. As McIlwain highlighted, its picture of an undiverse sovereign people and uniform institutions has become a universal norm to which demands for constitutional recognition must conform if they are to be taken seriously. Yet to accept it uncritically as an impartial standard is to fail to do justice to two alternative traditions of constitutionalism Paine opposed.

First, the argument of Thomas Jefferson in the Declaration of Independence (1776) is that sovereignty would devolve to the people as members of the thirteen states after the war of independence. Since the people had governed themselves through their colonial assemblies for a century, the new republic would be a confederation of thirteen sovereign states, *ex uno plures*, each continuing their ancient constitutions and ways, as he had explained earlier in *A summary view of the rights of British America* (1775). This confederal or 'anti-federalist' constitution (as it is called in contrast to the centralised federalism of the *Federalist papers* of 1788) was provisionally established in the Articles of Confederation of 1778 (arguably partially modelled on the oldest living constitutional confederation on Great Turtle Island: the *Haudenosaunee* or Iroquois Confederation).

In the final constitutional settlement of 1787, the anti-federalist constitution was defeated and that of Paine and the *Federalist papers* was victorious. The new constitution, which was passed without the consent of the people in all the state legislatures, established the Continental Congress, and so the federal government, as the body which represents the sovereignty of the undifferentiated people of all the states. In his pamphlet of 1781, the *Public good*, Paine demonstrates how his general theory vindicates the sovereignty of the Continental Congress over the states. He contends that sovereignty did not devolve from the Crown to the recognition of the sovereignty of pre-existing state legislatures, but directly to the Continental Congress, as the legitimate representative of all the people, to which the states are subordinate.

The reason why Paine pressed this argument lies in the subtitle of the *Public good*: *an examination into the claims of Virginia to the vacant western territory, and the right of the United States to the same.* He was a shareholder in the Indiana Company, a land speculation company which laid claim to vast tracts of land in the Ohio Valley to the west of Virginia. Virginia claimed jurisdiction over these lands by virtue of its colonial charter and the assertion of its sovereignty by Jefferson served to protect Virginian land speculators against the competing claims of the Indiana Company. By locating sovereignty in the federal government, directly representing the people, Paine ensured that the Congress, and not Virginia or any other state, had jurisdiction over the western lands, thereby vindicating the claim of the Indiana Company. The claim of Virginia to sovereignty over western territory by devolution and the continuity of its ancient constitution, he asserts, was either fictitious to begin with or discontinued by the war of independence.

The error in accepting Paine's theory as authoritative is not, let me emphasise, that it overrules the absurd land claim of Virginia or the later claims of the slave-owning states to autonomy. These unilateral claims would be properly defeated by the first step of mutual recognition in any fair constitutional dialogue. Rather, the error is to accept a partial framework in which the anti-federalist tradition of interpretation and its two hundred years of demands for recognition – from the popular opposition of the 1780s to abolitionists, suffragettes, labourites, African Americans and the politics of cultural recognition today – cannot be given a fair hearing. It presumes what the anti-federalists challenge: that *e pluribus unum* is the only form of association.

Second, as Robert Williams demonstrates in *The American Indian in Western legal discourse*, Paine does not satisfactorily explain how the United States acquired sovereignty over the 'vacant' western territories. The Ohio Valley and all of America west of the thirteen colonies were occupied by Aboriginal nations. The Shawnee and Delaware persistently denied that either the United States or the individual states had sovereignty over their independent nations. The Cayuga, Seneca, Oneida, Onondaga, Mohawk and Tuscarora nations of the Iroquois Confederation sought recognition as sovereign nations time after time. From the Creek, Choctaw, Chickasaw and Cherokee nations in the south to the Ottawa and Wyandot in the north, the Aboriginal peoples fought as nations against the invasion of their territories. The Cherokee later drew up their constitution and petitioned to be admitted as an independent state in the new Union. Yet, in the *Public good*, the sovereignty of the United States is said to extend over their 'vacant' territory without so much as a mention of their existence or their claims to recognition.

The authors of the *Federalist papers* present a constitutional theory similar to Paine's. John Jay observes in the second paper, presumably in one of his more short-sighted moments, that the American people are culturally homogeneous by ancestry and the experience of war:[41]

Providence has been pleased to give this one connected country to
one united people – a people descended from the same ancestors,
speaking the same language, professing the same religion, attached
to the same principles of government, very similar in their manners
and customs, and who, by their joint counsels, arms, and efforts,
fighting side by side throughout a long and bloody war, have nobly
established their general liberty and independence.

It follows in the next seven papers that a uniform federation
with a sovereign federal government is the appropriate form
of constitution. Any form of confederation that recognises
constitutive differences and aspects of co-ordinate sovereignty
among the states will lead inevitably to internal dissension
and disunity, and so to weakness in the face of the republic's
enemies. Hence, the federalist constitution is identified with
a *'united America'* and the anti-federalists with a *'disunited
America'*.[42]

A prime example of the disunity that is sure to come with
any other form of association, Madison later amplified, is foreshadowed in the contentions of the sovereign states over their
competing claims to the western lands under the Articles of
Confederation. The solution is to realise, as does Paine, that
jurisdiction over the western lands passed to the Congress
after victory over the British, and they became, in Hamilton's
phrase, 'the common property of the Union'. Only a constitution in which this power is lodged in a central authority
will enable the union to overcome what Madison calls the
'perplexity and contention' and so deal with 'the savage tribes
on our Western frontier', who, Hamilton writes, 'ought to be
regarded as our natural enemies'.[43]

Once a constitution modelled on the theories of Paine and
the *Federalist papers* was established in 1787, it provided a
'license for empire' over the Aboriginal territories as the
United States expanded westward.[44] Various justifications
were advanced for the removal, assimilation or extermination
of the Aboriginal peoples in what Richard Slotkin calls
Regeneration through violence, Roy Harvey Pearce, *Savagism and
civilization* and Richard Van Alstyne, *The rising American empire*:
the right of conquest, Lockean arguments, treaties, the

superiority of a modern society or simply manifest destiny. These arguments and policies tended to take place within the undoubted *imperium* of the constitution and its modern conventions for, as we have seen, the Aboriginal peoples had already been dispossessed and debased within them. In the most authoritative document of the new republic, the Declaration of Independence, Jefferson recognised the Aboriginal nations on the frontiers as 'the merciless Indian Savages, whose known rule of warfare, is an undistinguished destruction of all ages, sexes and condition'.[45] This had been, as you will recall, the language used to justify war since the time of Locke.

As the 'fraud, politics, and the dispossession of the Indians' unfolded in the wars of expansion of the 1780s,[46] Thayendanegea (Joseph Brant), a Mohawk leader, saw his homeland invaded, burnt and occupied and the Iroquois Confederation attacked, divided and driven into exile in Canada. At roughly the midpoint of the destruction, 1786, Thomas Eddy, a commissioner of Indian Affairs, wrote to Brant to ask if 'civilization is favourable to human happiness', pointing out that there are 'degrees of civilization', from 'Cannibals to the most polite of European nations'.

Brant replies that he was born and raised 'among those whom you are pleased to call savages'. He reminds Eddy that he had been educated in the classics at Moor's Charity School (now Dartmouth College) and had travelled extensively in America and Europe, meeting the great leaders of the civilised world. Nevertheless, 'after all this experience, and after every exertion to divest myself of prejudice, I am obliged to give my opinion in favour of my own people'. The reason for this is, 'in the governments you call civilized, the happiness of the people is constantly sacrificed to the splendor of empire'.

Brant illustrates his thesis by surveying the major institutions of European and European–American societies and comparing them with the ways of Aboriginal societies. Although Aboriginal peoples lack many of the institutions Europeans exalt as the marks of civility – 'no prisons', 'no pompous parade of courts', 'no written laws' – justice is 'as much regarded' and citizens perform 'brave and worthy' actions in service to their 'nation'. He finds himself obliged to reverse the conventional Eurocentric judgement in every comparison. The reason why happiness is sacrificed to empire in European societies, he explains, is that liberty, which exceeds property 'as the light of the sun does that of the most twinkling star', is placed on the same level as property, 'to the everlasting disgrace of civilization'. As a result, 'the estates of widows and orphans' are 'devoured by sharpers' and, as he well knew, 'robbery takes place under the colour of law'.

More fundamentally, the elevation of property in order to drive the expansion of empire requires an undergirding institution incompatible with liberty and unknown to Aboriginal societies: the prison, and especially long and cruel imprisonment for debt. 'Here', he exclaims, 'description utterly fails.' 'But for what are many of your prisoners confined? – for debt! – astonishing! – and will you ever again call the Indian nations cruel?' 'Cease, too', he concludes, 'to call other nations savage, when you are tenfold more the children of cruelty than they.'[47]

In conclusion, the language of modern constitutionalism that has been forged in constitutional theory and practice over the last three hundred years is a partial forgery. While masquerading as universal it is imperial in three respects: in serving to justify European imperialism, imperial rule of former colonies over Indigenous peoples, and cultural imperialism over the diverse citizens of contemporary societies. When members of the authoritative schools today write about constitutionalism, whether they claim to be universal, historical or transcendental, they do so within the conventions of universality, history and transcendence of this captivating map of mankind. They (and this often includes myself) think that they are tracing the contours of humanity's constitutions, yet they are merely tracing round the 'splendorous' frame through which they look at them.

In his 'On ethnocentrism: a reply to Clifford Geertz',

Richard Rorty writes that the tasks of a liberal democracy are 'divided between the agents of love and the agents of justice'. The agents of love are the 'connoisseurs of diversity' who 'insist that there are people . . . whom society has failed to notice'. Their job is to make these 'candidates for admission visible' by showing that their odd behaviour, currently regarded as 'stupidity, baseness, madness' and the like, can be seen as unfamiliar but none the less 'coherent'. The agents of justice are the 'guardians of universality' who ensure that once these people 'have been shepherded into the light by the connoisseurs of diversity, they are treated just like all the rest of us'.[48]

I have tried to suggest in this chapter that this well-meaning response is inadequate and more than a little threatening from the perspective of those of us who are to be 'shepherded'. To treat the candidates for admission 'just like all the rest of us' is not to treat them justly at all. It is to treat them within the imperial conventions and institutions that have been constructed to exclude, dominate, assimilate or exterminate them, thereby ignoring the question the politics of recognition raises concerning the universality of the guardians and the institutions they guard.

Many communitarian and critical theorists are no less imperious. When they ask the crucial question of 'whose justice?' and 'which rationality?' the answers are always the same: some European, male traditions of interpretation set within the stages view of intellectual history; never a dialogue with any of the non-European traditions set within non-European views of history, that have been authoritative for millennia in the very places where they write their books. A change in Greek syntax from Homer to Aristotle or a change in the Scottish university curriculum in the seventeenth century appears to be of utmost significance. The long contests of Aboriginal and non-Aboriginal cultures and of all the other non-authoritative traditions and their histories that have been fought on the ground they occupy and have shaped the society in which they live, go unnoticed and forgotten.[49]

This is the tyrannical blindness of Oedipus and the injustice of Creon, of refusing to heed Tiresias and hear the claims of others in their own voices and cultural ways. It precludes the first post-imperial step of mutual recognition we need to take on board *The spirit of Haida Gwaii*: *audi alteram partem*.

Despite all the attempts to grind cultural diversity uniform, its wonderful multiplicity has remained, as the passengers of the black canoe are here to remind us. For the cultural diversity modern constitutionalism tries to efface in theory and reform in practice is not the epiphenomenal mask of underlying and allegedly universal processes and interests, as the modern theorists followed Bernard Mandeville in claiming. This is modern constitutionalism's imperial fable. Rather, cultural diversity is the living face of human beings. In the next chapter, we shall turn to the kind of constitutionalism that developed in encounters where the agents of justice recognised and sought to accommodate this constitutive aspect of the human condition.

CHAPTER 4

The historical formation of common constitutionalism: the rediscovery of cultural diversity, part I

The hidden constitutions of contemporary societies

In this chapter I approach the labyrinth of contemporary constitutionalism by another path; from the perspective of the struggles to gain recognition of diverse cultures over the last four centuries. In the course of these intercultural encounters, contemporary constitutionalism has been shaped in various aspects to recognise and accommodate cultural diversity. Specifically, the three conventions of the common language of constitutionalism arose in these contests. Of course, modern constitutionalism continues to reign in its imperial splendour, but the aspects I will now sketch are not simply minor disturbances on the frontier of modern constitutionalism, destined to disappear as it progresses. They only appear that way from its perspective. That is 'the thing about progress', Nestroy discerned over a century ago, 'it appears much greater than it actually is'.[1]

The recognition and accommodation of cultural diversity in the broader language of contemporary constitutionalism discloses what might be called the 'hidden constitutions of contemporary societies'. They are hidden by the rule of modern constitutionalism and the narrow range of uses of its central terms. As contemporary societies begin to enter a post-imperial age, a vast undergrowth of cultural diversity and its partial recognition in constitutions has begun to come to light as the shadow of the imperial epoch begins to recede. This discovery flies in the face of the seven features of modern constitutionalism: diversity is not a thing of the past, it does not conform to the stages view of historical development and modern constitutionalism did not trickle down unchanged from the European centre to the non-European periphery.

The first sites where hidden constitutions appear are in the writings and constitutional arrangements of the agents of justice who have sought to come to terms with powerful, non-European cultures, immigrants, women and linguistic and national minorities fighting for cultural survival. On the inter-cultural common grounds between the relentless momentum of modern constitutionalism and the tenacity of other cultures one finds 'contrapuntal ensembles' of three conventions which facilitate the recognition and accommodation of cultural diversity. No doubt, these grounds are deeply distorted by relations of domination and inequality and shot through with broken promises and fraudulent designs. Yet for all that, they are places where ancient reluctant conscripts have said 'enough', stood their ground or taken the ruins of their culture with them in exile, and so bent the yoke of constitutionalism to fit their diverse necks.

The second places where hidden constitutions have been discovered are in the applications of constitutional law in particular cases, especially but not exclusively in the common law of Commonwealth countries and international law. This 'casuistry' of cultural differences and similarities is a remark-able aspect of contemporary jurisprudence. Rather than forcing citizens and institutions to fit the uniform of modern constitutionalism, the language of constitutionalism has been shaped to fit the cultural diversity of citizens and institutions in practice. To put this in a slightly different way, the genres or forms of reasoning developed in the common law to deal with the customary diversity of the ancient constitutions of pre-modern European societies did not disappear with the rise of modern constitutionalism. They have continued to evolve in practice, and others have been added, despite the official view in theory that they should have been replaced by the more abstract form of reasoning typical of the modern theorists.

The discovery of these two aspects of contemporary consti-tutionalism was marked by the establishment in the 1980s of a new interdisciplinary field of anthropology, history, law and political philosophy called legal pluralism. Legal pluralism is the study of the variety of ways contemporary constitutions recognise and accommodate cultural diversity. It began with the discovery by Clifford Geertz, Sally Falk Moore and others that post-colonial societies are constituted by a wide variety of legal and customary systems of authority that cannot be accurately represented in the language of modern constitutionalism. Scholars such as Roderick MacDonald, Jon Elster and John Griffiths then turned their attention to modern European societies and discovered a variety of normative orders and ways of accommodating struggles for recognition that exist in practice despite the reign of modern constitutionalism. As a result, Clifford Geertz and the many scholars who have been moved by his long and involved journeys have begun to explore the post-imperial landscape of cultures and constitutions which I introduced in the first chapter.

Permit me to frame my survey of the hidden constitutions with two images of constitutionalism. The first comes from René Descartes at the beginning of modern constitutionalism. Descartes is often thought of, especially in this century, as almost the founder of the kind of reform and rationalisation that drives the classic vision of modern constitutionalism. Yet nothing could be further from the truth. In the *Discourse on the method*, he goes out of the way to show that the kind of radical reform he advocates for his own thoughts should be contrasted with his attitude towards constitutional change. He writes that, at first sight, thorough and systematic reform in accord with a central plan appears more reasonable than adjustment and accommodation to the assemblage of customs and laws that already exist:

Thus we see that buildings undertaken and completed by a single architect are usually more attractive and better planned than those which several have tried to patch up by adapting old walls built for different purposes. Again, ancient cities which have gradually grown from mere villages into large towns are usually ill-proportioned, compared with those orderly towns which planners lay out as they fancy on level ground. Looking at the buildings of the former individually, you will often find as much art in them, if not more than in those of the latter; but in view of their arrangement – a tall one here, a small one there – and the way they make the streets crooked and irregular, you would say it is chance, rather than the will of men using reason, that placed them so.

The presumption of reform and regularisation in accord with a single plan is further enforced by the vision of Christianity, for 'the constitution of the true religion, whose articles have been made by God alone, must be incomparably better ordered than all the others'. Furthermore, he writes, we tend to favour reform and uniformity because we have the image of classical political philosophy before our eyes, in which 'the basic laws [are] laid down by some wise law-giver'. Moreover, this classical ideal is further reinforced by the image of Sparta, which is admired 'because [all the laws] were devised by a single man and hence all tended to the same end'.

Yet, for all that, 'we never see people pulling down all the houses of a city for the sole purpose of rebuilding them in a different style to make the streets more attractive'. And, Descartes goes on to infer that it would be 'unreasonable for an individual to plan to reform a state by changing it from the foundations up and overturning it in order to set it up again'. He therefore concludes that in politics it is better to accommodate the assemblage of customs and ways of the people than to radically reform them:[2]

Any imperfections [political associations] may possess – and their very diversity suffices to ensure that many do possess them – have doubtless been much smoothed over by custom; and custom has even prevented or imperceptibly corrected many imperfections that prudence could not so well provide against. Finally, it is almost always easier to put up with their imperfections than to change them, just as it is much better to follow the main roads that wind through mountains, which have gradually become smooth and convenient through frequent use, than to try to take a more direct route by clambering over rocks and descending to the foot of precipices.

You will say that these are 'reactionary' reasons for accommodating diversity, whereas my first chapter made the politics of cultural recognition look 'progressive'. My response is to say that the uses of the terms 'reactionary' and 'progressive' here are fixed by the seven features of the language of modern constitutionalism I am trying to question in this book. In chapter 6, I will discuss ways of conceiving diversity and reasons for affirming it other than those advanced by Descartes.

What would Descartes' picture of the constitution of a city look like after three hundred years of modern constitutionalism? The answer is given, I believe, by Wittgenstein, who is often taken to be Descartes' greatest philosophical opponent. In one of the most famous passages of the *Philosophical investigations*, Wittgenstein, thinking of his two homes, Vienna and Cambridge, compares language to an ancient city:[3]

Our language can be seen as an ancient city: a maze of little streets and squares, of old and new houses, and of houses with additions from various periods; and this surrounded by a multitude of new boroughs with straight and regular streets and uniform houses.

This picture of the constitution of a city is strikingly similar to Descartes'. The difference is that, after three hundred years, constitutional reform has made its inroads. The ancient city, with its multiplicity of old, new and overlapping additions is now surrounded by 'a multitude of new boroughs with straight and regular streets and uniform houses'. Constitutional uniformity is not the 'soul' of the city, as Pufendorf and other modern theorists suggested it should be. Neither Kant's nor Paine's republican constitution determines every aspect of the whole. Rather, the newer uniformity and regularity of modern constitutions forms a surrounding multitude of new boroughs around a maze of old and new formations and patchwork arrangements from many periods.

Understanding constitutionalism: Wittgenstein and Hale
Wittgenstein introduces the analogy between language and an ancient city to illustrate the understanding of language one comes to acquire by working through all the examples

carefully assembled in the *Philosophical investigations*. Since this concept of understanding will enable us to understand the language of constitutionalism, let me review his main points. Language, like a city, has grown up in a variety of forms through long use and practice, interacting and overlapping in many ways in the endless diversity and strife of human activities. Like a city, it does not have a uniform constitution imposed by a single lawgiver, although, of course, areas of it have been made regular by reforms, just like some newer neighbourhoods of a city. Wittgenstein often just lists examples of 'the multiplicity of language games' played with even the most seemingly univocal concepts to make his point, just as a civic guide would point to different boroughs, then to the diverse styles within each borough, then to the overlapping additions from various periods to make the analogous point.[4]

Consequently, the grammar of words is too multiform to be represented in a theory or comprehensive rule that stipulates the essential conditions for the correct application of words in every instance, just as there is no such comprehensive view of the constitution of a city. 'We do not *command a clear view* of the use of our words', not because the definitive theory has yet to arrive, but because language 'is lacking in this sort of perspicuity'. Like *The spirit of Haida Gwaii* or a constitutional association, language is aspectival: 'a labyrinth of paths. You approach from *one* side and know your way about; you approach the same place from another side and no longer know your way about.'[5]

The analogy holds for the language of constitutionalism that is woven into the practices and institutions of contemporary societies. It is a labyrinth of terms and their uses from various periods, including the surrounding regular ways and uniform institutions of modern constitutionalism surveyed in chapter 3. The theorists and citizens who inhabit these modern suburbs are accustomed to their straight and narrow ways, characteristic forms of thought and relatively stable uses, and they tend to presume that their ways should determine the whole. The presumption is that the identity of modern constitutions consists of some combination of seven essential features. These features provide the comprehensive rule by which all political associations and their institutions are identified and ranked on a scale of historical development. This form of representation is not taken as one arrangement of the data of constitutionalism from the parochial perspective of a few members of one neighbourhood, to be compared and negotiated in dialogue with others, but the way the data are arranged by historical processes of modernisation. The only range of disagreement in understanding constitutionalism is over the interpretation and application of this great map by the three authoritative schools. This map is then projected over the whole, hiding the diversity beneath.

Wittgenstein calls the presumption of such a comprehensive theory 'the craving for generality'. The craving has its source partly in 'our preoccupation with the method of science'. It is accompanied by a 'contemptuous attitude towards the particular case'. The idea that 'to get clear about the meaning of a general term' it is necessary 'to find the common element in all its applications' has 'shackled' philosophy: 'for it has not only led to no result, but also made the philosopher dismiss as irrelevant the concrete cases, which alone could have helped him to understand the usage of the general term'. The image of an ancient city graphically illustrates the way that the craving for generality overlooks and generates a contemptuous attitude towards the irreducible multiplicity of concrete usage that defeats its aspiration. This illustration is backed up with two lines of argument in the *Philosophical investigations* that expose the mistake in the presumption and present the correct way to understand general terms.[6]

The first argument shows that understanding a general term is not the theoretical activity of interpreting and applying a general theory or rule in particular cases. By using examples of signposts and maps, Wittgenstein shows that such a general rule fails to account for precisely the phenomenon we associate with understanding the meaning of a general term: the ability to use a general term, as well as to question its accepted use, in various circumstances without recursive doubts. No matter how elaborate such a rule might be, it is always possible to interpret and apply it in various ways. 'Does the sign-post leave no doubt open about the way I have to go? Does it shew which direction I am to take when I have passed it; whether along the road or the footpath or cross-country?'[7]

If I am in doubt about how to interpret and follow the rule, or if I can interpret it in endless ways, then the rule and its interpretation 'do not determine meaning'. So, even if a theorist could provide a theory which specified the exhaustive conditions for the interpretation and application of the general terms of constitutionalism in every case, as modern theorists from Hobbes to Rawls have sought to do, this would not enable us to understand constitutionalism. For interpretative disagreements would arise over how to apply and follow the conditions, as indeed they do over the interpretation of the classic and contemporary theories, thereby pragmatically proving Wittgenstein's point.

Rather, understanding a general term is nothing more than the practical activity of being able to use it in various circumstances: 'there is a way of grasping a rule which is *not* an *interpretation*, but which is exhibited in what we call "obeying the rule" and "going against it" in actual cases'. Such a grasp is not the possession of a theory, but the manifestation of a repertoire of practical, normative abilities, acquired through long use and practice, to use the term and go against customary use in actual cases. The uses of general terms, he concludes, are intersubjective 'practices' or 'customs', like tennis or the 'practice' of law. Our understanding of them consists in the 'mastery' of a 'technique' or practical skill 'exhibited' in being proficient players in the particular cases or 'language games' in which they are used.[8]

As Charles Taylor summarises in his article, 'To follow a rule', Wittgenstein's argument has led to a revolution in philosophy and the human sciences. Nevertheless, some theorists, such as Peter Winch, have gone on to infer that people using general terms in the everyday activities of life are still following rules. The rules are said to be 'implicit' or background 'understandings' embedded in practice and shared by all members of a culture or community. The role of the theorist is then to make explicit the implicit rules embodied in practice in a culture or community. We have seen Rawls take this turn in his recent work, and many of the communitarians and nationalists mentioned in chapter 2 have done the same in order to try to resurrect grand theory from the ashes left by Wittgenstein's first argument. In so doing, these theorists of practice have uncritically retained the older assumption of cultures and communities as homogeneous wholes and insouciantly carried on with a contemptuous attitude towards particular cases. They have neglected Wittgenstein's second argument that the 'grasp' exhibited in 'obeying' or 'going against' a rule in actual cases cannot be accounted for in terms of following general rules implicit in practice because the multiplicity of uses is too various, tangled, contested and creative to be governed by rules.

Wittgenstein introduces this second line of argument with the example of the general term 'game' in sections 65 and 66. He runs through various examples of games, showing that there is no one feature or set of features, such as 'amusement', 'skill' or 'winning and losing', common to all, but various 'similarities' and 'relationships' among them. Some features are shared by a number of games, such as board games, but then pass to card games, where 'the common features drop out and others appear'. 'I am saying', he writes, 'that these phenomena have no one thing in common which makes us use the same word for all.' As he moves through many examples, the upshot is not the discovery of a comprehensive rule implicitly followed in all cases, but 'a complicated network of similarities overlapping and criss-crossing: sometimes overall similarities, sometimes similarities of detail', like the constitution of an ancient city.

If, Wittgenstein asks his interlocutor, 'observation does not enable us to see any clear rule', and the person using a general term 'does not know it himself', then what 'meaning is the expression "the rule by which he proceeds" supposed to have left to it here?' 'The application of a word', he roundly concludes, 'is not everywhere bounded by rules.' If the freedom of language use still must be described in terms of rules, then, he suggests, it is like a game 'where we play and – make up the rules as we go along', or 'one where we alter them – as we go along'.[9]

Accordingly, the way to understand a general term is not to look in vain for implicit rules but, like tennis or law, to acquire the complex abilities to use it correctly in practice by working through and becoming proficient in various examples until one is able to go on oneself. Is the knowledge of a general term like 'game', he asks, 'somehow equivalent to an unformulated definition', as the theorists of practice presume? He then presents his revolutionary reply:[10]

Isn't my knowledge, my concept of a game, completely expressed in . . . my describing examples of various kinds of game; shewing how all sorts of other games can be constructed on the analogy of these; saying that I should scarcely include this or this among games; and so on.

Hence, like many practical activities that are mastered by examples more than by rules, understanding a general concept consists in being able to give reasons why it should or should not be used in any particular case by describing examples with similar or related aspects, drawing analogies or disanalogies of various kinds, finding precedents and drawing attention to intermediate cases so that one can pass easily from familiar cases to the unfamiliar and see the relation between them. For example, in the first chapter I arranged the six examples of the politics of recognition so you could see three similarities among them. Section 66 on the general term 'game' illustrates the technique and Wittgenstein then employs it throughout the *Philosophical investigations* to solve philosophical problems.

The aim of this sort of language game with the general term in question – 'the language game with the word "game"' in Wittgenstein's example – is to employ intermediate examples which make manifest a connection with other cases so that a person understands why or why not the term should be used in this case. As the game proceeds and examples are assembled in various ways, the players come 'to regard a particular case differently', to 'compare it with *this* rather than *that* set of pictures' and hence to change their 'way of looking at things', so they notice the aspects which render the case an instance of the general term or not. Wittgenstein explains, 'if I correct a philosophical mistake', I 'must always point to an analogy according to which one had been thinking, but which one did not recognize as an analogy'. He calls the analogical activity of finding intermediate cases the giving of 'further descriptions' and compares it to the way reasons are given in a court of law for and against a particular case.[11]

Wittgenstein does not mean that the exchange of descriptions and redescriptions of examples to illuminate similarities and differences is some sort of preliminary exercise to the formulation of a general rule under which the concrete case can be subsumed, for, as we have seen, there is none:

One gives examples and intends them to be taken in a particular way. – I do not, however, mean by this that he is supposed to see in those examples the common thing which I – for some reason – was unable to express; but that he is now to *employ* those examples in a particular way. Here giving examples is not an *indirect* means of explaining – in default of a better.

'The work of the philosopher', he simply states, 'consists in assembling reminders for a particular purpose.'[12]

The final aspect of Wittgenstein's two arguments I wish to draw to your attention is that his examples of understanding a general term by assembling examples always take place in dialogue with others who see things differently. The dialogical character of understanding is one of the many things he wishes to convey by calling the activity of understanding a 'language game', for, like playing tennis, we grasp a concept by serving, returning and rallying it back and forth with other players in conversations. Indeed, it is precisely the analogy between the use of words in dialogue and games like tennis that Wittgenstein thought of emphasising by selecting as a possible motto for the *Philosophical investigations*, the line 'I'll teach you differences' uttered by Kent to Oswald in *King Lear*, for the dialogue between them, in which the differences are taught and learned, is based on the analogy between word play and tennis play.[13]

Since there is no comprehensive view of the uses of a general term, any monological view is always partial to some degree – noticing some aspects of usage at the expense of overlooking others. Any one description of examples, no matter how elaborate, will always be one heuristic way of characterising the case in question among others, not a 'preconceived idea to which reality *must* correspond'.[14] This is the point of his dictum that you approach from one side and know your way about; you approach the same place from another side and no longer know your way about. To understand a general term, and so know your way around its maze of uses, it is always necessary to enter into a dialogue with interlocutors from other regions of the city, to listen to their 'further descriptions' and come to recognise the aspects of the phenomenon in question that they bring to light, aspects which go unnoticed from one's own familiar set of examples. Since there is always more than one side to a case, one must always consult those on the other side. As a result of exchanges of views by denizens from various neighbourhoods and the finding of examples which mediate their differences, a grasp of the multiplicity of cases is gradually acquired. Understanding, like the *Philosophical investigations* itself, is dialogical.

These two lines of argument are presented in condensed form in section 122. After stating that a single, comprehensive view of the meaning of a general term is unobtainable, he introduces his alternative philosophy of the dialogical comparison and contrast of examples in actual cases as a *ubersichtliche Darstelling* – a 'perspicuous representation' or 'survey' – that 'produces just that understanding which consists in "seeing connexions"'. 'Hence the importance,' he continues, 'of finding and inventing *intermediate cases*.' He then underlines the importance of his discovery in an exceptionally direct remark:

The concept of a perspicuous representation is of fundamental significance for us. It earmarks the form of account we give, the way we look at things. (Is this a 'Weltanschauung'?)

Wittgenstein's philosophy is an alternative worldview to the one that informs modern constitutionalism. First, contrary to the imperial concept of understanding in modern constitutionalism discussed at the end of the second chapter, it provides a way of understanding others that does not entail comprehending what they say within one's own language of redescription, for this is now seen for what it is: one heuristic description of examples among others; one interlocution among others in the dialogue of humankind. Second, it furnishes a philosophical account of the way in which exchanges of views in intercultural dialogues nurture the attitude of 'diversity awareness' by enabling the interlocutors to regard cases differently and change their way of looking at things.

Finally, it is a view of how understanding occurs in the real world of overlapping, interacting and negotiated cultural diversity in which we speak, act and associate together. As a result, if we care to understand *The spirit of Haida Gwaii*, Wittgenstein's philosophy explains why we must listen to the description of each member of the crew, and indeed enter the conversation ourselves, in order to find redescriptions acceptable to all which mediate the differences we wish each other to recognise. This is a way of doing philosophy and reaching mutual understanding fit for a post-imperial age of cultural diversity.

The general terms of the language of contemporary constitutionalism – constitutions, nations, societies, cultures, recognition, citizens, rights, sovereignty, justice, institutions, the common good, ancient and modern – are like games. David Kahane has corroborated Wittgenstein's second argument by exposing the poverty of attempts to explain the use of these concepts in particular cases by recourse to implicit rules and shared understandings. They are to be understood by surveying the actual cases of their use and the reasons given for and against their application, not only in the regular and uniform uses of modern constitutionalism, where the arrangement of examples has become fossilised, but also in the much broader range of uses in other neighbourhoods and boroughs. Of special importance will be sites where disputes and struggles have occurred and the dominant uses have been challenged and altered. The dialogues of Baron de Lahontan, the comparisons of Joseph Brant and the further descriptions of other 'marginal' writers will be canonical examples for us. This book is but one example of this form of survey which gradually loosens the grip of the theories of modern constitutionalism and discloses the diversity of contemporary constitutions and cultures that they conceal.

Wittgenstein suggests that the diverse similarities among instances of general concepts like games can be thought of as analogous to 'family resemblances', for 'the various resemblances between members of a family: build, features, colour of eyes, gait, temperament, etc., etc., overlap and criss-cross in the same way'. Games 'form a family'.[15] In an analogous fashion, the constitutions and cultures of the world form a family – the criss-crossing Aboriginal and non-Aboriginal constitutions, new and old, provincial and federal, general agreements on trade and tariffs, global codes of human rights and environmental treaties, international laws of Aboriginal peoples and so on. Moreover, within any constitutional association, the rights, institutions and laws are not identical in every case, but vary with the interacting cultural diversity of the members, again forming a family; except, of course, in those areas where the overwhelming force of modern constitutionalism has crushed the agonic interplay of law and cultural freedom.

The direct relevance of Wittgenstein's arguments to our topic is confirmed by Wittgenstein himself. He first presented them in his 'Remarks on Frazer's *Golden Bough*' (1930). In the early decades of the twentieth century, the anthropologist James George Frazer, like the theorists of modern constitutionalism, sought to understand a number of 'primitive'

practices of various 'savage' societies by arranging them in the
progressive scheme of historical development and judging
them relative to the scientific practices of contemporary
European societies. As a consequence, Wittgenstein remarks,
Frazer 'is more savage than most of his savages'. Much as the
African scholar V. Y. Mudimbe was to comment decades
later in *The invention of Africa*, Wittgenstein objects that it is
'impossible' for him 'to understand a different way of life from
the English one of his time!' What Frazer does not realise is
that 'an explanation' in the form of 'an hypothesis of development is only *one* kind of summary of the data'. The purpose of
this arrangement of the data, or any other, is heuristic and
mediatory – 'to sharpen our eye for a formal connection'
among them. It is not, as Frazer assumes, a preconceived idea
to which reality must correspond.

Wittgenstein then presents his alternative approach. The
'factual material [the various practices]' can be arranged 'so
that we can easily pass from one part to another and have a
clear view of it – showing it in a perspicuous way'. This cryptic
remark is immediately followed by the first draft of the
passage which became section 122 of the *Philosophical investigations* seventeen years later. In his notebooks, he is even more
insistent that his approach be regarded as an alternative to
the progressive and scientific form of thinking typical of
modern European civilisation. Therefore, there is no question
that he intended his arguments to be employed as I have used
them: to question the imperial and monological form of
reasoning we have found to be constitutive of modern constitutionalism.[16]

Since the practical form of reasoning Wittgenstein
describes is akin to the reasoning in individual cases at the
common law, as Stephen Toulmin and Albert Jonsen have
substantiated, it is not surprising that similar arguments were
presented by one of the greatest common lawyers, Chief
Justice Matthew Hale, against one of the founding theorists of
modern constitutionalism, Thomas Hobbes. As we noticed in
chapter 3, Hobbes presents his modern theory as a solution
to what he saw as the disunity and irregularity of ancient

constitutionalism. The metaphors he employs to persuade his readers are, as we might expect, almost the opposite of Descartes'. If the people expect their association to be anything other than 'a crasie building, such as hardly lasting out their own time', then it must be constructed by 'the help of a very able Architect'. Rather than accommodating the constitution to the cultural diversity of the citizens, as Descartes recommends, '*every man* is to strive *to accommodate himself to the rest*'. The architect is to view the diverse subjects he must render 'plain' and 'sociable' as 'stones brought together for building of an Aedifice'. 'For as that stone which by the asperity, and irregularity of Figure, takes more room from others, than it selfe fills; and for the hardnesse, cannot be easily made plain, and thereby hindereth the building, is by the builders cast away as unprofitable and troublesome.' Even more revealing is the kind of theoretical knowledge the architect needs and *Leviathan* provides. 'The skill of making, and maintaining Common-wealths consisteth in certain Rules, as doth Arithmetique and Geometry; not (as Tennis-play) on Practise onely.'[17]

Hale's trenchant reply is that the skill of making and maintaining a constitutional commonwealth is not a matter of a solitary, clever person deducing general rules from essential definitions. Rather, it is a practical skill that 'must be gained by the habituateing and accustomeing and Exercising of that Faculty [of reasoning] by reading, study and observation', as well as by 'Conversation between man and man'. The reason why it is a practical skill acquired by 'use and exercise' is that 'actions, and the application of remedyes to them' are 'so various', 'different' and 'diversified from another' that abstract rules are a hindrance rather than a help 'when it comes to particulars'. A man, like Hobbes, who has 'a prospect' of 'a few things may with ease enough fitt a Lawe' to 'those things'. But, he continues, 'the texture of Humane affaires is not unlike the Texture of a diseased bodey labouring under Maladies, it may be of so various natures that such Phisique as may be proper for the Cure of one of the maladies may be destructive in relation to the other'.[18]

Over three hundred years later, Albert Jonsen and Stephen Toulmin, commenting on the theories of Bentham and Rawls in the course of their history of reasoning by cases, draw much the same conclusion:[19]

If general, abstract theories in moral philosophy are read against their historical and social backgrounds, they will need to be understood not as making *comprehensive and mutually exclusive* claims but, rather, offering us *limited and complementary* perspectives on the whole broad complex of human conduct and moral experience, personal relations, and ethical reflection. So interpreted, none of these theories tells us the whole truth . . . Instead, each of them gives us part of the larger picture.

In *Reason and rhetoric in the philosophy of Hobbes*, Quentin Skinner shows that Hale's common-law view is typical of the Renaissance humanist culture against which Hobbes constructed his scientific alternative. The reasons that Renaissance humanists give for the practical and dialogical character of moral and political philosophy are similar to Wittgenstein's. One should always, they argue, listen to the other side (*audi alteram partem*) because it is always possible to speak on either side of a case (*in utramque partem*). The reason why this is always possible is that the criteria for the application of moral and philosophical concepts are so various and circumstantial, rather than essential and universal, that any case is always open to more than one description and evaluation, by means of comparisons and contrasts with other cases (what they call *paradiastole*). Therefore, the correct attitude or worldview is a willingness to exchange and negotiate alternative descriptions.

Hobbes sought to overcome the 'uncertainty' of humanist moral and political philosophy and put it on a scientific and monological footing by setting out essential definitions and deducing general rules that any rational person would be compelled to accept. He thus initiated, as Quentin Skinner concludes, 'the shift from a dialogical to a monological style of moral [and political] reasoning'. The theorists of modern constitutionalism followed in Hobbes' footsteps so that 'the very idea of presenting a moral or political theory in the form of a dialogue has long since lost any serious place in philosophy' (even though, ironically, the successive monological theories have been accompanied by debate and disagreement that only the humanist approach can explain).[20]

This historical shift from a humanist to a scientific worldview turns on the assumption of essential definitions which Wittgenstein challenged three hundred years later. As a result, although Wittgenstein's arguments can be seen as the progenitor of a shift to post-modern humanism, as Dennis Patterson recommends, they can also be regarded as akin to the earlier common-law humanism that has been, like the trials of Rita Joe, covered over but not cast away by the architects of modern constitutionalism.

The great tragedy of the modern constitutionalism is that most European philosophers followed Hobbes and turned their backs on dialogue just when non-European peoples were encountered and dialogue and mediation were needed to avert the misunderstanding and inhumanity that followed. Let us now turn to examples of those few who listened to and negotiated with the others they encountered.

Examples of the three conventions: the Aboriginal and common-law system and the conventions of mutual recognition and consent
The following examples of the recognition and accommodation of cultural diversity illustrate the multiplicity of uses of the concepts of contemporary constitutionalism and disclose the hidden constitutions of contemporary societies. They also bring to light the three conventions of common constitutionalism: mutual recognition, continuity and consent. Constitutional 'conventions' in this common-law sense are norms that come into being and come to be accepted as authoritative in the course of constitutional practice, including criticism and contestation of that practice. They gradually gain their authority by acts in conformity with them and by appeals to them by both sides, as warrants of justification, when they are transgressed. These three conventions form the sturdy fibres of Ariadne's thread through the labyrinth of conflicting claims to cultural recognition which currently block the way to a

peaceful twenty-first century. If they guide constitutional negotiations, the negotiations and resulting constitutions will be just with respect to cultural recognition.

The first and most spectacular example is the mutual recognition and accommodation of the Aboriginal peoples of America and the British Crown as equal, self-governing nations. This form of mutual recognition was worked out in the early modern period in a common association of 'treaty constitutionalism'. I would like to discuss it in some detail because it exhibits clearly the three conventions that ought to guide any diverse constitutional association. Once they are grasped in this case, it is easy to see how they can be applied analogously in different cases.

The problem of mutual recognition is classically formulated by John Marshall, the first Chief Justice of the Supreme Court of the United States, in his final and definitive judgement on US–Aboriginal relations in *Worcester v. the State of Georgia* of 1832 (Samuel Worcester's lawyers presented the case for Cherokee sovereignty):[21]

America, separated from Europe by a wide ocean, was inhabited by a distinct people, divided into separate nations, independent of each other and the rest of the world, having institutions of their own, and governing themselves by their own laws. It is difficult to comprehend the proposition, that the inhabitants of either quarter of the globe could have rightful original claims of dominion over the inhabitants of the other, or over the lands they occupied; or that the discovery of either by the other should give the discoverer rights in the country discovered, which annulled the pre-existing rights of its ancient possessors.

If the Aboriginal peoples of America are recognised as 'independent nations', as Marshall argues, the initial conditions of constitutional theory and practice in North America are not any of the three formulations of popular sovereignty employed by the authoritative schools of modern constitutionalism surveyed in the previous lecture. Rather, the situation is a continent of over five hundred sovereign Aboriginal nations governing themselves by their own institutions and authoritative traditions of interpretation for

roughly twenty thousand years before Europeans arrive in
the seventeenth century. The Europeans refuse to become
immigrants of the existing Aboriginal nations, as the US and
Canadian governments would certainly insist today in an
analogous situation, and demand instead that their nationhood be recognised and accommodated so they may govern
themselves by their own laws and traditions.

The question is how can the people in this diverse form
reach agreement on a constitutional association just to both
parties. The answer was worked out through hundreds of
treaty negotiations between agents of the Crown and the
Aboriginal nations from the 1630s to 1832. In *Worcester*,
Marshall reviewed the history of treaty making and presented
a synopsis of the customary system of treaty constitutionalism
that evolved over the previous two centuries. He took as a
major precedent the Royal Proclamation of 7 October 1763, in
which the Crown set out its understanding of the relations
between British North America and the Aboriginal nations.
The Proclamation, in turn, was based on a review of treaties
since 1664, Royal Commissions on Indian Affairs since 1665,
Royal Instructions to colonial administrators since 1670, the
Board of Trade's recognition of Aboriginal sovereignty in 1696
(when Locke was a member) and in the case of the Mohegan
nation versus Connecticut of 1705 (which John Bulkley
attacked with Locke's arguments), and the advice of the
Superintendent of Indian Affairs in North America, Sir
William Johnson (Joseph Brant's step father). In addition,
similar accounts of the treaty system were written by participants in treaty negotiations, such as Samuel Wharton, *Plain
facts: being an examination into the rights of the Indian nations of
America to their respective territories* (1781), which Paine attacked
in *The public good*, Cadwallader Colden, *The history of the five
Indian nations of Canada* (1747), and Benjamin Franklin's collection of treaties (1762). The oral accounts of the treaties by
members of the *Haudenosaunee* or Iroquois Confederation are
partially recorded in *The redman's appeal for justice: the position of
the six nations that they constitute an independent state* (1924).
Despite the efforts of the builders of modern constitutional-

ism to extinguish it, this ancient constitution is part of US constitutional law and Commonwealth common law, and remnants of it endure in practice down to this day.

The first convention of constitutional negotiations is to agree on a form of mutual recognition. In this case, it involves the mutual recognition of both parties as independent and self-governing nations. The initial reason Crown negotiators recognised the Aboriginal peoples as nations is that they did not redescribe the Aboriginal peoples in the forms of recognition constructed by the armchair European theorists. Instead, they simply listened to how the Aboriginal negotiators presented themselves in countless meetings. As William Johnson, the chief Crown negotiator, explained to the Lords of Trade in 1763:[22]

The Indians of the Ottawa Confederacy . . . and also the Six Nations, however their sentiments may seem misrepresented, all along considered the Northern parts of North America, as their sole property from the beginning; and although the conveniency of Trade, (with fair speeches and promises) induced them to afford both us and the French settlements in their Country, yet they never understood such settlement as a Dominion, especially as neither we, nor the French ever made a conquest of them.

'They have even repeatedly said at several conferences in my presence', Johnson goes on to recount, that 'they were amused by both parties [the British and French] with stories of their upright intentions, and that they made War for the protection of the Indians rights, but that they plainly found, it was carried on to see who would become masters of what was the property of neither the one nor the other.'

The 'Indians', Johnson summarises, are not 'subject to' 'our Laws' and they 'consider themselves as a free people'. In 1761, the Chippewa leader Minivavana enlightened the English trader Alexander Harvey at Michilimackinace in the following typical manner:[23]

Englishman, although you have conquered the French, you have not yet conquered us. We are not your slaves. These lakes, these woods and mountains, were left to us by our ancestors. They are our inheritances; and we will part with them to none.

The second reason why Crown negotiators applied the term 'nation' and 'republic' to the Aboriginal peoples is that the forms of Aboriginal political organisation they observed, while not identical, were similar in a number of respects to European nations. They did not apply criteria that only seventeenth-century European nations met and conclude that Aboriginal peoples were savages at the lowest stage of development. As the terms of Marshall's description neatly illustrate, they were able to see the cross-cultural family resemblances between Aboriginal and European forms of political association. Whereas long use and occupation of a territory gave them jurisdiction, as the 1665 Royal Commission had ruled, the ability to govern themselves in accord with their own laws and ways for a long time and to have their independence recognised by other similarly organised peoples gave them nationhood.

The very term 'nation', Marshall explains, 'so generally applied to them, means "a people distinct from others"'. 'The constitution' of the United States, 'by declaring treaties' to be 'the supreme law of the land', admits 'their rank among those powers who are "capable of making treaties"':

The words 'treaty' and 'nations' are words of our own language, selected in our diplomatic and legislative proceedings by ourselves, having each a definite and well understood meaning. We have applied them to Indians, as we have applied them to the other nations of the earth. They are applied to all in the same sense.

For emphasis, he states that the United States stands to the Aboriginal nations just as it does to 'the crowned heads of Europe'.[24]

The reason why the agents of justice applied these looser criteria of nationhood, rather than the biased criteria of modern constitutionalism, is that they are the customary criteria used to recognise nationhood throughout Europe ever since Bartolus of Sassoferrato employed them to bring the Holy Roman Empire to recognise the independence of the Italian city states in the early fourteenth century. Marshall, for instance, was able to draw connections with intermediate examples of European nationhood and treaty making to make his case. In recognising the sovereignty of Aboriginal nations, therefore, the Crown was doing no more than applying to them the same standards European nations applied to each other. These common criteria of nationhood have persisted in the great struggles for national liberation in the nineteenth and twentieth centuries, against the attempts of existing nations to apply the restrictive criteria of modern constitutionalism, and they have regained currency in recent international law and the proposed law of Indigenous peoples.

The negotiators were quite aware that the Aboriginal peoples did not have European-style states, representative institutions, formalised legal systems, prisons and independent executives. They observed the conciliar and confederal forms of government, consensus decision making, rule by authority rather than coercion, and customary law. Yet this did not cause them to situate the Aboriginal peoples in a lower stage of development. Quite the contrary. They were constantly instructed by the Privy Council to study and respect their constitutions and forms of government, ensure that they 'not be molested or disturbed' and punish the 'great frauds and abuses' committed against them by the settlers. Observers such as Cadwallader Colden, Benjamin Franklin, Baron de Lahontan and Joseph-François Lafitau repudiated the judgement of the modern theorists and sided with Joseph Brant. They suggested that Europeans were at a lower and more corrupt stage of development and that Aboriginal nations, with their participatory governments, service to the public good and great diplomacy, were similar in stature to the classical republics.

The reasons why the Aboriginal nations reciprocally recognised the Europeans as nations are similar. The Aboriginal peoples who encountered Europeans in the first two centuries had long traditions of recognising each other as nations and entering into various forms of treaty alliances and confederations. This is especially true of the *Haudenosaunee* confederacy, whose constitution, the Great Law of Peace (*Gayaneshakgowa*), dates from the 1450s. It is none the less true of the Cherokee, Shawnee, Delaware, Mohegan, Pequot, Ottawa, Huron, Mi'kmaq and many others. When Europeans demanded recognition as nations and sought accommodation, Aboriginal peoples took up the demand in their customary forms of nation to nation recognition and adapted them, in the course of the negotiations, to the peculiarities of the case. Francis Jennings and his former students have shown in *The history and culture of Iroquois diplomacy* that the Europeans in turn accommodated their ways to the elaborate diplomatic practices of negotiation the Aboriginal leaders insisted on following. Like the European negotiators, Aboriginal peoples did not view this as a great founding moment, marking a transition from the state of nature to constitutional society, but as one link in a chain of multinational constitutional agreements that stretched back long before the newcomers arrived on Great Turtle Island and would long outlast their transgressions and disruptions of it. Aboriginal scholars Gerald Alfred and Mark Dockstator have shown that this continues to be the attitude of many Aboriginal people today.

Although both parties are recognised as nations, the Aboriginal nations are prior or 'First Nations', as they are called in Canada, since they were in North America when the Europeans arrived. Once this form of mutual recognition was worked out, the only just way that the Crown could acquire land and establish its sovereignty in North America was to gain the consent of the Aboriginal nations. The convention of consent is the very one we have seen Locke and his followers finesse: *quod omnes tangit ab omnibus comprobetur*, 'what touches all should be agreed to by all'. Enshrined in the codex of Roman law, *q.o.t.* is the most fundamental constitutional convention. It applies to any form of constitutional associ-ation, ensuring that a constitution or an amendment to it rests on the consent of the people, or the representatives of the people who are touched by it. The way it should be applied depends on how the 'people' are recognised.

Marshall rejects the anti-constitutional arguments of Locke and Kant that consent is unnecessary, as well as the question-begging view of other modern theorists that the Aboriginal people could be treated as individuals or cultural minorities within sovereign European institutions and traditions of interpretation. The right of 'discovery' of a part of America by an European government did not give that European nation any rights over the Indigenous people, but only an exclusive right against other European nations to settle and acquire land from the Aboriginal occupants. It was simply a right that the European powers had agreed to among themselves. Applying *q.o.t.*, Marshall infers that it 'could not affect the rights of those who had not agreed to it'; that is, 'those already in possession, either as aboriginal occupants, or as occupants by virtue of a discovery before the memory of man'. Repudiating his earlier judgement in *Johnson and Graham's Lessee v. M'Intosh* (1823) that the Crown gained title by conquest, he states that the wars against the Indians were defensive and did not convey title.

Moreover, he mockingly asks, did 'sailing along the coast', or 'occasionally landing on it' give 'property in the soil, from the Atlantic to the Pacific; or rightful dominion over the numerous people who occupied it?' Or, ridiculing Locke and Vattel, 'has nature', or 'the Great Creator of all things, conferred these rights over hunters and fisherman, on agriculturalists and manufacturers?'[25]

The form of consent should always be tailored to the form of mutual recognition of the people involved. In this case, Marshall concludes, this is the form of 'mutual consent' the Crown established in the treaty system and the United States inherited after the war of independence. In this system, the Crown negotiated, and continues to negotiate, with the First Nations to purchase territory from them, to gain their recognition of Crown government in America, and to work out various relations of protection and co-operation over time. In one of the most generous acts of recognition and accommodation in history, the Aboriginal nations in turn negotiated, and continue to negotiate, to cede land and settle boundaries, recognise the legitimacy of Crown governments and work out relations of protection and co-operation. However, they consent to this on the condition that the Crown governments and their successors always respect the equal and prior sovereignty of the Aboriginal nations on the territories they reserve to themselves.

In treaty negotiations, Marshall notes, a 'boundary is described, between nation and nation by mutual consent. The national character of each, the ability of each to establish this boundary, is acknowledged by the other.' The treaties 'manifestly consider the several Indian nations as distinct political communities, having territorial boundaries, within which their authority is exclusive'. Hence, the treaty system is expressly designed not only to recognise and treat the Aboriginal people as equal, self-governing nations, but also to continue, rather than extinguish, this form of recognition through all treaty arrangements over time. Indeed, the legitimacy of *non*-Aboriginal governments in America depends on this continuity, for it is the condition of Aboriginal consent to recognise them. The proof of the Crown's commitment to continuity, Marshall claims (presumably in one of his more idealistic moods), is in the examples of its practice. Following closely the authoritative exposition of the Royal Proclamation by Superintendent Stuart of Indian Affairs for the southern division of British North America in Mobile in 1763, he writes:[26]

Certain it is that our history furnishes no example, from the first settlement of our country, of any attempt on the part of the crown to interfere with the internal affairs of the Indians, farther than to keep out the agents of foreign powers, who, as traders or otherwise, might seduce them into foreign alliances. The king purchased their lands, when they were willing to sell, at a price they were willing to take; but never coerced a surrender of them. He also purchased their alliance and dependency by subsidies; but never intruded into the interior of their affairs, or interfered with their self-government, so far as respected themselves only.

The Aboriginal and common-law system and the convention of continuity
The continuity of both parties' independent nationhood illustrates the third and final constitutional convention. The

mutually recognised cultural identities of the parties continue through the constitutional negotiations and associations agreed to unless they explicitly consent to amend them. The convention of the continuity of a people's customary ways and forms of government into new forms of constitutional associations with others is the oldest in Western juris-prudence. As we discussed in chapter 3, it is the spirit of ancient constitutionalism, expressing the view that customs and ways of peoples are the manifestation of their free agree-ment. To discontinue them without their explicit consent would thus breach the convention of consent.

In the early modern law of nations, the convention holds even in the case of conquest. The customs and ways of a conquered people continue until the conqueror expressly discontinues them. If the conqueror recognises them, either expressly or by long acceptance, then his imperial right to discontinue them must yield to continuity. As Marshall knew and we shall see in chapter 5, the convention was applied in many of the most important constitutional agreements of the eighteenth century. The protection of Aboriginal govern-ments in Royal Instructions and the Royal Proclamation is an example of the convention in practice.

The convention of continuity stands in opposition to the doctrine of discontinuity in, for example, Norman law. On this view, a new constitutional association, whether it is based on conquest or consent, discontinues or 'extinguishes' the pre-existing customs and ways of the people, and they are, as Marshall explains in *Johnson v. M'Intosh*, not 'governed as a distinct people', but 'incorporated with the victorious nation' and 'blended with the conquerors', so 'they make one people'.[27] Hobbes presented the classic theory of consti-tutional discontinuity in *Leviathan* and many modern theorists followed suit in order to trump the resulting irregularity and assemblage of peoples and their ways the convention protects.

Therefore, no matter how many relations of protection and interdependency the Crown (and later, the US and Canadian governments) and Aboriginal governments enter into as a result of treaty making over the centuries, the identity of both parties as equal and sovereign nations continues, just as it does in other cases of international treaties. 'The very fact of repeated treaties with them', Marshall writes, 'recognises it.' For example, the Aboriginal governments consent from time to time to delegate conditionally certain powers of self government and to share powers of resource development. Neither of these complex constitutional arrangements, which now span over one thousand agreements across Great Turtle Island, affects their status as equal self-governing nations. Marshall explains how the convention of continuity applies to Aboriginal sovereignty throughout the treaties with the United States in the following way:[28]

[T]he settled doctrine of the law of nations is, that a weaker power does not surrender its independence, its right of self-government, by associating with a stronger, and taking its protection. A weak state, in order to provide for its safety, may place itself under the protection of one more powerful, without stripping itself of the right of self-government, and ceasing to be a state. Examples of this kind are not wanting in Europe. 'Tributary and feudatory states', says Vattel, 'do not thereby cease to be sovereign and independent states, so long as sovereign and independent authority are left in the administration of the state'.

In this remarkable passage, the modern view that a constitutional association must give rise to one uniform sovereign state that is unlimited by external and internal interdependency is unceremoniously shown to be inadequate to the concrete cases of constitutionalism. The treaties give rise to a constitutional association of interdependence and protection, but not to discontinuity or subordination to a single sovereign. Marshall makes his point first by citing the convention of continuity then, surely with intended irony, by citing examples drawn from Emeric de Vattel, one of the advocates of the discontinuity of Aboriginal governments whom Marshall repudiated earlier. It does not bother him that the examples he cites are selected from 'ancient' constitutionalism. Indeed, his point seems to be that feudal constitutions, in recognising forms of constitutional association that accommodate types of self rule, are more liberal than the modern theories of liberal heroes like Vattel.

Seen in this unfamiliar light, the decision by the Crown and its representatives to recognise and continue the cultures of the Aboriginal nations appears as one of the most enlightened acts of the eighteenth century. The contrary tendency to discontinue and extinguish their cultural ways, justified in the imperial language of modern constitutionalism, appears regressive – the application of the doctrine of the Norman conquest. Yet the axis of this reversal of vision is not the post-modern deconstruction of constitutionalism, but the ancient convention of continuity. The convention continues the so-called ancient constitutions into the modern world, thereby rendering the constitutions of contemporary societies different from modern constitutional representations of them.

Let us now try to approach the treaty system from an Aboriginal point of view. Of course, the descriptions of the conventions will differ from Marshall's and mine, for there is no universal language of description, but if we can see family resemblances among them, then we are on the common ground.

The Two Row Wampum Treaty of the *Haudenosaunee* confederacy is one of the most famous exemplars of treaty constitutionalism between Aboriginal and non-Aboriginal peoples in America. The constitutional negotiations and relations between them are symbolised by belts of wampum beads exchanged at treaty discussions from 1664 to the negotiations between the *Haudenosaunee* confederacy and the Canadian and Québec governments at Kanehsatake, Québec, in 1990. The two row wampum belt is the diplomatic *lingua franca* of Aboriginal and non-Aboriginal constitutionalism, recording the form of agreement reached and expressing the good will the agreement embodies.

A background of white wampum beads symbolises the purity of the agreement; that is, the convention of consent. Two rows of purple beads represent the nations involved in the dialogue. Three beads separating the two rows stand for peace, friendship and respect; the values necessary to an uncoerced and lasting agreement. The two parallel rows of purple beads, Chief Michael Mitchell explicates,[29]

symbolize two paths or two vessels, travelling down the same river together. One, a birch bark canoe, will be for the Indian people, their laws, their customs and their ways. The other, a ship, will be for the white people and their laws, their customs and their ways. We shall each travel the same river together, side by side, but in our own boats. Neither of us will try to steer the other's vessel.

Aboriginal peoples and European Americans are recognised as equal and co-existing nations, each with their own forms of government, traditions of interpretation and ways. This is the convention of *kahswentha*, the mutual recognition of equality. While not in the same canoe, as in the Haida symbol, the people are in the same river. They agree to co-operate in various ways – travelling 'together', presumably mentioned twice for emphasis. But, notwithstanding the agreements they reach, their status as equal and co-existing nations continues. It is never part of the agreement to try 'to steer the other's vessel', or, in Marshall's description, 'to interfere with the internal affairs' of the other. For example, the treaty signed at Canandaigua, New York, in 1794 between President George Washington's official agent, Colonel Timothy Pickering, and the six chiefs of the *Haudenosaunee* recognises the confederacy as a sovereign nation and guarantees that the United States will never encroach on their remaining lands in western and central New York.[30]

The capacity to delegate to, or share various powers of self government with the protecting government (either the United States or Canada) while retaining their sovereignty is extremely important to the Aboriginal peoples. It enables each Aboriginal nation to work out by mutual consent the degree of self government appropriate to their population, land base and particular circumstances, without fear of subordination or discontinuity.

The convention of continuity through relations of protection and interdependency is also a common feature of Aboriginal constitutionalism. Article 84 of the constitution of the *Haudenosaunee* confederacy of six nations, for example, states that, 'whenever a foreign nation has been conquered or has by their own will accepted the Great Peace [confederated with the other nations], their own system of internal government may continue, but they must cease all warfare against other nations'.[31] True to form, each of the six nations of the confederacy has its own language, customs and government. The confederation itself was founded by the mediation of Deganawidah, who brought the original five warring nations together and guided them to reach agreement through dialogue on a form of association to protect their differences and similarities.

The Aboriginal and common-law system of constitutional dialogue

The concluding aspect of this example is the way in which the constitutional dialogue itself is guided by the three conventions. As the Royal Proclamation states, the negotiations take place in public, to minimise force and fraud, between representatives of the Crown and Aboriginal nations, thereby instantiating their mutual recognition as nations, and without pressure, so that the agreement will be uncoerced. The negotiations are intercultural. Each negotiator participates in his or her language, mode of speaking and listening, form of reaching agreement, and way of representing the people, or peoples, for whom they speak. These features are simply the application of the convention of continuity and the duty of *audi alteram partem* to the dialogue itself.

Over the last three hundred years, elaborate genres of presentation, speaking in French, English and Aboriginal languages, exchanging narratives, stories and arguments, translating back and forth, breaking off and starting again, striking new treaties and redressing violations of old ones have been developed to ensure that each speaker speaks in her or his cultural voice and listens to the others in theirs. The negotiations can be very diverse, such as the multinational and multilingual Great Peace of 1701, which brought over twenty nations together. In the Charlottetown constitutional negotiations of 1992, four Aboriginal negotiators (two women and two men), representing six hundred First Nations, the Métis, Inuit and Aboriginal people living off reserves, along with a national association of native women on the sidelines, met ten provincial premiers, two territorial leaders and a prime minister, all on equal footing.

When the multicultural negotiations end for the day and transcripts and translations are checked, this is only the beginning of the dialogue. The negotiators must turn to their diverse constituents, explain what has transpired, listen to their objections in their terms, reach agreement in the appropriate way on an acceptable response, and then return to the negotiations. This can take many forms, as the consultations surrounding the multilateral constitutional negotiations in Canada in 1992 illustrated. In the early years of the treaty system, William Johnson, for example, would have to explain his provisional agreement with the Aboriginal nations to Whitehall and fourteen very different colonial governments. The great Aboriginal negotiators, such as Canasatego, Shamokin, Tecumesh or Pontiac, would in turn have to reach agreement in the appropriate ways with six *Haudenosaunee* nations, the Shawnee, Delaware, Miami and Ottawa, each with their own internal diversity. In 1992 Ovide Mercredi, the Chief of the First Nations, had to leave the talks and try to reach consensus with the six hundred chiefs for whom he spoke, who, in turn, had to reach agreement with their constituents. Ellen Gabriel, the brave Mohawk negotiator at Kahnesatake, Québec in 1990, kept a consensus among Mohawk citizens as she negotiated in the face of the force of the Canadian army ranged against her.

As Richard White explains in his fascinating study, *The middle ground: Indians, empires, and republics in the Great Lakes region 1650–1815,* the system can deal with issues other than boundaries, military alliances and commerce. Marriages between catholic *canadiennes*, or *canadiens*, and Cree (which gave rise to the Métis nation), European Americans in Aboriginal nations and vice versa, and a host of other intercultural issues were recognised and conciliated in the common system. He has been unable to find one case where the negotiations were between two internally homogeneous cultures.

The three schools of modern constitutionalism disregard the hidden diversity of actual constitutional dialogue not only by laying down simplistic concepts of popular sovereignty and constitutional association as premises, but also by their corresponding concepts of constitutional dialogue. In recent work (still written in monological form), two concepts of dialogue predominate: the participants aim to reach agreement either on universal principles or on norms implicit in practice and, in both cases, to fashion a constitutional association accordingly. Both concepts are, for example, present in the work of Jürgen Habermas.

The presupposition of shared, implicit norms is manifestly false in this case, as well as in any case of a culturally diverse society. Also, the aim of negotiations over cultural recognition is not to reach agreement on universal principles and institutions, but to bring negotiators to recognise their differences and similarities, so that they can reach agreement on a form of association that accommodates their differences in appropriate institutions and their similarities in shared institutions. (In the case at hand, the appropriate institutions are, respectively, self government and co-operative arrangements for protection, resource development, health care and the like.) The presumption of an implicit consensus or a universal goal mis-identifies the *telos* of this type of constitutional dialogue, filtering out the diverse similarities and differences the speakers try to voice. Universality is a misleading representation of the aims of constitutional dialogue because, as we have repeatedly seen, the world of constitutionalism is not a universe, but a multiverse: it cannot be represented in universal principles or its citizens in universal institutions.

The responsibility of listening to others is also bypassed by misconceiving the diversity of modes of speaking. In some theories, it is assumed that the claims of various speakers can be framed in a purportedly universal genre of argument. A good illustration of the diversity blindness of this monological assumption is *Delgamuukw v. the Queen* (1991). The Gitskan and Wet'suwet'en nations of the northwest coast of Great Turtle Island brought forward their claim for recognition of their nations and territories. Gisday Wa and Delgam Uukw carefully outlined Aboriginal concepts of evidence, history, government and argument, contrasting these with European understandings and finding intermediate examples to help the judge understand. They then explained their claim to territory and self rule, based on their forms of governance and use long before the Europeans arrived, in their own terms and compared it with analogous European concepts, calling on respected anthropologists to support their claims.

Chief Justice Allan McEachern ruled that their forms of presentation, oral evidence and title did not measure up to the standards of the court and dismissed their claim. What the court's evidence certainly shows, he fulsomely concluded, is that the 'plaintiffs' ancestors had no written language, no horses or wheeled vehicles, slavery and starvation was [sic] not uncommon, wars with neighbouring people were common, and there is no doubt, to quote Hobbes, that aboriginal life in the territory was, at best, "nasty, brutish and short"'.[32]

Writers such as Seyla Benhabib are critical of the mono-logical theories of dialogue and argue that a democratic constitutional discussion in a culturally diverse society will involve a multiplicity of speech genres. Nevertheless, she goes on optimistically to suggest that we will always be able to put ourselves in the shoes of others and understand things from their point of view, 'either by actually listening to all involved or by representing to ourselves imaginatively the many perspectives of those involved'. In her path-breaking paper, 'Communication and the other', Iris Young deepens our understanding of the value of speaking in and listening to a variety of speech modes in such a discussion. 'Free and open communication enables different groups each to learn of their own partiality by learning something about other perspectives on their collective problems and on themselves.' However, she is sceptical of Benhabib's claim that the participants could reach full reciprocity and symmetry of understanding. There remains 'much about the others that they do not understand'.[33]

This seems to be an unduly pessimistic view of the possibility of understanding among culturally diverse human beings. It is certainly true that we cannot understand culturally different others simply 'by representing to ourselves imaginatively the many perspectives of those involved', any more than I can master tennis by imagining various exchanges. Understanding comes, if it comes at all, only by engaging in the volley of practical dialogue. We need the dialogue itself to become aware of all the aspects of our association that ought to be recognised and accommodated in the constitution. It is also true that the diversity awareness one comes to acquire in dialogue does not consist in being able to replace the other person and speak for him or her. Much remains opaque. However, there is no reason to believe that the participants in the dialogue could not come to 'understand' each other.

The reason it is possible to understand one another in intercultural conversations is because this is what we do all the time in culturally diverse societies to some extent. The everyday mastery of the criss-crossing, overlapping and contested uses of terms is not different in kind (but of course in degree) from the understanding demanded by constitutional dialogue. If one thinks of understanding in the way I presented it in the previous section, the connection becomes clear. The dialogue in such constitutional negotiations usually consists in the back and forth exchange of speech acts of the form, 'let me see if I understand what you said', 'let me rephrase what you said and see if you agree', 'is what you said analogous to this example in my culture', or 'I am sorry, let me try another intermediate example that is closer', or 'can you acknowledge this analogy?' 'Now I think I see what you are saying – let me put it this way for I now see that it complements my view.' The participants are gradually able to see the association from the points of view of each other and cobble together an acceptable intercultural language capable of accommodating the truth in each of their limited and complementary views and of setting aside the incompatible ones.

Reading the transcripts, I find it difficult to doubt that Aboriginal negotiators failed to understand William Johnson. The transcript of *Delgamuukw* makes it clear that the Gitskan and Wet'suwet'en understood the concepts that the Chief Justice used to dispossess them under the colour of law, and so were able to launch an appeal. Israeli and Palestinian negotiators over self rule surely understand one another. The Cree, Naskapi and Inuit negotiators understood the Québec and Canadian participants in the James Bay and Northern Québec Agreement of 1975 all too well. Those who participated in the constitutional negotiations and broad consultations in Canada from 1991 to 1992 came, as a result, to understand one another fairly well and temper their earlier views. Those who refused to participate, on the contrary, insisted that their own views were comprehensive and exclusive, held the most extreme positions and, consequently, misunderstood the others. Of course, one cannot fully grasp 'where the others are coming from' and so cannot speak for them, but one can, by intermediate steps, understand what they are saying about the ancient city we share.

Young may take a sceptical stance towards reciprocal intercultural understanding because she believes that, if it is possible, then dialogue might be reduced to a mere stepping stone to a monological and universal overview of the ensemble. This concern is suggested by her conclusion that only the 'preservation of difference and the recognition of asymmetry – the non-reciprocity – of social positions can preserve publicity and the need for continued communication'.[34] But this path out of the world of cultural diversity is closed, not by the inability to understand one another, but by the constitution of the phenomenon we are trying to understand. It is lacking in this sort of perspicuity as a result of the three features of cultural diversity. Understanding it consists in being able to move about within the dialogue, passing from one neighbourhood to the next, exchanging stories and noticing our similarities and differences *en passant*, not by transcending the human condition.

Further evidence for this mundane point is that written constitutions which have arisen out of such constitutional dialogues are intercultural, without even a pretence of transcultural status. The 'partnership' constitution of Aoretera–New Zealand, the Waitangi treaty, is written in Maori, the language of the *tangata whenua* (the original inhabitants) and in English, the language of the newcomers. Both are authoritative and have distinct traditions of interpretation, with different conceptions of history, evidence, argument and government. The non-Aboriginal Canadian constitution is written in French and English. Both are authoritative and have distinct traditions of interpretation. The fundamental constitution of North America, the treaties of the Aboriginal and common-law system, should be the same.

In modern theories of constitutionalism, the agreement reached in dialogue is seen as foundational, universal and the fixed background to democracy. This Platonic image reinforces the attitude that the agreement must be comprehensive and exclusive. In the Aboriginal and common-law system, the agreement is seen as one link in an endless chain, stretching back to what one's ancestors have done before and forward to what one's children will do in the future. The present link, while appropriate to the circumstances at hand, is in line with the whole chain as far as one can see. In addition, the link is always open to review and renegotiation in a future dialogue if it is not as fitting as it appeared at the time. As a result of this more flexible and pragmatic image, the concept of 'reaching agreement' is different from the modern one and the corresponding attitude of the participants is more open to mutual understanding, accommodation and conciliation.

Mohawks call the practice of meeting to review how well an agreement fits, either amending or reaffirming it, 'repolishing' the chain. They see the periodic reflection on the constitution as a necessary ingredient of a healthy and untarnished association, just as we noted among the members of the black canoe. This democratic constitutionalism does not, as one might object from the modern viewpoint, lessen the veneration with which they hold an agreement. Each one is sacred and sworn to last 'as long as the sun shines and the waters flow', unless a new agreement is reached in accordance with the three conventions. It is, after all, not they who have broken the chain innumerable times and allowed it to tarnish but, rather, those who swore that 'peace and friendship' would subsist 'through all succeeding generations'.[35]

As the settlers gained the upper hand in the nineteenth century, the Aboriginal and common-law system was overwhelmed by the theory and practice of modern constitutionalism. Within its horizons, the relationship of protection, which continued Aboriginal self government according to Marshall, was reinterpreted. Treaties were said to be mere private contracts and Aboriginal rights mere individual rights to hunt and fish on Crown land. The European–American governments were unilaterally recognised as superior guardians whose burden it was to protect Aboriginal people who were recognised as inferior wards incapable of consent and whose primitive ways had to be discontinued and reformed for their own good. When the wards resisted, they were depicted as 'obstacles to progress' and removed to disappear, by neglect, starvation or, as at Wounded Knee, by slaughter.

Although the Aboriginal nations protested throughout this century of the 'gradual civilisation of the Indian tribes', it is only in recent decades that their claims for recognition have started to be effectively heard. They have revived the Aboriginal and common-law system hidden beneath the empire of modern constitutionalism to reclaim self government and control of their territories. From 1972 to 1975, the first contemporary treaty constitution was negotiated between the Cree, Naskapi and Inuit nations and the Québec and Canadian governments. The James Bay and Northern Québec Agreement, while far from ideal, is a precedent that has helped to set the 'world reversal' in motion. Since then, the justice of Aboriginal claims for recognition has begun to be acknowledged in the courts of common-law countries and in the United Nations draft Declaration on the Rights of Indigenous Peoples. In this post-imperial dawn, treaties and agreements have begun to take on some of their former lustre and the Crown has started to discern its fiduciary responsibility in the relationship of protection. Even the mighty leviathans who have extended their empire of modern constitutionalism over 'stolen continents' are being instructed once again by Royal Commissions to see themselves as the Royal Commission of 1664 recommended: as equal 'partners in confederation' with the Aboriginal nations who have survived and continued through the usurpation.[36]

These partnerships will take many forms, depending on the arrangements the partners reach in discussions guided by the three conventions. By calling these agreements 'treaty constitutionalism' and using the example of the Two Row Wampum Treaty, I do not mean to imply that only one form is possible. This would be another kind of imperialism. The appropriate degree of interdependency and the best sort of agreement vary with the very different circumstances of Aboriginal and non-Aboriginal partners on this earth. Even in Canada, the differences within and among First Nations, Inuit and Métis are legion. As Augie Fleras and Jean Elliot suggest in *The nations within*, a new discipline, the comparative politics of Aboriginal nations, is needed to study the variety of appalling social, economic and political conditions of Aboriginal nations and to assist the negotiators.

Of course, one might object, only a rough balance of power in the early modern period among the Aboriginal nations, France, England and the colonial governments caused the Crown to enter into treaty constitutionalism and occasionally abide by it. As constitutional scholars such as Milner S. Ball, Patrick Macklem, Brian Slattery and Joseph Singer, as well as historians such as John Tobias, Vine Deloria Jr. and Russell Barsh, have shown, the three conventions have been abused many times over the centuries. The treaty of Canandaigua, for example, has never been honoured, despite two centuries of protest. In addition, the Crown has imperiously proclaimed, in the language of Hobbes, the treaties to be a 'burden' tolerated solely at its 'pleasure'. As a result, Aboriginal peoples, as Oren Lyons and John Mohawk protest, have been 'exiled in the land of the free'.

The practice of treaty constitutionalism is not the ideal speech-situation or the heteroglossia of the scholars. The 'kind of scrubbed, disinfected interlocutor' in these theoretical models of dialogue, Edward Said writes, 'is a laboratory creation, with suppressed, and therefore falsified, connections to the urgent situation of crisis and conflict that brought him or her to attention in the first place'.[37] The treaty system is a living human practice in which, by great effort, the battle for recognition by arms has been transformed into the conflict of words. This does not end the strategies of fraud and deceit humans play under the colour of the conventions. It only stops the killing, and this only as long as the participants continue to listen to each other.

Nevertheless, the point of this book is that when Aboriginal peoples claim injustice has been done and demand redress, they appeal to the three conventions to justify their case, arguing that their status as nations has been misrecognised, their powers of self rule discontinued and their consent bypassed. The agents of justice on the other side appeal to the same norms of justification. They argue that they have recognised Aboriginal people appropriately, that they consented to discontinue their powers or that consent can be ignored in this case. The three conventions of common constitutionalism are immanent in this practice – and in the practices of constitutionalism to follow – as the norms of justification, in spite of the efforts of modern constitutionalists to bury them.

It is possible to expose the biases and specious arguments, and see the justice of the practice, not by creating an ideal model to which reality must correspond but, as we are engaged in doing, by surveying it from Aboriginal and non-Aboriginal perspectives. And this practical activity of critical reflection can be extended by drawing comparisons with other examples of common and modern constitutionalism, gradually acquiring a critical understanding of contemporary constitutionalism as we approach this labyrinth from one path after another. In this way, as Wittgenstein recommends, we extend our concept of constitutionalism, as 'in spinning a thread we twist fibre on fibre. And the strength of the thread does not reside in the fact that some one fibre runs through its whole length, but in the overlapping of many fibres.'[38]

CHAPTER 5

The historical formation of common constitutionalism: the rediscovery of cultural diversity, part II

Diverse federalism and the conventions of mutual recognition, continuity and consent

The next example of a constitutional association based on the three conventions I wish to discuss is 'compact' or, as I prefer, 'diverse' federalism. In the first chapter we saw that one of the major causes of conflicts and civil wars over cultural recognition is the inability of modern constitutionalism to tolerate multinational constitutional associations with a diversity of often overlapping legal and political cultures. The requirements of one sovereign people (in one of three forms), one nation and one uniform order of modern legal and political institutions make the recognition and accommodation of diversity impossible. The only options available within these parameters are either assimilation or secession, neither of which resolves the problem of recognition under conditions of cultural diversity. The former Yugoslavia is one of the most tragic examples, as Noel Malcolm has argued in his exemplary case study, and the break up of Czechoslovakia is another, non-violent but extremely expensive instance.

Diverse federalism is a means of conciliation because it enables peoples mutually to recognise and reach agreement on how to assemble or federate the legal and political differences they wish to continue into the association. A good example is the confederation of the provinces of Nova Scotia, New Brunswick, Lower Canada (Québec) and Upper Canada (Ontario) to form Canada in 1867. The discontinuity and uniformity school interprets confederation as the subordination of the provinces to the sovereign federal government and the creation of uniform provinces. The continuity and diversity school interprets it as the creation of a federal government by the delegation of some provincial powers and the continuity and co-ordinate sovereignty of the diverse provinces.

The best presentation of the diverse federalism interpretation is by a Québec jurist, Justice Thomas-Jean-Jacques Loranger, in *Lettres sur l'interprétation de la constitution fédérale: première lettre* (1883). First, the four provinces recognised each other as autonomous, self-governing constitutional associations under British rule. 'These provinces', Loranger writes, were 'in the enjoyment of their complete political and legislative autonomy.' Their pre-existing status was 'guaranteed to them by treaties and Imperial statutes' of the previous century. As Chief Justice Dorion had explained in 1874, 'we have responsible government in all the provinces, and these powers are not introduced by legislators, but in conformity with usage', that is 'founded on the consent and recognition of those principles which guide the British Constitution'.[1]

The second or 'compact' feature is that the act of confederation consisted in reaching agreement, by the consent of the four colonial governments through three years of negotiations, on which powers they would delegate to constitute a federal government to govern their common affairs. The 'provinces did not attribute to the federal government powers of a nature different from those that each before possessed. They delegated to it a portion only of their local powers to form a central power, that is to say, they allowed it the management of their affairs of a general character, but retained their own government for their local affairs.'[2]

As a consequence, finally, the political and legal institutions of the provinces – their cultures of self rule – continued through the confederation. 'In constituting themselves into a confederation, the provinces did not intend to renounce, and in fact never did renounce their autonomy. This autonomy with their rights, powers and prerogatives they expressly preserve for all that concerns their internal government.' Hence, there is no subordination to the federal government, but rather, 'an equality between them or rather a similarity of powers, and that each of the two powers is sovereign within its respective spheres'. This is, he concludes, the same in the 'Helvetian and Germanic confederations and in all other possible confederations', including, he claims, the United States:[3]

the central government has only those powers which are conferred on it by the states and the latter retain the remainder, for the very simple reason, that the central government is the creation of the several governments that have given it the form and totality of powers which they deemed suitable, and no more.

Let us draw out the implications of this form of constitution. Since the pre-existing forms of provincial government are bound to be various, and since the citizens will amend them from time to time, the resulting federation is an irregular and multiform assemblage. The equality it embodies is not the identity of political and legal institutions, but the equal recognition and autonomy of the diverse forms of provincial self government. The irregularity of the federation will also increase as other provinces join, as in the case of Canada, so the resulting assemblage will have the appearance of diversity that Descartes commended and Pufendorf condemned.

Since the consent of each province is required for confederation and any subsequent amendment that touches their legal and political culture, some provinces may agree to delegate powers to the federal government that others choose to retain until they see how economically the federal government exercises them, or perhaps to experiment with a different model themselves. For example, Québec has its own pension plan whereas the other provinces have delegated this power to the federal government. Such an association also varies in character depending on which powers are delegated, shared and retained. Some federal powers apply directly to citizens; others to the provinces. Hence, it is difficult and pointless to apply the rigid concepts of federation and confederation to an association like Canada, as Jennifer Smith shows, or, say, India, for they exhibit features of both. The citizens are the sovereign people of two political associations, with overlapping political identities and loyalties. *Ex uno plures* is thus an appropriate motto for such an association.

Compact federalism does not require unanimity on every amendment, only the consent of the people of the provinces affected, or their provincial representatives, in accord with *q.o.t.* The provinces can also agree on an amending formula short of unanimity, provided that one agreement is unanimous. This is analogous to the individual case in liberal theory, where each individual consents on entering a political society to be governed by the majority principle. There are also many informal arrangements in the federal tradition to ensure that members are properly protected. An amendment that affects the individual citizens of the entire federation requires the consent of the majority through their federal representatives or a referendum. Those who find these checks and balances too onerous want a warrant to ram through their monological vision of the constitution without the difficult but rewarding activity of becoming aware of the diversity of their partners and of reaching agreement by constitutional dialogue. Their attitude belongs to the imperial age.

The final feature is the liberal character of compact federalism. Loranger explains that an association of this kind is based on a combination of the conventions of continuity of self rule and of consent to any alteration. He states that a 'right or a power can no more be taken away from a nation than an individual, except by a law which revokes it or by a voluntary abandonment'.[4] The analogy he draws between a nation and an individual brings out its liberal pedigree. In early modern liberal theories, such as Locke's, individuals enter into a constitutional association with pre-existing rights which are mutually recognised. This culture of individual rights is continued into the association except for those rights which they, or their representatives, consent to delegate to constitute a government. Loranger's point is that the same principles apply whenever the people who form the association have pre-existing forms of self government as well as pre-existing individual rights, which is, despite the counterfactual conception of the people in modern constitutionalism, almost every time.

If so, why is not compact federalism a constitutive feature of modern liberal theory? In a decision that affirms Loranger's interpretation, Lord Watson of the Privy Council draws a sharp contrast with the discontinuity interpretation which puts this question in focus:[5]

The object of the Act of Confederation was neither to weld the provinces into one, nor to subordinate provincial governments to a central authority, but to create a federal government in which they should all be represented, entrusted with the exclusive administration of affairs in which they had a common interest, each province retaining its independence and autonomy.

The difficulty from the point of view of Loranger and Watson is to understand why any people would weld themselves into a union or subordinate themselves to a federal sovereign. In the most searing passage in the text, Loranger asks why any people, after struggling for centuries to govern themselves by their own laws and ways, would do such a thing:[6]

Why should the Province of Quebec, for example, have, on an inauspicious day, with utter want of thought, abandoned its rights the most sacred, guaranteed by treaties and preserved by secular contests, and sacrificed its language, its institutions and its laws, to enter into an insane union, which, contracted under these conditions, would have been the cause of its national and political annihilation? And why should the other provinces, any more than Quebec, have consented to lose their national existence and consummate this political suicide?

The answer from the other side is that the refusal to do so offends against just about every feature of modern constitutionalism. To see the difference, let us return to Hobbes' extreme formulation of the opposing view:[7]

where there be divers Provinces, within the Dominion of a Commonwealth, and in those provinces diversity of Lawes, which commonly are called the Customes of each severall Province, we are not to understand that such Customes have their force, onely from Length of time; but that they were antiently Lawes written, or otherwise made known, for the Constitutions, and Statutes of their Soveraigns; and are now Lawes, not by vertue of the Praescription of time, but by the Constitutions of their present Soveraigns.

The general principle is that 'all Lawes, written and unwritten, have their Authority, and force, from the Will of the Common-wealth; that is to say, from the Will of the Representative'. On this view, the provinces were not autonomous and did not have the authority to enter into constitutional negotiations in 1867. They derived their authority from the imperial Crown. After confederation, sovereignty gradually devolved in the course of decolonisation to the federal government, for there can be only one will of the commonwealth, and the provinces are subordinate to it. Furthermore, as the three undifferentiated concepts of popular sovereignty came to be authoritative, the authority of the provinces was further reduced, if not entirely dis- regarded. Québec then appears as nothing more than a large number of French-speaking individuals in one region or some kind of ethnic minority asking for special status against the norm of uniformity. The very idea that Loranger was trying to get across – that Québec is a sovereign and co-ordinate constitutional society that has governed itself by its laws and ways for centuries and is multicultural in composition – is impossible to express in this framework.

Diverse federalism and continuity: the Québec Act and the ancient constitution

To understand how the modern framework came to be widely accepted, and diverse federalism relegated to the margins, we need to retrace our steps. The continuity of the provinces' ways of self government was also recognised, as Loranger notes, in earlier constitutional acts: the Constitution Act of 1791, which established the provinces of Lower and Upper Canada, and the Québec Act of 1774, which brought Québec (or Canada, as it was then called) into the British Empire after the capitulation of France in 1760.

The Québec Act guaranteed that the Roman catholic

religion, French language, seigneurial property system and the customary laws and forms of government from the French period would continue until a legislature was established. The Québec legislators could then alter these old forms as they saw fit. The protestant religion, English language and schools, and the right to use English in the courts and legislature were also recognised and protected for the English-speaking immigrants. In defending this most enlightened example of continuity, William Knox, a whig undersecretary, gave one of the best analyses of the pros and cons of continuity and discontinuity, as well as an example of how a constitutional dialogue can be approximated even in a case of capitulation. I will let Knox speak for himself.

In *The Justice and policy of the late act of parliament* of 1774, Knox explains, although the 'free exercise of their religion' and 'the full enjoyment of their property' were guaranteed to the *canadiens* by the capitulation of 1760 and the subsequent treaty of Paris, these were temporarily discontinued in 1763 and an English legal system imposed. It 'is difficult to conceive the misery and distress in which the poor Canadians found themselves involved by the operation of these new and unknown laws'. Foreshadowing Joseph Brant's candid assessment of the English legal system twelve years later, Knox writes, 'we shall cease to wonder, that the Canadians are not in rapture with the English laws of arrests, and be less amazed at the obstinate prejudice they maintain for their own laws and customs', if we only realise that 'there is no country under heaven, where the recovery of debt is attended with more circumstances of cruelty, misery and slavery than our own'.[8]

The citizens of Québec petitioned for the restoration of their 'former laws and customs'. Instead of drawing up a theory, the 'king's servants' listened, for they 'were not inattentive to the state of Quebec, or deaf to the cries of the Canadians'. Mr Morgan was sent 'to collect the laws and customs which had prevailed or been in force in Canada under the French government'. A commission was instructed to examine the whole and transmit their opinions, 'how far those laws and customs were fit to be adopted in any general plan for the regulation of the province, and fully to report their sentiments of the nature of the constitution, which was most likely to give content and satisfaction to the inhabitants, and attach them to the English government'.

The opinions were then studied and a number of conflicting plans were proposed. To find a resolution they then examined earlier examples that could serve as 'precedents'. Ireland was selected as a case of discontinuity and Minorca of continuity. In the case of Ireland, 'the capitulation of Limerick was the only assurance' for Irish catholics of 'the enjoyment of their property or the exercise of their religion'. This continuity affected only a few. The 'vast majority of that wretched people, were at the mercy of the victorious protestants'.

A regime of discontinuity and reform was imposed. The Irish catholics were 'by law rendered incapable of purchasing, inheriting or even obtaining the security of a mortgage upon a land estate'. To encourage the discovery and 'detention of offenders against these laws, as well as to promote refor-mation, the informers are rewarded with a grant of the lands, which, upon conviction of the owner, become forfeited to the crown'. Besides the legal disabilities, the Roman catholics are deprived of 'all weapons offensive or defensive', and it is 'penal for them to cut their victuals with knives exceeding a certain length'. They are debarred from giving their children any education 'unless under protestant masters', and if the profits on their farms 'exceed one third of the rent, their leases become voidable'.

It 'is difficult to imagine', he reflects, 'what more can be done by severe treatment to extinguish a sect, or deprive its followers of all spirit or ability to disturb the government'. Yet, the effect of these policies of discontinuity and reform has been precisely the opposite. After almost a century, 'such is still the malignant hatred borne by the papists to the protestants', that, 'although the protestants now bear the pro-portion of two to five to the Roman catholics, are in possession of all the offices of the state, the land owners of nearly the whole island, and protected' as well 'by the whole power of England, they think themselves in the utmost danger of being massacred by the papists, if, even in time of peace, there should happen to be a less number than twelve thousand effective troops remaining in the island'. What 'success may we hope for from the like methods in Canada, where the Roman catholic inhabitants are five hundred to one protestant, and those Roman catholics ten years ago were subjects of France, and every man bearing arms against England?'

Turning to the example of continuity in Minorca, Knox writes, 'the effects of lenity' were 'more promising' and 'more to the point'. The inhabitants of Minorca were Spaniards 'hostile to England', yet they were 'permitted the full enjoyment of their religion and properties, from the cession of the island to Great Britain by the treaty of Utrecht to the present hour'. Although 'we have had two wars with Spain in that time, and the island has once been conquered by France, the inhabitants have shewn no impatience under English government'. Therefore, he concludes, the planners were induced 'to adopt a plan of lenity and indulgence' towards Québec, 'from the comparison of the advantages with which that mode of treatment had been attended in Minorca, with what had been the result of the severe system' in Ireland. Another policy consideration, he adds, was the other thirteen hostile colonies would seize on any 'discontent' that such a severe system would surely cause.

So far, he continues, I have 'argued the point upon the opposition's ground', and 'made it appear, to the conviction of every unprejudiced mind, that the plan, which benevolence and humanity recommend, is consonant with the soundest policy'. But, there is still the consideration of *'justice'*, which ought to prevail even over 'impolicy, if that could be proved'. In this case, justice and policy coincide, for the treaty of Paris guarantees the Roman catholic religion and the pre-existing system of property, 'which his majesty is not by his prerogative enabled to abolish'. The Roman catholics in Canada, in addition, are not subject to the disabilities, and penalties, to which Roman catholics in this kingdom are subject', because the Acts of Parliament which imposed them 'do not extend to Canada'.

The Canadians 'are also capable of and entitled to all the rights of British subjects in that province' to hold public office, serve on juries, hold elections and have an assembly. The continuity and expansion of their rights of governing themselves by their own laws and ways is 'founded upon the principles of humanity'. In summary, the 'Quebec Act' secures 'the enjoyment of their properties and civil rights; and the re-establishment of their ancient laws and customs, subject to such alterations as the legislature of the province may think fit to make'.

The reason why the conventions of continuity and consent were familiar to and embraced by eighteenth-century whig loyalists like William Knox and Lord Mansfield is that they are the normative foundations of their whig philosophy of the 'ancient constitution'. On this widespread early modern view, reconstructed by John Pocock in *The ancient constitution and the feudal law*, when William conquered England and imposed the Norman yoke of feudal law, he could not discontinue the pre-existing ancient constitution of Anglo-Saxon local government, trial by jury, independent property and individual liberties. These early beginnings of the common-law liberties of a free people survived the conquest and were authoritative in virtue of their long use and practice. Although whig and republican writers would often speak of these liberties of self rule as 'natural' and derive them from 'reason' alone, they would almost always, as Mark Goldie and Richard Ashcraft have shown, make the complementary argument that they could also be derived from the history of the ancient constitution. As a consequence, the very civil liberties and forms of self government that the whigs championed were based on the conventions of the ancient constitution as they applied to the Norman conquest of England.

As we might expect, Matthew Hale presents a classic exposition of the ancient constitution in *The history of the common law of England*. The conquest by King William was not, he opens his famous discussion, 'such a conquest as did, or could alter the Laws of this Kingdom, or impose Laws upon the People *per Modum Conquestus*'. Contrary to Hobbes, the prevailing laws have authority from their 'usage and custom'. The primary reason why the laws and religion of a country are continued through a conquest is on 'Account of Humanity, thinking it a hard and over-severe thing to impose presently upon the conquered a Change of their Customs, which long Use has made dear to them'.[9]

In his chapter on conquest in the *Two treatises*, Locke defends the ancient constitution, but he redescribes it in terms of rights in a manner which eliminates the convention of continuity. Even 'if William had a right to make War on this Island', '(as by the History it appears otherwise)', his dominion by conquest would 'reach no farther, than to the *Saxons* and *Britains* that were then Inhabitants of this Country'. He lays it down in successive sections that even a just conqueror 'gets no power but only over those, who have actually assisted, concurr'd, or consented to that unjust force, that is used against him'. Conquest gives him '*no right of Dominion*' over those who did not fight against him, or even of the posterity of those that did: they 'are free of any subjection to him'. Secondly, a conqueror has a right to the amount of property necessary to make up for damages, but this 'will scarce give him a *Title to any Countrey he shall Conquer*'. He 'has not thereby a Right and Title to their Possessions'. Hence, the inhabitants of 'any country' who 'derive a Title to their Estates from those, who are subdued, and had a Government forced upon them against their free consent, *retain a Right to the Possession of their Ancestors*':[10]

> For the first *Conqueror never having had a Title to the Land* of that Country, the People who are the Descendents of, or claim under those, who were forced to submit to the Yoke of a Government by constraint, have always a right to shake it off, and free themselves from the Usurpation, or Tyranny, which the Sword hath brought in upon them, till their Rulers put them under such a Frame of Government, as they willingly, and of choice consent to.

A conqueror has no rights over the prevailing system of property and form of government unless the people consent to its alteration. If he cannot gain their consent, he is constrained to recognise the continuation of both, as William presumably did, or face justified revolution. 'Who doubts', Locke concludes, 'but the Grecian Christian descendents of the ancient possessors of that Country may justly cast off the Turkish yoke which they have so long groaned under when ever they have the power to do it? For no Government can have a right to obedience from a people who have not freely consented to it.'

In this powerful and revolutionary doctrine, the convention of consent does all the work. The prevailing system of property and government has no authority from the normative force of custom and usage, but solely from the people's refusal to consent to the conqueror's system. This reformulation is consistent with Locke's modern account of custom we considered in chapter 3. Locke thought that the doctrine would have very little use because he mistakenly assumed, as most modern theorists have done, it 'seldom happens' that the 'Conquerors and Conquered never incorporate into one people, under the same laws and freedom'.[11] Looking back from the end of the twentieth century, it is obvious that he was wrong, not only in the long run, but almost immediately.

For, if a conqueror cannot alter the property or government of a conquered people without their consent, then a colonial people, who have not even been conquered, must enjoy at least as much freedom from their imperial government. Locke's close friend, William Molyneux, wasted no time in drawing this inference, to Locke's disapproval, in his influential defence of the autonomy of the Irish protestant legislature from Imperial interference, in *The case of Ireland being bound by the Acts of the Parliament of England* (1698). He did not, we may note, apply it mutually to Irish catholics. Molyneux's argument complemented the older view that the four nations of England, Scotland, Wales and Ireland constituted a confederal or 'multiple' kingdom.

Within thirty-five years, John Norris, in *The liberty and property of British subjects* (1726), used the *Two treatises* to justify colonial resistance to the imperial constitution of Carolina that Locke himself had helped to draft. In the *Rights of the*

British colonies asserted and proved (1764), James Otis combined Locke's convention of consent with his sections on the beginnings of political societies to protest that the British government could not interfere with colonial property without the consent of the colonial legislatures. Even though Locke argued that the convention of consent did not apply to Aboriginal peoples, Samuel Wharton, whom we met earlier, used the *Two treatises* to defend their property and government in *Plain facts* (1781).

Diverse federalism, the three conventions and the American revolution

The most effective interpretation and selective application of the conventions of the ancient constitution is *A summary view of the rights of British America* by Thomas Jefferson in 1775. In the pamphlet, Jefferson sets out the main justification for the revolution: the British government passed laws and interfered with colonial property without the consent of the colonial legislatures. The 'universal law' the British government has violated is, 'a right which nature has given to all men, of departing from the country in which chance, not choice, has placed them, of going in quest of new habitations, and of there establishing new societies, under such laws and regulations as to them shall seem most likely to promote public happiness'.

The first British settlers in America applied this law in the same manner as 'their Saxon ancestors had' long ago in leaving northern Europe and possessing 'themselves of the island of Britain', which was 'then less charged with inhabitants'. The Saxons then 'established there that system of laws which has so long been the glory and protection of that country'. Their mother country in northern Europe exerted no claim over them, and, if it were to do so now, the present subjects of Great Britain 'have too firm a feeling of the rights derived to them from their ancestors, to bow down the sovereignty of their state before such visionary pretensions'.

With this venerable precedent firmly in place, Jefferson draws the inescapable analogy. As for the British settlers in America, 'for themselves they fought, for themselves they conquered, and for themselves alone they have right to hold'. Great Britain offered no assistance whatsoever. The emigrants then freely chose 'to adopt that system of laws under which they had hitherto lived in the mother country, and to continue their union with her by submitting themselves to the same common sovereign, who was thereby made the central link connecting the several parts of the empire'.[12]

Great Britain violated this imperial chain of sovereign parts linked together by consent. The British Crown and parliament transgressed the authority of the colonial assemblies to draw their own boundaries and establish the common-law system of allodial property allotment, which the colonies introduced by collective assemblies of the people, or 'by their legislature, to whom they may have delegated sovereign authority', or by the Lockean rule that 'each individual of the society may appropriate to himself such lands as he finds vacant, and occupancy will give him title'. Instead, the Crown seized control of land grants by the 'fictitious principle that all lands belong originally to the king', and the settlers, being farmers not lawyers, 'were early persuaded' and 'accordingly took grants of their own lands from the crown'.

The fiction is based on the principle, 'first introduced' by 'William, the Norman', that 'all lands in England were held either mediately or immediately of the crown'. But this system could only be rightly applied to 'those who fell in the battle of Hastings'. Although this comprises 'a considerable proportion of the lands of the whole kingdom', it does not include the land 'left in the hands of his Saxon subjects: held of no superior, and not subject to feudal conditions'. In the same way that 'Norman lawyers' sought to impose further 'feudal burdens' on the common-law property of free born Englishmen under the guise of the Norman fiction of discontinuity, successive 'princes' sought to usurp property in America and, among other methods,[13]

parted out and distributed among the favourites and followers of their fortunes, and, by an assumed right of the crown alone, were erected into distinct and independent governments; a measure which it is believed his majesty's prudence and understanding would prevent him from imitating at this day, as no exercise of such a power, of dividing and dismembering a country, has ever occured in his majesty's realm of England.

The problem Jefferson and the other revolutionaries faced is, if the conventions of continuity and consent apply in their case and justify their cause, then, by the convention of mutual recognition and parity of reasoning, they apply as well to the Aboriginal nations, as the Crown recognised in the Royal Proclamation of 1763, and to the colony of Québec, as the Crown recognised in the Québec Act of 1774. All we need to do to see this is to view Jefferson's confederal empire of sovereign societies, linked together by the consent of the parts, from each neighbourhood. In turn, as some loyalists were willing to concede to avoid revolution, the Crown was equally constrained to recognise the co-ordinate status of the colonial assemblies, as it somewhat belatedly did in the Balfour Declaration of 1927. However, as Jefferson's account of the 'conquest' and 'allotment' of America foreshadows, the revolutionaries had no intention of mutually recognising the claims of others. Instead, they invaded Canada to the north and the Indian lands to the west.

The justification for not recognising the continuity and consent of others is presented in the Declaration of Independence of 1776. The Aboriginal nations, as we have seen, are redescribed in the progressive language of modern constitutionalism as savages in a state of war. The Royal Proclamation protected the Aboriginal nations to the west and outlawed colonial claims to their lands by the very system Jefferson condemned in 1775. It is alluded to, as one of the 'long train of abuses and usurpations' which evinces a design to introduce 'absolute despotism', under the grievance of 'raising the conditions of new Appropriation of Lands'. The Québec Act is redescribed as a grievance, for 'abolishing the free system of English Laws in a neighbouring Province, establishing therein an Arbitrary government, and enlarging its boundaries so as to render it at once an example and fit instrument for introducing the same absolute rule into these

Colonies'. The so-called 'free system of Laws' that was 'abolished' refers to the system of English laws that was imposed in 1763, in violation of the treaty of Paris and the convention of continuity, and rescinded in 1774![14]

This hostile condemnation of Canada as an enemy is explained by Charles Metzger in terms of the religious intolerance of the revolutionaries. Be this as it may, the contrast between 'free' English and 'arbitrary' *canadien* governments suggests that the convention of continuity has been replaced by the modern intolerance of different forms of government. The grievance that Canada's borders were enlarged in order to introduce a similar form of 'arbitrary' government in the colonies points to a further reason. In explaining the Québec Act two years earlier (1774), William Knox reminds his readers that the Royal Proclamation of 1763 established a boundary down the western backs of the colonies. It limited 'settlements under grants from the old provinces', excluded 'all provinces from jurisdiction in the interior of Indian country', and regulated all 'trade with the savages'. The colonists violated the boundary, 'emigrants in great numbers flocked thither' and they 'took possession of vast tracts of country without any authority, and seated themselves in such situations as pleased them best'.

Fortunately, Knox continues, the *canadiens* had a string of trading posts along the entire boundary which they had built up over the previous century and one half. Therefore, to stop the intrusion on Indian land, 'the whole of the derelict country is, by the first clause of the [Québec] act, put under the jurisdiction of the government of Quebec, with the avowed purpose of excluding all further settlement therein, and for the establishment of uniform regulations for the Indian trades'.[15] Therefore, for the revolutionaries to recognise that the constitutional conventions which they applied in their own case applied mutually to Québec, would be, *eo ipso*, to concede that they applied as well to the Aboriginal nations.

In these examples, the three conventions are abused to undermine the diverse federations they would entail and to establish uniform constitutional associations in their place. However, as McIlwain once argued, the patriots who fought the revolution continued to think about constitutionalism in the terms of these three ancient conventions, even when they applied them partially.[16] What brought many to abandon them altogether, and to embrace the new constitution of the United States in 1787?

The constitutional convention was unable to gain the unanimous consent of the state legislatures to the new constitution. Yet, the revolution, as Jefferson explained above, was fought in the name of the sovereignty of the state legislatures, delegated to them by the citizens of the states, and this was affirmed in the Articles of Confederation. Any alteration in the constitution that touched them would require their consent, for, again, this was the justification for the rebellion against Great Britain and the principle of the Articles of Confederation. To proceed without the consent of the states would be to abandon the convention on which the new republic rested.

Madison takes up the constitutional impasse in number forty of the *Federalist papers*. The dilemma is, he writes, not hiding his preference: 'whether it was of most importance to the happiness of the people of America that the Articles of Confederation should be disregarded, and an adequate government be provided, and the Union preserved; or that an adequate government should be omitted, and the Articles of Confederation preserved'. The criterion for deciding constitutional cases such as these is that, 'where the several parts cannot be made to coincide, the less important should give way to the more important part; the means should be sacrificed to the end, rather than the end to the means'.[17]

On Madison's view, 'the establishment of a government adequate to the national happiness was the end', to which the Articles of Confederation ought, 'as insufficient means, to have been sacrificed'. Accordingly, the ancient convention of consent was reduced to an expendable means and the new constitution established. The new, modern convention, which he weaves into his formulation of the dilemma, is the 'happiness of the people of America'. The 'people of America' are not the citizens of states, who fought the revolution for the recognition of their forms of government, but the unconstituted members of the entire republic. The justification for overriding and subordinating the states in this way, he retroactively argues, is that in many cases 'the powers of the [new] Confederation operate immediately on the persons and interests of individual citizens'. Once the people are seen in this unconstituted light, then it is undemocratic not to proceed when the convention had the consent of nine of the thirteen states with a majority of the population, or to consider 'the absurdity of subjecting the fate of twelve states to the perverseness or corruption of a thirteenth'.[18]

The arguments prove, Madison concludes, 'that the charge against the convention of exceeding their powers' has 'no foundation to support it'. Even 'if they had violated both their powers and their obligations', as he concedes, 'this ought nevertheless to be embraced, if it be calculated to accomplish the views and happiness of the people of America'. By abandoning the conventions on which the revolution had been fought, and by employing arguments noticeably similar to the ones used earlier by British loyalists against the demands of the colonial assemblies, the new constitution with its modern conception of the people was laid over the old confederation and its ancient articles. The constitutional *'coup d'état'*, as Charles Beard called it, was complete.[19]

As the *Haudenosaunee* image of the chain is meant to remind us, such celebrated constitutional acts appear greater in theory than they are in practice. Much of the old sovereignty of the states continued into the new federation and, as Calvin R. Massey reminds us, the sovereign states have used it to create a diverse federation of legal and political pluralism in practice, unknown to the theorists and similar in some aspects to Canada.

The modern attack on diverse federalism: the Durham report and its followers

The problem with the three conventions from a modern point of view is that they bring into a new constitutional association

forms of government from a lower stage of historical development, make reaching agreement difficult and obstruct
progressive consolidation and uniformity. Now, we have just
seen the exemplary arguments employed to discredit the
convention of consent and replace it with 'the happiness of
the people'. Abuses of the convention of mutual recognition
are too numerous to recall. This leaves the convention of
continuity. In what circumstances was it redescribed in
the language of modern constitutionalism as an obstacle to
progress, and the policy of discontinuity and reform applauded
as enlightened constitutionalism? One of the most influential
instances is the report on Canada by the liberal Lord Durham
in 1840.

In 1791 Canada was constituted into two provinces with their
own legislatures: Lower Canada (Québec) and Upper Canada
(Ontario, the former *pays d'en haut*). French was the majority
language in Lower Canada and English in Upper Canada.
In addition, the languages, religions and rights to use both
French and English in the courts and legislatures were
continued and guaranteed for the English minority in Lower
Canada and the French minority in Upper Canada. The
recognition of the governments and territories of Aboriginal
nations in the Royal Proclamation was reaffirmed in Royal
Instructions and treaty making. In 1837–8, several Lower and
Upper Canadians, both French and English, decided it was
time to do what the thirteen other colonies had done: overthrow British rule and establish independent republics. The
popular rebellions were defeated and Durham was sent to
report.

Given what the rebels had actually said, especially in Lower
Canada, Durham writes that he 'expected to find a contest
between a government and a people': that is, a contest of
Canadians against British rule. This expectation was
furthered by the fact that 'the French', who led the rebellion
in Lower Canada, 'have been viewed as the democratic party,
contending for reform', and 'the English as a conservative
minority, protecting the menaced connexion with the British
Crown'. Moreover, some 'vague expectation of absolute

independence still seems to delude them'. Their 'national vanity' induces 'many to flatter themselves with the idea of a Canadian Republic', and the name of the leader, 'Mr. Papineau', 'is still cherished by the people'. The presumption of a struggle for decolonisation was also reinforced by what Durham's editor calls 'foolish vapouring about Canadian Independence and a Canadian Republic in 1837–8'.[20]

Despite the testimony of these voices, the idea of the people seeking their political freedom is a complete misconstrual of the situation according to Durham. He proceeds to construe the conflict in a manner that will be entirely familiar not only to *québécois(es)* and Canadians, but also to anyone who reads Western media reports of conflicts over cultural recognition today. That is to say, he presents it as an ethnic or racial conflict, caused by the continuity of pre-modern ways.

He begins by stating that he 'found a struggle, not of principles, but of races', a 'deadly animosity that now separates the inhabitants of Lower Canada into the hostile divisions of French and English'. The source of the animosity is the differences between the two races. The French-speaking colonists were governed in the old regime by a 'central, ill-organised, unimproving and repressive despotism'. Uneducated and dominated by priests, they became 'a race of men habituated to the incessant labour of a rude and unskilled agriculture' and so on. They 'remained the same uninstructed, inactive, unprogressive people'. In sum, they 'clung to ancient prejudices, ancient customs and ancient laws, not from any strong sense of their beneficial effects, but with the unreasoning tenacity of an uneducated and unprogressive people'.[21]

The race of English settlers who arrived after 1760, in contrast are superior in every respect. They have 'a great respect for popular rights' and include 'hardy farmers and humble mechanics'. The 'active and regular habits of the English capitalist drove out' the 'careless competitors of the French race', creating employment and profits that 'had not previously existed'. They purchased seigneurial lands of the French settlers, and 'full half of the more valuable seigniories are actually owned by English proprietors'. The English farmer 'carried with him the experience and habits of the most improved agriculture in the world', so overtaking 'the worn-out and slovenly farm of the habitant'.

Even though he notes that the French were the first non-Aboriginals to explore the continent and establish continent-wide trade routes, he reports that the English have 'developed the resources of the country', 'constructed or improved its means of communication', and 'created its internal and foreign commerce'. As a consequence, the 'large mass of the labouring population are French in the employ of English capitalists'. Although a 'few of the ancient race smarted under the loss occasioned by the success of English competition', he cautions, perhaps concerned about how this narrative might be interpreted in England, this is not to be 'represented as a contest of classes', but, 'in fact, a contest of races'. And, drawing the obvious conclusion, in this contest of races the 'superior political and practical intelligence of the English cannot be, for a moment, disputed'.[22]

The problem is that, although the rights of the English minority are protected, they are outnumbered by the French majority in the Assembly. 'That a race which felt itself thus superior in political activity and intelligence, should submit with patience to the rule of a majority which it could not respect, was impossible.' In particular, the 'jealousy and dislike' of the majority in the Assembly was blocking the English minority's ambition to acquire and speculate in land. Trumpeting the theme of property and empire that Joseph Brant and William Knox discerned earlier, Durham explains that the 'enterprising' English population,[23]

looked on the American Provinces as a vast field for settlement and speculation, and in the common spirit of the Anglo-Saxon inhabitants of that continent, regarded it as the chief business of the Government, to promote, by all possible use of its legislative and administrative powers, the increase of population and the accumulation of property.

A superior and progressive race is thus held in 'check' by an inferior and static race. The cause is that the ancient ways of the French settlers were continued after the Conquest in 1760. The 'continued negligence of the British Government left the mass of the people without any of the institutions that should have elevated them in freedom and civilization'. If these English institutions had been forced on them, 'that would have assimilated their character and habits, in the easiest and best way, to those of the Empire of which they became a part'. But, this was not done and they 'remain an old and stationary society, in a new and progressive world'.

Turning directly now to the convention of continuity, he explains that there 'are two modes by which a government may deal with a conquered territory': either 'respecting the rights and nationality of the actual occupants' or

treating the conquered territory as one open to the conquerors, of encouraging their influx, of regarding the conquered race as entirely subordinate, and of endeavouring as speedily and rapidly as possible to assimilate the character and institutions of its new subjects to those of the great body of its empire.

In the case of Canada, where there is a vast land and a small population, the conqueror should not consider 'the few individuals who happen at the moment to inhabit a portion of the soil', but, rather the modern criterion of the people as a whole – 'those of that comparatively vast population' that will populate it in the future. He should 'establish those institutions which would be most acceptable to the race by which he hoped to colonize the country'. To remove any doubt, Durham adds that the vast population will undoubtedly be 'Anglo-Saxon', for the 'English race' is sure to predominate, 'even numerically in Lower Canada', as 'they predominate already, by their superior knowledge, energy, enterprise and wealth'. Therefore, he concludes, the fundamental cause of the conflict in Canada is neither imperialism nor exploitation, as the participants claimed, but the archaic convention of continuity. The 'error' to which 'the present contest must be attributed, is the vain endeavour to preserve a French Canadian nationality in the midst of Anglo-American colonies and states'.[24]

Having dismissed the oldest convention of Western constitutionalism, he recommends the union of Lower Canada with the more populous Upper Canada so the French Canadians could be completely assimilated to the superior English ways. The union should be neither a mere 'amalgamation' nor a federation of two equal provinces, but one which ensures the 'end of out-numbering the French'. The 'change of a language' over 'a whole people' will take some time, but the 'alteration of the character of the Province ought to be immediately entered on, and firmly, though cautiously followed up'. Lower Canada 'must be governed now, as it must hereafter, by an English population'. The justification for discontinuity and assimilation is a 'comprehensive view of the future and the permanent improvement of the Province'.[25]

In this example, the ways of property acquisition and empire building are attributed to a dominant race and palmed off as universal and modern, to which all others must be subjected and gradually assimilated in the name of progress. Resistance to this modern form of usurpation is construed as the reaction of ethnic backwardness. With arguments such as these, the policies of discontinuity and reform surveyed in chapter 3 found their modern justifications. As Bhikhu Parekh points out, John Stuart Mill 'enthusiastically welcomed the Durham Report, calling it an "imperishable memorial of that nobleman's courage, patriotism and enlightened liberty"'.[26] He hoped to see a similar policy in India. The Act for the Gradual Civilization of the Indian Tribes of 1857 was written in the same spirit of imperial expansion and racial superiority. Sir John Seeley presented similar arguments for a culturally homogeneous British empire in *The expansion of England* in 1884.

Québec struggled successfully against the union that followed Durham's recommendation and, as Loranger explained, agreed to the diverse federation of 1867 on the grounds that its three conventions would protect Québec from any future attempts at usurpation. No constitutional amendment touching Québec's political culture was put through without the consent of the provincial government until 1982, when the Canadian Charter of Rights and Freedoms was enacted with the express dissent of the Québec Assembly. The amendment transferred considerable jurisdiction over property and civil rights from the provinces to the federal courts, whereas this jurisdiction was guaranteed to the provinces by the 1867 constitution and, in the case of Québec, by the Québec Act of 1774.

The Québec government had no objection to the individual rights in the Charter (except for the touchy issue of linguistic rights which I will come to in a moment), for Québec already had its own Charter of Rights. The objections the Québec government raised in the courts, as we can now anticipate, were that the amending procedure violated the convention of consent and the amendment violated the convention of continuity, the very principles on which the federation and the consent of the Québec people to it, rests. If these violations are not rectified and Québec's co-ordinate sovereignty recognised through constitutional negotiation, then Québec has the right to secede.

The defenders of the imposition of the Charter on Québec without consent disregarded the language of diverse federalism from Hale, Locke, Molyneux and Jefferson to Knox and Loranger in which the people of Québec, through their representative assembly, voiced their appeal. They covered over the breach of consent and continuity with arguments similar to those of Madison in 1787: unanimous consent is impossible, the Charter has the approval of a majority of the provinces and the population of Canada, and it is a necessary feature of a modern society. Furthermore, they redescribed Québec's claim to political continuity as an illiberal demand of a backward ethnic minority for special status in an otherwise uniform Canadian society based on the sovereignty of the (English-speaking) majority. In so doing, they reproduced the assimilative arguments of Durham without so much as listening to the other side.

After fourteen years of further conflict, there is no sign that the protagonists understand each other's point of view.

Indeed, it is a textbook illustration of the phenomenon of constitutional disintegration we are studying. The words and deeds of one side are redescribed and adjudicated in the monological framework of the other, thereby providing further evidence for the correctness of their comprehensive and exclusive view from the safety of the sidelines. Not surprisingly, those courageous citizens who have taken the *beau risque* of engaging in the constitutional dialogue on the common ground, either in constitutional negotiations or the public conversation surrounding them, have become aware of the partial justice in each other's views and, as Jeremy Webber nicely puts it, are 'reimagining' their association in its unassimilable diversity.

These examples of diverse federalism are not unusual. As Michael Burgess and Alain-G. Gagnon argue in *Comparative federalism and federation*, legal and political pluralism is the norm rather than the exception in contemporary societies. Many are more akin to Canada, India and the United Kingdom than to the norm of a uniform state in modern constitutionalism and its three authoritative schools of interpretation. They are federations of more or less self-governing and overlapping political associations with somewhat dissimilar legal and political ways.

Once the recognition and accommodation of this diversity is seen to rest on three defensible conventions of contemporary constitutionalism, they no longer appear as unenlightened and *ad hoc*, as they do from the monolithic perspective of modern constitutionalism. Quite the opposite. The exclusive reign of modern constitutionalism appears as the continuation of the ancient Norman yoke by other means. When contemporary societies are seen in this post-imperial light, one cannot help but see that, if the three conventions were accepted as the norms of constitutional negotiations over, for example, Northern Ireland and Palestine, the dialogues would proceed more fairly than they have under the constraints of the conventions of modern constitutionalism, as William Knox pleaded long ago.

Linguistic minorities and the three conventions: the form of reasoning
appropriate to mutual recognition and accommodation
So far, we have surveyed examples of how the three conventions can be employed by large members of the black canoe to
mutually recognise each other, providing the norms by which
the bears, eagle and wolf can work out ways of paddling
together. There are also smaller members of the crew: the
frog, the dogfish woman, the mouse woman, the beaver,
the bear cubs and the ancient reluctant conscript. There is
also the raven, the individual member of any culture, small or
large, who wishes to dissent from all the others and express
him- or herself in a distinctive way.

These passengers are more vulnerable because they cannot
claim their own political institutions to protect their cultures.
The members of minority cultures must seek recognition
and accommodation within the institutions they share with
members of the majority cultures of contemporary societies.
They ask to use their languages in the public sphere, to have
appropriate schools and access to the media, to be acknowledged and affirmed in the curricula and narratives of the
societies they have helped to build, and to be able to live in
accord with their cultural ways without discrimination, so they
too can participate in the governance of the constitutional
association without oppression. I have a partiality for these
minority members because I see things from such a standpoint
myself.

Furthermore, acknowledging another aspect of the black
canoe, there are the female members of all cultures, large and
small, who comprise one half of the citizens of any contemporary society: the bear mother, the dogfish woman, the
mouse woman, the raven half the time, and *laana augha*,
the village mother. As we have seen in chapter 2, their many-
splendoured voices deserve to be heard and recognised in
appropriate and equitable ways.

Our survey has shown that the constitutions, institutions
and traditions of interpretation of contemporary societies
have not been, to say the least, established to recognise and
accommodate, let alone affirm, the cultural differences of

these members. If the three conventions do not support the just demands of women and cultural minorities to amend these imperial institutions, they are useless, for these are the intercultural citizens whose cultures criss-cross, overlap and interact the most and pose the toughest challenge to contemporary constitutionalism. Indeed, it is often asserted, even by a scholar as sensitive to these issues as Edward Said, that the recognition and accommodation of the 'overlapping territories' and 'intertwined histories' of the more 'nomadic' citizens is incompatible with the analogous treatment of larger members: interculturalism clashes with nationalism and federalism.[27] If our account cannot recognise the claims of individuals, women, linguistic minorities and intercultural citizens – such as African, Hispanic, Asian, Japanese, Caribbean, Indian, Turkish, Arab and Jewish citizens of the United Kingdom, European Union, United States and Canada – then it will be an inadequate guide to constitutionalism in a post-imperial age of cultural diversity.

The argument of this section is that the three conventions are adequate to this task. The conventions of mutual recognition, consent and continuity can be adapted to these complex cases and applied analogously to recognise and accommodate the cultural diversity of these citizens in just ways. As in the earlier examples, the three conventions are also already to some extent the norms of justification appealed to by both sides in these struggles. The same sorts of reasons advanced by the larger members to resist imperialism and gain liberty are now used, as I pointed out in chapter 1, in analogous ways to defend this third movement of anti-imperial struggles for appropriate cultural forms of self rule within the shared institutions of contemporary societies.

I expect that many readers will see the connections between the earlier examples and these cases, and so be able to go on to apply the three conventions and the concepts of constitutionalism without further ado. None the less, a brief survey will not be superfluous. As we pass through the examples, carefully applying the convention of mutual recognition in each case, our understanding of the nationalist and federalist claims of the larger members will be correspondingly extended, enabling us to see that the apparent conflict is caused by the restrictive and non-aspectual uses of constitutional terms, not by the character of cultures themselves.

The first example is of small linguistic minorities, such as the French-speaking minorities in the English-language provinces of Canada and the English-speaking minority in Québec. Their demands for schools and the use of their languages in the courts, legislatures and public sphere of their respective provinces have been defended in common-law countries on the same grounds as the claims of the majority cultures. If Québec and the English-language provinces seek the constitutional recognition and continuity of their cultural ways, then, by parity of reasoning, they must apply all three conventions in the appropriate manner to the linguistic minorities in their midst. Recognition, to be just, must be mutual.

The argument was presented in an exemplary fashion by Ernest Lapointe in the federal parliament in 1916. He was (unsuccessfully) defending the French-speaking minority in Ontario against the policy of the provincial government to discontinue their French-language schools. Stating the convention of continuity first, he writes that, 'it has long been the settled policy of Great Britain that whenever a country passed under the sovereignty of the Crown by treaty or otherwise, to respect the religion, usages and language of the inhabitants'. Then, 'while fully recognising the principle of provincial rights', which, as we have seen, rests as well on continuity, he goes on to 'respectfully suggest to the legislative assembly [of Ontario] the wisdom of making it clear that the privileges of the children of French parentage of being taught in their mother tongue not be interfered with'.[28]

In 1932, Lord Sankey of the Privy Council made it clear that the conventions of recognition and continuity on which confederation rests apply mutually to the English and French minorities:[29]

it is important to keep in mind that the preservation of the rights of minorities was a condition on which such minorities entered into the federation, and the foundation upon which the whole structure was subsequently erected. The process of interpretation as the years go on ought not to be allowed to dim or to whittle down the provisions of the original contract upon which the federation was founded.

Of course, their minority rights have been dimmed and whittled down many times. The French-speaking settlers of Acadia were driven into exile by British troops in 1755. French schools were outlawed in Nova Scotia in 1864, New Brunswick (1871), Prince Edward Island (1877), Manitoba (1890), Northwest Territories (1892), Albert and Saskatchewan (1905), Keewatin (1912), Ontario (1912), Manitoba (1916) and Saskatchewan (1930). Alberta and Saskatchewan continue to defy Supreme Court rulings upholding the rights of their French-speaking minorities. In spite of the continual policies of discontinuity and assimilation, the French-speaking minorities have courageously survived and, in the course of their legal and political appeals, common-law justices have developed a form of reasoning which applies the conventions of recognition and continuity in an even-handed manner to claims of linguistic minorities and majorities. This is the form of reasoning involved in the application of constitutional law in particular cases which I mentioned earlier; a casuistry of cultural differences and similarities which shapes the language of constitutionalism to fit the cultural diversity of contemporary societies.

One particularly illustrative example is a recent case concerning the English-speaking minority in Québec. They have been vastly better treated than the French-speaking minorities. As the Durham report shows, they could once command the most powerful empire in the world to impose their will on the whole of Québec. Since the quiet revolution in the 1960s, the French-speaking majority has gained political and economic power and sought to defend its popular sovereignty in, or, if necessary, outside the Canadian confederation. Although the democratic majority has continued to protect the language, schools and social services of the minority, following the guarantees agreed to in the 1867 constitution, after 1976 the government passed a law proscribing the use of English on commercial signs and prescribing the use of French only, as part of wider legislation to protect and promote the French language and *visage linguistique* of Québec. To adapt Durham's report to these changed circumstances, a 'few of the' English-speaking citizens 'smarted under the loss occasioned by the success of' the 'competition' of their fellow French-speaking citizens.

A group of English-speaking shopkeepers appealed to the courts that the law violated their individual right of freedom of expression guaranteed in both the Québec and federal charters of rights. The Québec and federal courts ruled in their favour. Politicians and commentators immediately hailed or condemned the case as a great conflict between individual and group rights, or between individual and community. Scholars unhesitatingly and habitually interpret it in these terms, thereby proving the captivity that the language of modern constitutionalism continues to exert over the way we look at constitutional issues.

However, as Avigail Eisenberg demonstrates in her careful survey of this and related cases, the federal court justices did not take up the case in these terms, but, rather, in the language of cultural recognition. They reasoned over the value of 'identity related differences'. The 'notion of difference', she explains, 'denotes differences between people that play a constitutive role in shaping their identities. Culture, religion, language and gender are amongst the central differences that distinguish and help to determine the identities of people in Canadian society'.[30] That is, the sovereign people come already constituted in diverse ways by their 'identity related' or, in my terms, 'cultural' differences of language, religion and gender. If a valuable cultural difference is constitutive of the ways a person speaks and acts, then, like custom in ancient constitutionalism, not to recognise and accommodate it is the injustice of cultural imperialism, for it is to assimilate that person to different ways of speaking and acting without consent.

In their decision, the justices begin with the plaintiffs' side. They give full recognition to individual freedom of expression in public in the language of one's choice. 'Language is so intimately related to the form and content of expression', they write, 'that there cannot be true freedom of expression by means of language if one is prohibited from using the language of one's choice.' They then draw attention to a connection between the two sides. Language is not only 'a means by which a people may express its cultural identity', as the Québec charter of the French language indicates and the defendants submit, but also 'the means by which the individual expresses his or her personal identity and sense of individuality'.

Once language is shown to fit expression in the way form-line sculpture fits Haida myth creatures, they argue that freedom of expression in one's own language is essential to participation in a democratic society. It is necessary to individual 'development' and 'dignity', as well as to 'participation by the members of the society in social, including political, decision-making'. Once the value of the cultural difference in question is established by these criteria drawn from John Stuart Mill and shared by both sides, the only remaining question is whether the use of one's language in commercial signage is an area of free expression protected by the Charter. In a ground-breaking section, the justices conclude that it is, giving the English-speaking shopkeepers the most sympathetic hearing they could have imagined.

The justices then turn to listen to the other side, asking what could justify placing limits on such a valuable identity-related difference in a free and democratic society. The answer they gave is that if it threatens the preservation and enhancement of the French language. For, as we have seen in the above quotation, the French language is reciprocally recognised as the constitutive means in which the 'people' of Québec express their cultural identity. Hence, the French *visage linguistique* is a valuable cultural difference worthy of protection, especially in light of its vulnerability in the context of North America.[31]

After the two claims for cultural continuity are mutually recognised in these terms, the justices ask if there is a mode of accommodation suitable to the circumstances of the case. They answer that a commercial sign policy of French 'always' rather than French 'only' resolves the conflict. As long as the overall 'predominance' of the French language is ensured, bilingual signs should be permitted. The resolution, much like the later decision in France overturning the French only sections of the Toubon law, accommodates each claim for recognition. Moreover, the linguistic minorities in Québec, by expressing themselves on their signs in French and their first language, affirm the predominance of French language and give proportional public expression to the diverse languages that constitute aspects of the linguistic character of the society as a whole.

In coming to their decision, the justices explained that they used a heuristic test which can be applied in many cases of cultural recognition. It is not a set of universal rules and a calculus for its application in every instance. The heuristic test is more like Wittgenstein's 'object of comparison' which brings to light the cultural differences and similarities in a case and furnishes criteria for their mutual accommodation. It might be called the 'even-handed' test for mutual cultural recognition. Two requirements must be satisfied to establish that a legislative limit to a constitutional right, such as the freedom of expression, is justified in a free and democratic society. First the legislative objective, such as the preservation and promotion of the French language, must be 'of sufficient importance' and 'a pressing and substantial concern' to 'warrant' overriding the right. Second, the legislative means employed must be 'proportional to the ends'. The proportionality requirement, in turn has three aspects. The 'limiting measures must be carefully designed, or rationally connected, to the objective; they must impair the right as little as possible; and their effects must not so severely trench on individual or group rights that the legislative objective, albeit important, is nevertheless outweighed by the abridgement of rights'. The court adds that the proportionality test varies 'with circumstances' and that 'rigid and inflexible standards' should be avoided.[32]

Similar forms of reasoning in the language of common constitutionalism are applied in many cases of conflicting claims to cultural recognition. In adjudicating a conflict between Aboriginal and non-Aboriginal fishing rights on the west coast, for example, the court found that fishing a specific body of coastal water is constitutive of the cultural identity of the Aboriginal Musqueam nation, in a way that it is not for non-Aboriginal commercial fishers. Therefore, the limits on non-Aboriginal fishing rights do not apply in the same way to Aboriginal fishing rights. It does not follow, however, that there are no limits on Aboriginal fishing rights. The court concluded that 'conservation' is a good shared by both sides on the common ground, even though they understand it differently. Therefore, it can provide the 'pressing and substantial concern' to accommodate and limit differentially both rights.[33]

In *Thomas v. Norris*, the court rejected the claim by the Coast Salish nation that they had the collective right to coerce one of their members to participate in a spirit dance. When the plaintiff, Thomas, refused to take part in a spirit dance he was subjected to, he alleged, assault, battery and imprisonment by the Salish band council government. The court found, as Eisenberg puts it, 'that the Spirit Dance, and more specifically the involuntary aspect of it, was not a central feature of the Salish way of life'. Therefore, 'the group claim to involuntarily initiate participants into the Spirit Dance could not override' the individual members' 'rights to be protected from assault, battery and false imprisonment'.[34]

I would like to emphasise that in each of these cases rights are taken seriously. The question the justices ask is how to apply rights even-handedly so they do not discriminate against citizens' identity-related differences that can be shown to be worthy of protection. If rights were applied without taking these cultural differences into account, the result would not be impartial. The dominant culture would in fact be imposed in each case. Therefore, there are no grounds for complaint from a defender of rights, for rights are rescued from being a tool of cultural domination. Conversely, a critic of rights has no reason to complain, for the alleged blindness to cultural differences has been corrected, yet without abandoning rights.

In *Making all the difference: inclusion, exclusion, and American law*, Martha Minow shows that US courts employ the same sort of contextual and aspectual reasoning to accommodate identity-related differences, especially gender differences, in the interpretation and application of rights in some cases, and they should in others. Albert Jonsen and Stephen Toulmin trace the broad family of similar types of reasoning through European history from Aristotle to the present in *The abuse of casuistry*. My study of the forms of mutual recognition and accommodation in constitutional negotiations over cultural recognition in Canada, 'Diversity's gambit declined', suggests that similar modes of reasoning are involved. Earlier examples displayed related genres of reasoning in the practise of treaty constitutionalism and diverse federalism.

We may, if we please, redescribe these forms of reasoning on the common ground as the reconciliation of clashes between individual and collective rights, liberalism and nationalism, or, as Habermas reconstructs them, 'the individualistic design of the theory of rights' and the 'collective experiences of violated integrity'.[35] But these further descriptions in the abstract language of modern constitutionalism occlude the ways of reasoning that actually bring peace to the conflict. Projecting such a general scheme over particular cases is analogous to, Wittgenstein suggests, a pupil in geography bringing a mass of falsely simplified ideas about the course and connections of the routes of rivers and mountain chains. It shackles the ability to understand and causes us to dismiss as irrelevant the concrete cases which alone can help to understand how the conciliation is actually achieved. The perspicuous representation of the reasoning that mediates the conflicts over cultural recognition consists of dialogical descriptions of the very language used in handling actual cases.

A tragic example should, I hope, carry this message home.

Most readers will agree that if one wishes to understand the conflict in *Antigone*, the worst way to approach the text is in terms of the individual versus the state or some such grand scheme from modern constitutional theory. Rather, we carefully listen to Antigone's plea for recognition, the reasons she gives and the contrary arguments of Creon in the dialogue between them, paying particular attention to the words they use and how they handle them. Then, perhaps more importantly, we listen intently to the even-handed ways Haemon tries to reason with both sides: the further descriptions he offers, the analogies he draws and the conventions he appeals to in order to reach a form of accommodation that will avert the tragedy which follows.

This close attention to the handling of language is what we mean by the expression 'doing justice to the text', as Quentin Skinner has carefully explained over the last three decades. It is also what Wittgenstein means when he says that 'our only task is to be just. That is, we must only point out and resolve the injustices of philosophy, and not posit new parties – and creeds.' To avoid creeds, he continues in his notebook, one must 'in no way interfere with the actual use of language, with what is really said', but 'in the end only describe it'.[36] If we wish to do justice to the conflicts that surround us and lead to one tragedy after another, we can do *no better* than to keep the example of *Antigone* constantly in mind.

To resume, the government of Québec overrode the court's decision and continued to enforce the French only sign law. To protect the balance between the sovereignty of the people in their provincial parliaments and the unelected federal court, whose justices are appointed by the prime minister, the constitution allows a provincial parliament to override an unpopular federal court interpretation of the Charter for a period of up to five years. This balancing device of diverse federalism provides an opportunity to bring hot-headed democratic sentiment in line with the court's reasonable interpretation or, alternatively, to bring a biased court to see that its interpretation overlooked the respect-worthy regional circumstances that should have been taken into account. In this case, Québec parliamentarians considered themselves justified in invoking override not only because the sovereignty of the Québec parliament had been at the heart of Québec's struggle for recognition for over two hundred years, but also because the federal court's interpretation was based on the very Charter Québec had not consented to in 1981.

Notwithstanding any of these points, the sign legislation itself violates the conventions of mutual recognition and continuity, for it unilaterally recognises the French language to the exclusion of the minority English language, and this was confirmed by Québec's own provincial court. One might conclude that this proves the poverty of diverse federalism. A strong Hobbesian sovereign is needed to enforce unilaterally the federal court's rulings. This is to misunderstand how enforcement works in a culturally diverse society. Unilateral attempts of enforcement by the federal government are ineffective and they provoke disunity and secession. There will always be conflicts over mutual recognition in any free and diverse society. There is no final solution. The mutual checks and balances of the diverse members are a more effective and democratic method of enforcement than a central sovereign.

At the same time as the government of Québec overrode the court's decision, they were also negotiating a constitutional amendment to regain powers from the federal government. Even though their amendment, the Meech Lake agreement, contained a clause protecting the English-speaking minority, a majority of the citizens of the rest of Canada were sceptical. They rejected the proposed amendment on the express ground that the Québec government had failed to abide by the court decision. This expression of democratic will played a decisive role in defeating the amendment. Further pressure was applied by an English-speaking citizen of Québec who referred the offensive law to the United Nations.

These pressures helped citizens in Québec who were in favour of revising the sign legislation. The government of Québec initiated a public discussion and pluralistic nationalists published a *pacte linguistique* calling for the official recognition of the English language and the eleven Aboriginal languages as constituents of the linguistic character of Québec. As a result of public deliberation, the majority expressed themselves in favour of bringing the sign legislation in line with the court ruling and the law was changed. This illustrates the democratic and dialogical way in which mutual recognition can be enforced in diverse societies without recourse to a Hobbesian sovereign or any other unilateral device.

Intercultural citizens, gender differences and the three conventions

If the conventions apply to individuals and longstanding minorities, then, by the convention of mutual recognition, they apply analogously to the rainbow coalition of members of other cultures who have joined the constitutional association more recently or who have been oppressed in the past. Their cultural differences should continue into the constitutional association unless they consent to assimilate to the dominant culture. Given the migration patterns of the present century, this is a large percentage of the population of contemporary societies. The widespread persecution of cultural differences that often causes migration in the first place, and just as often awaits migrants in their new country, is one of the most explosive problems of the age. The way in which the three conventions should apply varies with the constitutional traditions of a given society and the forms of recognition demanded. The different situations of, say, Indian South Africans, African Americans, Asian Canadians or migrant workers in Japan are too great to draw any generalisations.

None the less, another example from my borough provides an illustrative example. Section 27 of the Charter protects the cultural differences of all citizens and ensures that they are recognised and affirmed in public life. Based on the convention of continuity, it states that the 'Charter shall be interpreted in a manner consistent with the preservation and enhancement of the multicultural heritage of Canadians'. Multicultural groups won this form of recognition in the constitutional negotiations of 1981. Since then, they have been able to use it to ensure that they have a say over legislation and constitutional amendments that adversely affect their identity-related differences. They have also used it to fight for public support of the preservation and enhancement of their cultural ways, to redress past discrimination and persecution, and to ensure that their histories are woven into the curricula and public narratives of Canadian society.

Protecting and enhancing the cultural differences and similarities of intercultural citizens involves more than just a continuation of the three conventions. They are Antigone's children, the citizens of the common ground created by European imperialism and the many resistances to it. These citizens, as Edward Said argues, bear the experience of intertwined histories and live the three features of cultural diversity to a greater degree than the other members of contemporary societies. Cultural diversity is their identity-related difference; the good they bring to the association. The recognition and accommodation of these suppressed and persecuted citizens on equal footing with other members of a society marks the transition to post-imperial constitutionalism. It requires more than the mutual toleration and respect that might have been sufficient in the earlier examples. It requires that the citizens affirm diversity itself as a constitutive good of the association. This is not a change in conventions but in civic attitude.

In the early modern examples of recognition, the conventions are extended to others on the ground of the golden rule of mutual recognition: you should do unto others what you would have them do unto you. The resulting diversity of the constitution is tolerated and respected, but it is not usually seen as a good in itself, except by Aboriginal peoples (as Jamake Highwater noted in chapter 1). In this post-modern example of recognition, diversity is itself affirmed as a good. The good of a constitutional association that recognises cultural diversity in its public life is, of course, that it engenders an attitude of diversity awareness among its citizens. This is a good specific to the post-imperial age – a good of *The spirit of Haida Gwaii* – which I explore further in chapter 6.

The final example is the struggles of women for the recognition and accommodation of their gender-related differences in the institutions and traditions of interpretation of contemporary societies. As we saw in chapter 2, these struggles are also intercultural. They involve coalitions of women of many cultures whose differences criss-cross with those of male citizens. To summarise, the claim advanced by cultural feminists is that, since constitutions and their traditions of interpretation have been established by men without the consent of women, it is not enough to have a say within them. Women must have an equal say 'in their own voice' in constitutional dialogues on the gender bias of contemporary constitutions.

This is to reconceive the concept of popular sovereignty in the same way we have done in earlier examples. It is to acknowledge, as Gilligan and Spelman have forcefully submitted, that the sovereign people come to any constitutional dialogue already constituted by their identity-related differences. In this case, the three conventions are applied to recognise and continue gender differences. Accordingly, for women to be treated fairly in discussing any constitutional issue, not only issues related to their gender difference, their culturally different ways of speaking and acting need to be recognised and accommodated in the dialogue itself. One aspect of any just constitutional negotiations will be to reach agreement on which gender differences are relevant and worthy of being constitutionalised. With this protection in place, women will be able to amend the political institutions they share with men so they can speak and act in their own ways on equal footing in everyday political struggles: that is, without assimilation to other ways of speaking and acting.

Many male and female sceptics doubt that there are identity-related differences of gender which require constitutional protection. However, cultural feminists have brought forward sufficient evidence of their differences and their constitutional domination by men to establish that their claim warrants a fair hearing. This is all that they need to claim, for the question cannot be decided in a monological theory. The only fair hearings will be periodic constitutional dialogues in which the gender bias of the constitution and traditions of interpretation are discussed and the three conventions applied to the male and female interlocutors. If the participants reach agreement that no significant differences remain that cannot be recognised and accommodated in the prevailing constitutional order, then the sceptics will be proven correct. If not, then they must agree that the cultural differences that remain after the discussion ought to be constitutionalised, just as in any other case, and subject to periodical review.

Mary Wollstonecraft voiced this argument over two hundred years ago. It would be the supreme indignity not to retell it in her own lucid words. M. Talleyrand-Périgord published a pamphlet extolling the rights of man that had been agreed on by the constitutional negotiators of *The Declaration of the rights of man and citizen* in 1789. In the pamphlet he notes in passing that women are excluded from the rights in the Declaration. Wollstonecraft writes to him, complimenting him for his astute observation. A 'glimpse of this truth seemed to be open before you when you observed', quoting Talleyrand-Périgord, 'that to see one-half of the human race excluded by the other from all participation of government was a political phenomenon that, according to abstract principles, it was impossible to explain'.

If this is so, she replied, 'on what grounds does your constitution rest'? 'If', she continues, 'the abstract rights of man will bear discussion and explanation, those of woman, by a parity of reasoning, will not shrink from the same test.' How, then, is the test to be carried out? First, men cannot discuss for women, for this surely would be unjust. Consider,

whether, when men contend for their freedom, and to be allowed to judge for themselves respecting their own happiness, it be not inconsistent and unjust to subjugate women, even though you firmly believe that you are acting in the manner best calculated to promote their happiness? Who made man the exclusive judge, if woman partake with him of the gift of reason?

Second, it is not enough for women to discuss by using the concepts that men have developed to describe them and their rights. As the entire *Vindication of the rights of woman* aims to demonstrate, these concepts have been designed by men to legitimate the subjugation of women. The dominant conceptions of men and women by male writers, from the creation of Eve out of the rib of Adam down to Rousseau's equally biased account, are only 'his invention to show that she ought to have her neck bent under the yoke, because the whole creation was only created for his convenience or pleasure'. Therefore, unless women are able to present their own arguments in their own voices the constitutional association will remain unjust:[37]

> But if women are to be excluded, without having a voice, from a participation of the natural rights of mankind, prove first, to ward off the charge of injustice and inconsistency, that they want reason, else this flaw in your NEW CONSTITUTION will ever show that man must, in some shape, act like a tyrant.

Again, a Canadian example illustrates how the three conventions serve to engender dialogues of this emancipatory kind. First, the major women's organisations applied the conventions of recognition, continuity and consent in the discussions among the culturally diverse members of their own organisations to ensure a multiplicity of perspectives on the conditions of women in Canadian society. Then, feminist activists and scholars amassed evidence to show the gender bias of Canadian political and economic institutions and their traditions of interpretation in law and parliament. Next, they fought hard for constitutional recognition and redress in 1981, securing two constitutional amendments.

The first clause, section 28 of the Charter, recognises their formal equality: 'not withstanding anything in this Charter, the rights and freedoms referred to in it are guaranteed equally to male and female persons'. Second, they struggled along with representatives of disadvantaged minorities to win an affirmative action amendment to redress substantive inequalities based on gender and cultural discrimination. This umbrella clause draws together the family resemblances of linguistic minorities, intercultural groups and women. Section 15, part 2, reads, individual equality before and under the law 'does not preclude any law, program or activity that has as its object the amelioration of conditions of disadvantaged individuals or groups, including those that are disadvantaged because of race, national or ethnic origin, colour, religion, sex, age or mental or physical disability'. Once these were in place, women could then appeal to them, not only to correct gender biases in Canadian society, but also to gain a better position to protect women in future constitutional negotiations.

These examples of how all the diverse members of *Haida Gwaii* are recognised and accommodated illustrate the multiplicity of ways constitutional actors can be guided by the three conventions of common constitutionalism. In modern constitutionalism, there is a tendency to think, following Hobbes, that this cannot be right, that there can be only one correct way of being guided by a rule. This leads us to think that conventions from pre-modern constitutionalism could not possibly guide constitutionalism in a post-modern age because the situations are so different. The inclination is to say, 'But being guided is surely a particular experience!' The 'answer to this' inclination, Wittgenstein replies, is 'you are now *thinking* of a particular experience of being guided'.

The use of the old common-law term 'convention' is intended to dispel this fixation. As the examples have shown, a constitutional convention, like Wittgenstein's 'rule', can be grasped in a variety of ways, 'in what we call "obeying the rule" and "going against it" in actual cases'. To bring his interlocutors to see that the concept of being guided can be extended in this aspectual way, Wittgenstein, unsurprisingly, invites them to imagine the following homespun examples of being guided:

You are in a playing field with your eyes bandaged, and someone leads you by the hand, sometimes left, sometimes right; you have constantly to be ready for the tug of his hand, and must also take care not to stumble when he gives an unexpected tug.

Or, again: someone leads you by the hand where you are unwilling to go, by force.

Or: someone takes you for a walk; you are having a conversation; you go wherever he does.

Or: you walk along a field-track, simply following it.

Then, he simply asks, all 'these situations are similar to one another; but what is common to all the experiences?'[38]

If interlocutors from other neighbourhoods and boroughs present their examples of struggles for recognition to complement the limited perspective of mine, as I trust they will, our concept of being guided by the conventions of common constitutionalism will be extended further. Such an endless dialogue of humankind will correct my tendency to write as if all the world is America, and the analogous tendencies of the other participants. In this dialogical way, the citizens of such a republic of words, speaking and listening in turn, could gradually become mutually aware of the cultural diversity that ought to be recognised and accommodated in the global family of constitutions and cultures. For now, however, you will be relieved to learn that, although one can 'demonstrate a method, by examples', fortunately, 'the series of examples can be broken off'.[39]

CHAPTER 6

Constitutionalism in
an age of cultural diversity

A summary of contemporary constitutionalism

The survey of the composite language of contemporary constitutionalism suggests that the constitutions of contemporary
societies are considerably different from the picture given by
the modern theories and the three authoritative schools.
Where the machinery of modern constitutionalism has not
clear-cut the living cultural diversity, because the sovereign
people have said enough and refused to submit, the resulting
common ground is a multiplicity. These constitutions are
based on the sovereignty of culturally diverse citizens here and
now, not on abstract forgeries of culturally homogeneous
individuals, communities or nations. The aspectival character
of the constitutions is not grasped by a comprehensive
representation, but by participation in a practical dialogue
where limited and complementary stories are exchanged.
Constitutional negotiations are not monologues in an
imperial voice, but intercultural dialogues where the post-
imperial majesty of *audi alteram partem* always has her final say.

These constitutions are not causal stages high above the
ancient ones of early modern Europeans or Aboriginal
peoples, but continuous with them. They preserve legal,
political and cultural plurality rather than impose uniformity
and regularity. There is not one national narrative that gives
the partnership its unity, but a diversity of criss-crossing and
contested narratives through which citizens participate in and
identify with their association. Constitutions are not fixed and
unchangeable agreements reached at some foundational
moment, but chains of continual intercultural negotiations

and agreements in accord with, and violation of the conventions of mutual recognition, continuity and consent. In sum, as the people remove modern constitutionalism from its imperial throne and put it in its proper place, what remains to be seen looks to me like the outlines of the black canoe in dawn's early light.

The six examples of the politics of cultural recognition in the first chapter can now be seen as the extension of this common constitutionalism. They comprise a third cluster of anti-imperial struggles against the seven features of modern constitutionalism and for the liberty to engage in self rule in accord with citizens' diverse cultural ways. It follows that the question posed at the outset can be answered in the affirmative. As I anticipated at the close of chapter 1, a contemporary constitution can recognise cultural diversity if it is conceived as a form of accommodation of cultural diversity. It should be seen as an activity, an intercultural dialogue in which the culturally diverse sovereign citizens of contemporary societies negotiate agreements on their ways of association over time in accord with the conventions of mutual recognition, consent and continuity.

In the course of the survey of examples, reasons have been given for amending or, in some cases, abandoning each of the seven features of modern constitutionalism. The contemporary constitutionalism that remains includes common constitutionalism and modern constitutionalism trimmed of its features that violate the three conventions. In a like manner, contemporary constitutionalism comprises the family of constitutions and traditions of interpretation of the world that are related by their common respect for the three conventions, such as the Aboriginal constitutions and traditions of interpretation we surveyed in chapter 4.

Contemporary constitutionalism is just because it rests on the three venerable conventions of justice that survived our critical survey. It is also worthy of our hearing, and perhaps allegiance, because it furthers the liberty of self rule. Since there is no greater value in Western civilisation, and perhaps in any civilisation, this is no small recommendation for the vision presented here for your consideration.

Moreover, the path from modern to contemporary constitutionalism was not taken lightly or without due consideration of the other side. To recall, Hobbes founded the comprehensive and exclusive authority of modern constitutionalism on its scientific status. Hale replied that the model of science is inapplicable to the tangled domain of constitutionalism. It cannot provide knowledge of how constitutional actors ought to be governed because they are not, and cannot be coerced to be, governed by comprehensive rules as the model presupposes. The hermeneutical sciences sought to restore comprehensive theory to office on the basis of rules implicit in practice. Nationalism, communitarianism and practice-based liberalism rested their comprehensive claims on this version of the model. Wittgenstein demurred, pointing out that this revised model is equally inappropriate to the aspectival domain of human action. The hundreds of voices heard in the survey support Hale and Wittgenstein in dethroning modern constitutionalism. The final irony of modern constitutionalism's long reign is that the model of science on which its authority rested is even a false representation of the natural sciences. As Clifford Geertz demonstrates, natural scientists too study individual cases, advance limited and competing sketches, draw analogies with other cases and discuss these with as many colleagues as possible.[1]

Instead of grand theory, constitutional knowledge appears to be a humble and practical dialogue in which interlocutors from near and far exchange limited descriptions of actual cases, learning as they go along. Accordingly, the language and institutions of modern constitutionalism should now take their democratic place among the multiplicity of constitutional languages and institutions of the world and submit their limited claims to authority to the three conventions, just like all the others.

Hence, in this post-imperial view of constitutionalism the value of progress is also preserved and transformed. Progress is not the ascent out of the ancient cultural assemblage until one reaches the imaginary uniform modern republic, from which one ranks and judges the less developed others on the rungs far below. Rather, it consists in learning to recognise, converse with and be mutually accommodating to the culturally diverse neighbours in the city we inhabit here and now. This is the reversal of worldview called for, as Jamake Highwater warns, citing the Mexican essayist Octavio Paz, if the family of humankind is to survive:[2]

What sets worlds in motion is the interplay of differences, their attractions and repulsions. Life is plurality, death is uniformity. By suppressing differences and peculiarities, by eliminating different civilizations and cultures, progress weakens life and favors death. The ideal of a single civilization for everyone, implicit in the cult of progress of technique, impoverishes and mutilates us. Every view of the world that becomes extinct, every culture that disappears, diminishes a possibility.

This quotation turns on a connection suggested by the term 'culture' itself. The value of continuing the overlapping, interacting and contested forms of life we call human cultures is analogous to the value of preserving the equally interdependent plant and animal cultures. Since both Aboriginal and non-Aboriginal ecologists concur that all forms of life are suspended in this delicately balanced labyrinth of biodiversity, the value is life itself. And, on the other side, there is a connection, as William Cronon, Carolyn Merchant, David Maybury-Lewis, Alfred Crosby and Julian Burger have shown beyond reasonable doubt, between the global spread of modern constitutionalism, with its policies of discontinuity and assimilation, and the ecological imperialism and destruction that continues to accompany it. The kinship between the recognition of human and ecological cultures is effortlessly expressed by Bill Reid in his meditation on the meaning of 'Haida':[3]

As for what constitutes a Haida – well, Haida only means human being, and as far as I'm concerned, a human being is anyone who respects the needs of his fellow man, and the earth which nurtures and shelters us all. I think we could find room in South Moresby [one of the islands of *Haida Gwaii*] for quite a few Haida no matter what their ethnic background.

Notwithstanding these arguments in support of contemporary constitutionalism, I have not responded directly to four objections voiced by the guardians of modern constitutionalism in the course of our survey. Contemporary constitutionalism conflicts with national integrity in nationalism, violates individual freedom and autonomy in liberalism, protects enclaves of anti-democratic rule and leads to disunity in practice. I address these legitimate concerns in the next section. A consideration of the two public goods of contemporary constitutionalism follows in the third section. A brief conclusion answers the question raised in chapter 1 of the identity of the chief of *The spirit of Haida Gwaii*.

Replies to four objections to contemporary constitutionalism
The post-imperial constitutionalism of this book is incompatible with the 'integrity' of the nation in nationalism in one sense of this term. If the integrity of the nation is a code word for an ethnic nation, then, as we saw in chapter 1, it is empirically false. Nations are, in William McNeill's phrase, polyethnic. This has not stopped the ideologists of the ethnic nation state from making their false claims. We saw a classic example in the *Federalist papers* in chapter 3. Anthony Smith explains that ethnicity has been a feature of the modern concept of a nation from the seventeenth century to the racial versions of the nineteenth and twentieth centuries. It is lodged in place by the broader assumption that cultures and nations constitute a world system of separate, closed and homogeneous units at various stages of development.

The integrity of the ethnic nation is more often a claim that the nation should be purified, rather than a claim that it is pure, although the two are often connected. The policies of 'forging' a nation in chapter 3 and the justifications of Lord Durham and John Stuart Mill in chapter 5 are classic examples of how modern nation states have attempted to construct dominant ethnic identities. These attempts to assimilate the ethnic citizens who fail to fit the mould have been, and continue to be, disastrous and abhorrent failures.

The abandonment of the set of assumptions that held

ethnic nationalism in place and the adoption of the more accurate picture of cultural diversity is certainly incompatible with ethnic nationalism and any other form of exclusive nationalism. However, it is not incompatible with the sense of belonging to a people or a nation who govern themselves by their own laws and ways. This aspiration to belong to a self-governing nation is and has been central to the politics of recognition, in spite of the attempts of Lord Durham and others to reduce it to an ethnic struggle. The type of nationalism which survives is conceived in awareness of the cultural diversity of any nation. The test is the application of the three conventions of common constitutionalism. The same conventions by which a people gain recognition, continuity and *q.o.t.* also recognise, continue and respect the consent of the other culturally different members of the association, right up to, as we saw in chapter 5, the individual who wishes to dissent from the rest.

A particularly promising example is the vision of diverse nationalism presented by a young generation of Québec nationalists. Following in the footsteps of Loranger, they apply the three conventions to the cultural diversity of Québec society. French language, culture and democratic institutions constitute a *lingua franca* of political life. By parity of reasoning, the eleven self-governing Aboriginal nations, the English language, schools and social services of the English-speaking minority, the languages and schools of the intercultural citizens, the charter of individual rights and the confederal relation of the diverse Québec nation to the rest of Canada are also recognised and continued. Another pertinent example is the way the Aboriginal scholars associated with the Canadian Royal Commission on Aboriginal Peoples conceptualise Aboriginal nationalism to recognise the cultural diversity of Aboriginal nations. These are surely two of the most important intellectual movements of contemporary constitutionalism.[4]

Let us now view contemporary constitutionalism from the perspective of modern liberals and their objection. A constitution ought to provide the foundation for the individual freedom and dignity of all citizens in both the public and private spheres. It should enable them to participate freely and with equal dignity in the governing of their society and to live their private lives in accord with their own choice and responsibility. In recent years, liberal philosophers have asked how these values of civic and private freedom and responsibility can be preserved in the culturally diverse societies of today. They argue that the social condition of being able to exercise individual freedom in both the civic and private spheres is that citizens are members of viable cultures. The reason for this is that a viable culture is a necessary and partly constitutive context for individual freedom and autonomy. Consequently, although liberals place no value on cultures in their own right, they are now classified as a primary good of a liberal society because they provide the support for liberal values.

The older imperial liberals agreed with this, but they presumed that modern European cultures were the superior cultural bases for individual freedom. Within their stages vision of history, they believed that these superior cultures developed as a causal result of the processes of modernisation, supplemented where necessary by policies of reform and socialisation. Accordingly, liberal governments could look on the destruction of the diversity of primitive cultures and the inculcation of European culture with moral approval.

In hindsight, some liberals now see the error of their ways. The imperial liberals from Locke to Mill were not only mistaken in their presumption that modernisation causes cultural convergence. As Daniel Weinstock, a liberal, explains in a dialogue on cultural diversity with a communitarian and a nationalist, they also overlooked the social preconditions of one of liberalism's primary goods: individual self respect. Citizens can take part in popular sovereignty, by having a say in constitutional negotiations, and exercise their civic and private freedom only if they have a threshold of self respect. Self respect is a sense of one's own value and the relatively secure conviction that what one has to say and do in politics and life is worthwhile. The social basis of this threshold sense of self respect is that others recognise the value of one's activities and goals; that there is an association in which individuals can acquire a level of confidence in the worth of what they say and do. Since what a person says and does and the plans he or she formulates and revises are partly characterised by his or her cultural identity, the condition of self respect is met only in a society in which the cultures of all the members are recognised and affirmed by others, both by those who do and those who do not share those cultures. A complementary argument, also starting from Rawls' concept of self respect, is advanced by Susan James from a liberal feminist perspective.

Consequently, a constitutional association whose members view the disappearance of the cultures of other members with moral approval or moral indifference, and who treat other cultures with condescension and contempt, destroys the self respect of those members. In so doing, the ability of those citizens to exercise their individual freedom and autonomy in constitutional negotiations, civic participation and private life is undermined. This is scarcely a new discovery. In *A vindication of the rights of woman*, Mary Wollstonecraft catalogued the debilitating effects on women of the degrading stereotypes and education upheld by men. The disastrous effects of policies of cultural destruction and assimilation on the self respect and self esteem of Aboriginal peoples proves this obvious but overlooked point beyond reasonable doubt.

If a liberal constitution is to provide the basis for its most important values of freedom and autonomy, it thus must protect the cultures of its members and engender the public attitude of mutual respect for cultural diversity that individual self respect requires. To put this differently, the primary good of self respect requires that popular sovereignty is conceived as an intercultural dialogue. The various cultures of the society need to be recognised in public institutions, histories and symbols in order to nourish mutual cultural awareness and respect. Far from being a threat to liberal values, the recognition and protection of cultural diversity is a necessary condition of the primary good of self respect, and so of the individual freedom and autonomy that it underpins, in a manner appropriate to a post-imperial age.

It is also worth noting that the protection of cultural diversity is compatible with the principle of liberal neutrality. As we have seen in many classic liberal theories, the feigned cultural indifference of the constitution served to reinforce the dominant, European male culture at the expense of all others. In hindsight, it is obvious that the stages view of cultural development served to prop up the self respect, and so the autonomy of the members of the dominant society and to undermine the self respect, and so the ability to participate fully of the other members. If a contemporary constitution is to be culturally neutral, it should not promote one culture at the expense of others, but mutually recognise and accommodate the cultures of all the citizens in an agreeable manner.

A closely related worry is that legal and political diversity will shield illiberal and undemocratic enclaves. The consistent application of the conventions of mutual recognition, continuity and consent renders such an outcome impossible for, as we have seen, the conventions which protect the provinces and nations of a multinational confederation also apply to the citizens within them. Nevertheless, I would like to answer the objection by taking up the case of the recognition of the sovereignty of Aboriginal peoples by the non-Aboriginal states that have been erected over them. If treaty constitutionalism does not lead to undemocratic forms of government, then the lesser degrees of self government necessary to accommodate cultural diversity in other cases are unlikely to as well.

Before proceeding, I would like to enter a disclaimer. The presumption that non-Aboriginal people may sit in judgement, from the unquestioned superiority of their constitutions and traditions of interpretation, and guard the transition of the Aboriginal peoples from colonialism to self government smacks of the imperial attitude that contemporary constitutionalism aims to dislodge. Given the historical record, it is not Aboriginal people who need guarding. To avoid this undignified stance, I will try to proceed in a way that leads non-Aboriginal readers to see their role, not as superior judges and guardians but as treaty partners in an intercultural dialogue.

Two of the primary goods of constitutionalism are civic participation and the civic dignity that accompanies it. They cannot be realised by assimilating Aboriginal peoples to non-Aboriginal forms of government. This is unjust and the cause of the alienation and resistance that come to any free people who are forcefully governed by alien laws and ways. Self government enables Aboriginal peoples, just as it enables non-Aboriginal peoples, to participate in governing their societies in accord with their own laws and cultural understandings of self rule, and so regain their dignity as equal and active citizens.

These two goods are not realised only in one canonical form of institution and charter. The practice of government should rest on the sovereignty of the people, enabling them to exercise their powers of self rule in culturally appropriate ways and to amend or overthrow the government if it thwarts their powers. Accordingly, the constitutional forms of democratic participation and citizen dignity vary with the cultures and circumstances of the peoples of the world. In many cases Aboriginal peoples, with their smaller, oral societies, tend to place greater emphasis on direct participation by all and government by consensus. As J. Anthony Long explains, in a large number of Aboriginal nations, political authority rests on the ability of the chief or council to sustain the continuous consent of the citizens. With their respect for family, tradition and place, the methods of election also vary. When consent dissipates due to distrust, the citizens often form sovereign bodies, such as healing circles, to reform defective practices and elect a new chief or council.

Although these forms of face to face government have often served as an ideal in Western political thought, modern theorists condemn them as primitive, ancient and incompatible with modern constitutions. Locke, Kant, Constant and their followers took the size and institutional formation of

European societies as the norm and held that representative government, aggregate majority rule, the concentration of sovereignty and compulsory obedience are essential features of a modern constitution. This was yet another hasty and parochial generalisation. The democratic goods of participation, free expression and reform are realised better for Aboriginal peoples in their culturally distinct forms of constitution. The attempt to impose European institutions would create resistance and undermine the democratic goods the institutions are meant to secure, just as earlier attempts have done for the last four centuries.

This response, however, does not address the immediate concern. The fear is that, as the administrative dictatorships over Aboriginal peoples are dismantled, they may leave a class of Aboriginal male elites in power. They may use their sovereignty to rule despotically over their own people and shield themselves from constitutional limits. They have gained so much power under the cloak of the Indian Act and other administrative arrangements that Aboriginal people may not be able to control them. This is a genuine concern that is also shared by many Aboriginal people, especially Aboriginal women who have suffered physical abuse and discrimination on reserves.

First, the patriarchal structures that the elites occupy were set up by colonial administrators. They destroyed the wide variety of forms of rule by women and men that Aboriginal peoples previously enjoyed. The existence of such elites, then, is scarcely an argument for continuing to subject Aboriginal people to non-Aboriginal rule. Quite the contrary. The solution is to ensure that Aboriginal peoples are able to draw on and innovate with their older constitutions and traditions in order to limit or overthrow the elites in the transition to self government. The character of sovereignty in contemporary constitutionalism makes this possible.

In the theories of Hobbes and Pufendorf, sovereignty signifies a single locus of political power that is absolute or autonomous. It is not conditioned by any other political power. A sovereign ruler or body of people (such as a legislature) exercises political power over others (subjects) but is not subject or accountable to the exercise of political power by others. Absolute sovereignty arose in the age of absolute monarchy and passed to absolute nation states in the eighteenth century. This sense of sovereignty generates the problem of undemocratic enclaves. However, it is a false depiction of sovereignty today.

The concept of sovereignty has undergone a change in the transition from Hobbes to contemporary constitutionalism. First, the exercise of political power is dependent on and limited by the consent or agreement of the people. This limit, required by the convention of consent, is marked by the phrase 'popular sovereignty'. It is the single most important condition of legitimacy in the contemporary world. No constitutional association is considered legitimate unless government rests on the consent, and so the sovereignty, of the people. Although the expressions sovereign 'nations' and sovereign 'states' continue to be used, they imply the proviso that the exercise of political power in them has the consent of the people. Popular sovereignty takes two forms: either the people exercise political power themselves or they delegate political power to their representatives. The people place more constraints on the exercise of political power by charters of rights.

Second, sovereignty is limited by a degree of interdependency on, but not subordination to, international relations of various kinds. All contemporary nations are involved in complex relations of interdependence, yet they are still recognised as sovereign. The Maastricht treaty, the North American Free Trade Agreement, the General Agreement on Tariffs and Trade, international laws, treaties, environmental accords and agreements on human and Indigenous rights all limit the exercise of political power. None the less, the continued use of the term 'sovereignty' signals that there are limits to external independence. These are hard to define and are always open to debate, but there seem to be two widely held conditions. As Chief Justice Marshall explained in chapter 4, the relations of interdependency should be voluntarily taken on and they should fall short of colonial dependency. If either of these two conditions of consent and continuity is not met, then it is standardly said that sovereignty has been lost.

Finally, political power is divided among a number of representative bodies, thereby forming varieties of federal and confederal associations, rather than being concentrated in one supreme body, as in the classic modern theories. As we saw in chapter 4, the majority of contemporary societies divide power in various ways to allow regions, peoples and nations to govern themselves to different degrees, as in Australia, the United Kingdom and Germany and, concurrently, to place checks on the corrupting tendency of concentrating power in a single, central body.

It does not follow from the demise of the absolute sense of sovereignty that 'the end of sovereignty' is near, as some scholars have hastily concluded.[5] Rather, a concept of sovereignty remains which incorporates these three limits and is appropriate to the contemporary age. Sovereignty in this non-absolute sense means the authority of a culturally diverse people or association of peoples to govern themselves by their own laws and ways free from external subordination. It is a concept of sovereignty that accords with the overlapping and interdependent terrain of constitutionalism we have discovered in the previous chapters. As the politics of cultural recognition continues to submit governments to the three conventions, it will be limited further.

Once it is realised that the recognition of sovereignty in a post-imperial age can mean no more than this, the normative problem of a despotic elite dissolves, for such an elite could not survive the application of the limits to sovereignty. This concept of sovereignty is not alien to Aboriginal constitution-alism, for it is the concept of sovereignty embodied in the treaty system. Furthermore, the argument applies analogously to any recognition of sovereignty in diverse federalism. No sovereign member is shielded from these limits, just as no independent country is, for they are prescribed by the three conventions which justify the recognition of their sovereignty.

The most common objection to the recognition and

accommodation of cultural diversity is that it will lead to
disunity. The connections between uniformity and unity on
one hand and diversity and disunity on the other are so firmly
forged in the language of modern constitutionalism that it
seems unreasonable to raise doubts. In the theories of Hobbes
and Pufendorf, uniformity leads to unity and so to the strength
and power needed to hold out in the competition with other
European powers over the wealth and labour of the non-
European world. Diversity leads to disunity, weakness, dissolution and death. The 'crasie house', Hobbes concluded, 'hardly
lasting out their own time, must assuredly fall upon the heads
of their posterity'.[6] We have noticed the same connection
drawn in the *Federalist papers* between uniformity, unity and
imperial expansion, this time over the Aboriginal nations,
and the disunity and weakness that would befall a diverse
confederation. Lord Durham in Canada was no less concerned
to insist that the unity created by cultural uniformity would
empower the British empire to expand across the continent.
In fact, it is difficult to find a classic text of modern constitutionalism which does not contrast uniformity, unity and
power to diversity, disunity and weakness.

Comparable arguments are bandied back and forth in the
current debates over the politics of cultural recognition. In *The
disuniting of America*, for example, Arthur Schlesinger voices
similar fears about the disunity and weakness caused by
diversity. In his review of the contest, Sheldon Wolin suggests
that the parable of the tower of Babel is the intermediate case
which enables us to see the connections among the arguments.
Because the men of the plain of Shinar all spoke one language
and had no cultural differences they were able to unite in
building a tower so powerful that it challenged the authority
of god. God saw what was happening and smashed the tower.
He scattered the people and introduced a multiplicity of
languages and cultures so they would forever remain disunited, weak and unable to challenge his omnipotence.

Although these imperial arguments were originally served
to us as reasons for uniformity, I humbly submit that they may
now simply be returned as reasons against it. Further, even if

cultural uniformity were necessary to unity, the only just way it can be obtained is through consent of those affected. More decisively, the inference is false. The imposition of uniformity does not lead to unity but to resistance, further repression and disunity. The proof is the dismal record in practice.

Knox's comparison of Ireland and Minorca remains as relevant today as it was in 1774, as we have seen in example after example. Aboriginal peoples are exemplary. Every imaginable means of destruction of their cultures and assimilation into uniform European ways has been tried. Yet, after five hundred years of repression and attempted genocide, they are still here and as multiform as ever. The other cultures I have mentioned have suffered suppression and assimilation as well. They too have resisted, like so many bent but unbreakable twigs, to use Sir Isaiah Berlin's phrase, for cultural recognition is a deep and abiding human need. The suppression of cultural difference in the name of uniformity and unity is one of the leading causes of civil strife, disunity and dissolution today.

Conversely, where cultural diversity has been recognised and accommodated in various ways, confrontation and conflict have eased and the members of a constitutional association have been able to work together on their common problems. As we have seen, resources of legal and political pluralism and culturally sensitive constitutional reasoning are available in the history of common constitutionalism to handle these situations. Their use demonstrates that the unity of a constitutional association derives from the protection and concordance, rather than the discontinuity and assimilation, of the cultural identities of its members. The strength of the constitutional fabric consists in the interweaving of different threads – a crazy quilt rather than a crazy house.

The mutual recognition of the cultures of citizens engenders allegiance and unity for two reasons. Citizens have a sense of belonging to, and identification with, a constitutional association in so far as, first, they have a say in the formation and governing of the association and, second, they see their own cultural ways publicly acknowledged and affirmed in the basic institutions of their society. No matter how diverse or confederal it is, these two features nurture a strong sense of pride in the association. There is no irreconcilable conflict between allegiance to the constitution and one's culture or cultures, for the constitution and its public institutions and traditions of interpretation are the protectors, rather than the destroyers, of the cultures and rights of the members. If these two conditions are not met, the association is experienced as an alien and imposed yoke that suppresses the members' liberty and cultural identities, causing resistance and disunity. As Said pragmatically replies to Schlesinger, 'it is better to explore history than to repress or deny it'. The 'fact that the United States contains so many histories, many of them now clamouring for attention, is by no means to be suddenly feared since many of them were always there, and out of them *an* American society and politics' were created. If the 'old and habitual ideas of the main group' are not 'flexible enough to admit new groups, then these ideas need changing, a far better thing to do than reject the emerging groups'.[7]

This is the oldest lesson of Western and Aboriginal constitutionalism. The politics of cultural recognition is the response to the flouting of the lesson in modern constitutionalism. If the twenty-first century is to be different from the devastating cultural conflicts of the late twentieth century, this lesson will have to be relearned. The courageous citizens of Palestine and Israel, including the dissidents, may prove in practice that this lesson can be learned even after long periods of bitter conflict and imperfect negotiations.

Two public goods of contemporary constitutionalism: belonging and critical freedom

Why, then, in the face of injustice and inefficacy, is modern constitutional politics dominated by the will to impose uniformity in the name of unity and power? Why is the first step of mutual recognition so difficult? There are many answers to this question. The pursuit of property and the splendour of empire, the misunderstanding and fear of others different from oneself and other explanations have been raised in the course of this book. Since I am dealing with language, I want to take up the reason why the *language* of modern constitutionalism disposes its users to uniformity.

We observed in chapter 4 that the language of modern constitutionalism is informed by the mistaken assumption that the general terms of constitutionalism are applied identically in every instance. This assumption predisposes the theorists and citizens who use the language to look for and insist upon a uniformity and unity that the diverse and aspectival constitutional phenomena it is supposed to represent do not exhibit. They predicate of the phenomena what lies in the language of representation. When the association and its constituents fail to live up to the ideal they are said to be suffering an identity crisis.

In the course of his many attempts to dislodge the assumption that a concept is identical to itself in every instance, Wittgenstein paused to suggest one explanation for the powerful hold of this widespread 'paradigm of identity'. His interlocutor insists, surely, 'a thing is identical with itself'. Wittgenstein replies, there 'is no finer example of a useless proposition, which yet is connected with a certain play of the imagination. It is as if in imagination we put a thing into its own shape and saw that it fitted.'[8]

This explanation applies to the concepts of modern constitutionalism, for the image of a thing fitting into its own shape is exemplified in the idea that there are necessary and sufficient conditions for the application of a general term of constitutionalism. When the identity of a constitutional association and its constituents is imagined in this way, it is thought of as identical to itself, for example, that a nation must fit into its own shape, like it fits into its borders on a map. The thought that it is not identical to itself, but a complicated network of similarities, overlapping, criss-crossing and open to negotiation offends against the imaginary unity of the nation. This play of the imagination is held in place and reinforced by the habitual use of the language of modern constitutionalism.

The captivating role of this imaginary paradigm of identity

in modern constitutionalism has been noted by many observers. Descartes mentions how the early modern constitutional reformers were driven by the classical images of the unity of Sparta and the vision of the mythical legislator who makes the constitution to fit his ideal plan. These republican images have been supplemented by the individualist and communitarian sovereign people of Locke and Rousseau, the modern constitutional monoculture of Kant and Constant, the veil of ignorance, the homogeneous community, the transcultural ideal speech-situation and the shared understandings of those who followed.

Quentin Skinner records how Hobbes' philosophy, which many imagine as the paradigm of a modern political philosophy, is an attempt to transcend the indeterminacy and lack of fit of the concepts of humanist constitutionalism. John Pocock explains how the constitutional philosophy of Hale, based on the study of different cases and the history of existing and ancient law, gave way to the ahistorical image of the stages view of human history, which, ironically, came to be called historicism. It consists in, he writes,

the habit of generalizing about the periods of history, of supposing each of them to have been governed by certain general characteristics, so that it could be further supposed that there was a certain logic about the way in which one period succeeded another, and that the dominant characteristics of one period might help to explain how it had been transformed into another or replaced.

By their willingness 'to engage in sweeping generalizations, many of which were naturally unsound', the modern theorists of constitutionalism 'converted history into a unified science, capable (at least in theory) of looking at the whole of human life from a standpoint distinctively its own'.[9] In case after concrete case, Pocock has gone on to survey how the Napoleonic manner in which the generalisations were spread swept over the complexity of the constitutional languages and critical contests in which real human beings strive to give meaning to their actions and settle their differences.

Adam Kuper, Johannes Fabian, Edward Said, Bruce

Trigger, Anthony Pagden, Calvin Luther Martin and many others present studies of how this great map of mankind continues to be foisted on the constitutional diversity of humankind long after it has been shown not to fit, as if the shape of human organisation must – somehow – fit into itself. John Dunn introduces an array of illustrations of how the uniform and homogeneous image of Athenian democracy continues to exercise a profound influence on the modern constitutional imagination. The ways in which the images of maps and sharp borders inform the imaginary community of modern constitutional theory and practice are brought to critical light by the research of Benedict Anderson. Sir Isaiah Berlin assembles reminder after reminder of how uniformity and unity dominate modern European political philosophy so thoroughly that diversity is scarcely ever even considered as anything but a threat to law and order. Seyla Benhabib, Peta Bowden, Christine Di Stefano, Jane Flax, Carol Gilligan, Jane Roland Martin, Susan Mendus, Martha Minow, Elizabeth Spelman, Iris Young and other feminist scholars, who are not unfamiliar with the psychological explanations of the image of shapes fitting into perfect receptacles, demonstrate the ways in which liberal, communitarian and nationalist theories exclude the contingency and differences of concrete others in the quest for an imaginary unity. Many more examples could be given.

It is not too extravagant to suggest, therefore, that the failure mutually to recognise and live with cultural diversity is a failure of imagination; a failure to look on human associations in ways not ruled by these dubious images.

I have invited you to see the terms of constitutionalism as never quite identical to themselves. I have described them as overlapping, interacting and negotiated in use because these are the ways they are handled in practice, thereby constituting the aspectival and diverse identity of the constitutional associations they describe. These descriptions free us to regard constitutionalism differently, providing an alternative 'paradigm of identity' and evoking a play of the imagination more congenial to recognising and negotiating cultural diversity in a post-imperial age.

The best evocation of this alternative play of the imagination is *The spirit of Haida Gwaii*. If contemporary constitutionalism is imagined in the light of this wonderful sculpture, the two public goods it harbours come into sharp relief. As chapter 2 foreshadowed, they are the critical freedom to question in thought and challenge in practice one's inherited cultural ways, on one hand, and the aspiration to belong to a culture and place, and so to be at home in the world, on the other. The differences between these invaluable goods have been settled in the black canoe. Their concord is indicated by Bill Reid's epigram, 'the boat goes on forever anchored in the same place', and by the various aspects of the constitutional organisation of the members on board. The stream of examples in this book has been arranged so that their mediation comes into view in the course of the voyage. Now that we have reached our destination it will not be amiss to recollect what we have seen.

In modern constitutionalism, critical freedom and adherence to custom are thought of as the mutually exclusive and irreconcilable goods which underlie the conflicts of our time over cultural recognition. The ancient constitution is said to have provided a sense of belonging, by the deference to custom, but excluded the critical freedom essential to modern identity. Modern constitutionalism enthrones the freedom of critical enquiry and dissent by excluding the authority of custom. This opposition between ancient authority and modern examination was at the heart of the great early struggles for modern constitutionalism and it continues to inform debates among liberals, nationalists, communitarians, post-moderns, cultural feminists and interculturalists today.

Chapter 3 exposed the caricature in this opposition. The sign law case in chapter 5 illustrated how the good of belonging to a secure culture and the freedom to dissent need not clash in a culturally diverse association based on the three conventions. Let us examine more carefully how they are conciliated in *The spirit of Haida Gwaii*, then in contemporary constitutionalism, by starting from the more familiar image of constitutional uniformity and working towards the less familiar image of diversity.

Imagine the large father grizzly bear at the bow of the canoe addressing the other passengers. He describes his vision of the constitutional association in his terms and traditions, explaining how bears exercise their rights, govern themselves, care for each other and relate to others. Instead of then listening to the others, becoming aware of and marvelling at the diversity of cultural ways, enjoying the reflective disequilibrium the dialogue engenders, and negotiating a peaceful arrangement of their similarities and differences, he unjustly demands that everyone adopt the ways of the bear clan, as male bears see them. He claims that the ways of the bear clan are superior to all the others in their civility or efficiency. Alternatively, he may claim that they are not bear ways at all, but universal ways that the bears, being at a higher stage, are able to discern. Or he confidently asserts that his articulation of the association comprehends and sublimates the constitutional ways of the others in a higher synthesis. The other passengers would accept these ways if they too were reasonable, if they would think through the following thought experiment, or if they would only speak in the language of constitutionalism he uses.

The injustice of not applying the conventions of recognition and continuity mutually is glaringly obvious. The various strategies of the bear manifest the imperial attitude of speaking for rather than with others, the anti-democratic attitude which informs the imperial features of modern constitutionalism. This attitude of superiority is supported by the background image that the association must exhibit uniformity, that some such vision must capture its identity. And, alas, if the other passengers accept his modern language, they too will find it difficult to imagine otherwise.

From the perspectives of *The spirit of Haida Gwaii*, it is unimaginable that this attitude could be seen as just. The passengers are arranged to subvert this imperial attitude at every turn. Of course, the bear ways are indispensable to the beauty of the canoe, but they would become monstrous if they were to gain hegemony and efface the living cultures of the other members. The beauty of the bear, and of any other member of the ensemble, comes from his place among the others. The aesthetic justice involved is precisely that of rendering each member his or her due.

As one walks around the sculpture and is drawn to imagine oneself aboard, one is constantly made aware that the passengers never fit into their own shape. The play of one's imagination is never allowed to settle on this possibility. This *Xuuya* play is orchestrated by the endless juxtaposition of these diverse and interrelated creatures, the identity of each consisting in the innumerable ways it relates to and interacts with the others. As the assemblage is viewed from one point of view, certain aspects are recognised and they give a vision to the whole. For example, take in the breathtaking view from the raven's position. Then view the multiplicity from the bear's locale. Other aspects and relations come to light, and a different vision of the whole. Now, look at how the mother bear, according to Bill Reid, appears to be cautioning her husband that his vision overlooks some important aspect of the confederation. Then walk around and see how each member and the ensemble are transformed from the neighbourhood of *hlkkyaan qqusttaan*, the frog, or the borough of *Qaganjaat*, the mouse woman. The imperious attempt to colonise this celebration of diversity in one form of recognition – whether of one passenger, of the comprehension of all passengers, or of a form which transcends their differences – is continually resisted and defeated by the play of the irreducible diversity of the work of art on one's imagination. *Xuuya*, the raven, is at the helm as a reminder that this play is the spirit of the voyage.

If we now view ourselves as members of the black canoe, the diversity of our fellow citizens evokes a sense of belonging to a constitutional association in which one's own culture (or cultures) is recognised as a constituent and interrelated part of the justice of the whole association. This specific sense of belonging and civic pride would be lost if one's culture were excluded, identified in isolation from the others or imposed on all the members. The sense of belonging comes from being associated with the other cultures.

The good of belonging typical of ancient constitutionalism is thus transformed in a manner appropriate to a culturally diverse age, as we foresaw in our discussion of the minor members of the black canoe in chapter 5. The sense of belonging and allegiance comes not only from the public recognition of one's culture, but also because one's culture is respected among others and woven into the public fabric of the association, gaining its strength and splendour from its accommodation among, and interrelations with, the others. This is more than a civic awareness that citizens of other cultures exist in one's polity. One's own identity as a citizen is inseparable from a shared history with other citizens who are irreducibly different; whose cultures have interacted with and enriched one's own and made their mark on the basic institutions of society. The loss or assimilation of any of the other cultures is experienced as an impoverishment of one's own identity.

I imagine that many citizens of the four nations of the United Kingdom have a very similar sense of belonging to their multiple kingdom. As interculturalists argued in chapter 5, the sensibility should be extended analogously to the other cultures of contemporary societies. Such a post-imperial understanding of belonging is incompatible with assimilation and the best bulwark against it. The pride of belonging to a culture that gains its splendour and reputation from its association with others encourages citizens to care for the survival and conservation of all cultures. The surviving cultural multiplicity constitutes the secure place of anchorage.

At the same time, the black canoe evokes a sense of estrangement from one's own cultural outlook by seeing it juxtaposed to a multiplicity of others. Although the myth creatures view the whole from their own individual points of view, their overlap, interaction and negotiation ensure that they cannot help but be aware that their own viewpoint is one among many, and that the others are not exotic and separate, but near at hand and interrelated to their own in a variety of ways. Their entangled arrangement, graphically highlighted by the wolf and eagle, creates the disequilibrium with respect to one's settled cultural self understanding.

The sense of being at home in the multiplicity yet at the same time playfully estranged by it awakes an attitude of wonder. The Haida myths Bill Reid retells in *The raven steals the light* overflow with examples of how the creatures of the black canoe revel in this wonderful cultural freedom. In our discussion of exchanging stories in Aboriginal constitutional dialogue in chapter 1, we noted that it is a highly prized and carefully nurtured achievement of many Aboriginal civilisations.

Now, the ability to free ourselves from what is most familiar and to wonder again at the sheer diversity of things is just as highly valued in contemporary, non-Aboriginal civilisations. However, as George Marcus and Michael Fischer submit in *Anthropology as cultural critique*, it is thought to require an exotic experience: atonal music, cubist or surreal painting, *Waiting for Godot* or, especially, an encounter with a primitive culture. The juxtaposition of the myth creatures reveals that this invaluable attitude of world reversal and wonder can be awakened just by doing what Wittgenstein does in the *Philosophical investigations* and what they do aboard the canoe: exchange and juxtapose their myths, narratives and further descriptions of their interrelated histories together. The wonderfulness of *The spirit of Haida Gwaii* thus ushers in the other public good of contemporary constitutionalism: the ability to see one's own ways as strange and unfamiliar, to stray from and take up a critical attitude towards them and so open cultures to question, reinterpretation, negotiation, transformation and non-identity.

The theorists of modern constitutionalism define critical freedom and dissent as their primary good. Yet, after a critical survey, the settled forms of critical freedom and dissent within modern constitutionalism and its three traditions of interpretation turn out to be much narrower than they first appear. They are exercised within the uncriticised horizons of seven features which look increasingly contingent and parochial as the vestiges of the imperial age recede. Moreover, the presumption of a comprehensive theory forecloses the possibility of an intercultural dialogue in which diversity awareness and broader critical freedom could be engendered and exercised.

A constitutional association which recognises and accommodates cultural diversity, in contrast, provides the social basis for critical reflection on and dissent from one's own cultural institutions and traditions of interpretation. Citizens are made aware of cultural diversity at home, as something related to and overlapping with their own culture, but nevertheless different. The possibility of crossing from one culture to another is available and unavoidable, for each citizen is a member of more than one culture. The diverse legal and political institutions of the association create an environment in which one's own institutions and traditions can scarcely be taken for granted. The mutual respect for and affirmation of cultural diversity in the civic life of a society further enhance a critical attitude to one's own culture and a tolerant and critical attitude towards others. An ethos of critical freedom is also sustained by the public acknowledgement that the constitution is open to review and that discussion of it is a valuable dimension of citizenship. Most importantly, engagement in intercultural dialogues on the constitution, like Aboriginal exchanges of stories, is itself the exercise of critical freedom, as citizens tell and mediate their stories of the association. In these and other ways, contemporary constitutionalism provides a broader and more cosmopolitan forum for a civic life of critical freedom than modern constitutionalism.

Hence, the goods of belonging and freedom support rather than oppose each other in a culturally diverse association based on the conventions of mutual recognition, continuity and consent. Critical freedom requires the presence of a diversity of living cultures and the accommodation of diverse cultures requires critical dialogue in accord with the three conventions.

While *The spirit of Haida Gwaii* presents a wonderful artistic symbol, is there an analogous written expression of the spirit of mutual recognition and accommodation? Many examples have been mentioned. The great speeches of negotiators in the Aboriginal and common law system are among the best. However, let me select a more recent example. In 1969 the prime minister of Canada, Pierre Trudeau, announced his plan to abolish the treaty system and assimilate all Aboriginal people into the modern Canadian society for the sake of their improvement. Harold Cardinal, an Aboriginal leader, responded with a short book, *The unjust society*, which has become a classic in Aboriginal struggles against the plan and for recognition. He evokes an unforgettable array of images and analogies to put into words the spirit of treaty constitutionalism as one male Aboriginal sees it.[10]

An Indian looks at nature and sees beauty – the woods, the marshes, the mountains, the grasses and berries, the moose and the field mouse, the soaring eagle and the flitting hummingbird, the gaudy flowers and the succulent bulbs. He sees an overall fitness, an overall collective beauty, but he looks deeper. He sees the beauty of the individual components of the big picture. He sees the diversity of the various elements of the entire scene. He admires the grace of a leaping deer, the straight-line simplicity of the pines the deer leaps through, the jagged, three-dimensional thrust into the sky of the rugged peaks, the quick silver flash of a trout on the surface of a wind-whipped lake. He turns a sensitive ear to the faraway eerie wail of the loon and the nearer snuffling grunt of a bear pawing at a ground-squirrel's den, and he blends them into the whispering of grasses and the bolder talk of the tall pines. He feels the touch of wind against his cheek and the coolness of the mist above the rapids. He surveys the diversities of nature and finds them good.

An Indian thinks this might be the way of people. He knows that whites and Indians are different. He knows that there are differences even within these groups, differences between Scot and Ukrainian, between Cree and Iroquois. He knows that there are differences between man and his brother, red or white.

To the Indian this is the natural way of things, the way things should be, as it is in nature. As the stream needs the grasses, so do peoples need of each other, and so can peoples find good in each other. Indians are close to nature, so it natural for them to see the bigger world in terms of the small world they do know. They know that men of different cultures and races have much to offer one another. We offer our culture; we offer our heritage. We know it is different from yours. We are interested in your culture and heritage; we want you to discover ours.

Now, try to imagine, as an *improvement*, a world in which this author and the culture which animates his writing have been completely assimilated to non-Aboriginal society. If the suggestion appears to be a contemptible affront to your dignity as a human being, then this book will not have been in vain, for you will have come to share the view of the passengers of the black canoe.

Conclusion: the philosophy and practice of contemporary constitutionalism

I have sought to outline both the philosophy and practice of constitutionalism informed by the spirit of mutual recognition and accommodation of cultural diversity. Both the philosophy and practice consist in the negotiation and mediation of claims to recognition in a dialogue governed by the conventions of mutual recognition, continuity and consent. This tradition of contemporary constitutionalism is a minor one in philosophy and practice. It does not recommend itself to the competing schools in theory or the clashing parties in practice. Their aim is to fit the constitution to the shape of their comprehensive theories of justice, whereas mine is to submit their partial claims to just negotiation and mediation. The similarities and differences of each which gain the acceptance of all in the dialogue are then accommodated in the constitution.

The tradition has few illustrious members. Deganawidah, the mediator of the *Haudenosaunee* Confederation in the fifteenth century, is a noteworthy exception in practice and Wittgenstein in philosophy. Many practitioners, like Haemon, have been silenced by the battles that engulfed their attempts at mediation or, like Hale, by the victory of monological forms of constitutionalism. How many people now even remember those who negotiated and mediated the constitutional agreement between Israel and Palestine, the South African constitution or the federation of Bosnian Croats and Muslims? How long will these fragile accommodations last? Those who negotiated a constitutional agreement in Canada in 1992 were voted down, thrown out of office and replaced by those who stood on the sidelines and took the most extreme positions.

The fate of Chief Justice Marshall is typical. After leading ruthless wars of slaughter against the Creek and Seminole, General Andrew Jackson, 'Sharp knife', was elected president in 1829. On hearing of Marshall's judgement in defence of the Cherokee nation, discussed in chapter 4, he flatly responded, 'John Marshall made his decision, let him enforce it.' President Jackson then ordered the forced removal of the five 'civilised' tribes (Cherokee, Choctaw, Chicksaw, Creek and Seminole) from their ancestral lands and their relocation eight hundred miles westward. Thousands of Aboriginal people were killed and starved to death during the brutal exodus. The Cherokee suffered the worst treatment. Over four thousand died in the final cleansing march, the 'trail of tears' of 1838–9. Their lands were stolen, possessions plundered and schools converted to taverns for the incoming settlers. The atrocities were so abhorrent that an enquiry was set up in 1841. It reported that, 'bribery, perjury, and forgery, short weights, issues of spoiled meat and grain, and every conceivable subterfuge was employed by designing white men'. The government did not release the report.[11]

Moreover, a tradition, which includes Sophocles and Bill Reid, Wittgenstein and Geertz, Joseph Brant and Ellen Gabriel, is unlikely to raise false hopes. Nevertheless, chapters 4 and 5 surveyed how this tradition of constitutional philosophy and practice has made a difference to the actual constitutional history of the last four hundred years. Even Marshall's decision continues to be used throughout the world to counter Jackson's many followers today. This book has also shown how recent practitioners have transformed the tradition to do justice to the more culturally diverse circumstances in practice and the advances in the understanding of cultures in philosophy. In each case, the accommodation is just because the three conventions of justice are held fast in and by the dialogue. On these conventions we, like the ancient reluctant conscript, stand fast, for they are the rules of the common ground on which we stand. Even transgressions by Locke, Kant, Herder, Publius and Mill are not tolerated. Furthermore, the two previous sections have provided a sketch of the goods that might accrue to the culturally diverse citizens of the twenty-first century if this tradition were taken more seriously than it is.

Finally, the philosophy and practice of contemporary constitutionalism offers a mediated peace. In both theory and practice this is seen as second best relative to a just peace. A just peace is a constitutional settlement in accordance with the comprehensive theory of justice. The argument of these lectures is that this is the most destructive illusion of our age. The just peace of the theorists and dogmatists is neither justice nor peace. It is always a limited and partial description of justice which, when imposed, galls the necks of others and leads to discord. On the contrary, a mediated peace *is* a just peace: just because it is a constitutional settlement in accord with the three conventions of justice and peaceful because the constitution is accommodated to the diverse necks of those who agree to it. If this view of constitutionalism came to be accepted, the allegedly irreconcilable conflicts of the present would not have to be the tragic history of our future.

How the wise members of *The spirit of Haida Gwaii* avoid this tragic fate is now as clear as day. We began with the question of the spirit appropriate to a post-imperial age of cultural diversity. As Vaclav Havel writes, 'if the world today is not to become hopelessly enmeshed in ever more terrifying conflicts, it has only one possibility: it must deliberately breathe the spirit of multicultural co-existence into the civilization that envelops it'. The 'basis' of this 'new spirit' is 'for different peoples, religions and cultures' to learn to 'respect each other', to 'respect and honour each others' differences'.[12]

This is the *spirit* of *Haida Gwaii*. The answer given by the black canoe is that, although the passengers vie and negotiate for recognition and power, they always do so in accord with the three conventions. Of equal importance to their pacific way of life, they also never fail to heed what is said by the chief whose identity has remained a mystery until this moment. She or he is the mediator.

Notes

I have cut the number of notes to the minimum so the book retains the character of lectures. All the authors and texts mentioned are listed in the bibliography. I have used notes only for direct quotations and for texts mentioned which require a specific reference. In the case of successive quotations from the same author or text, the references are gathered together in one note at the end of several quotations.

1 DEMANDS FOR CONSTITUTIONAL RECOGNITION

1 Isaiah Berlin, 'Return of the *Volkgeist*', *New Perspectives Quarterly*, 8, 4 (1991) 4–10, and 'The bent twig: on the rise of nationalism', *The crooked timber of humanity* (New York: Random House, 1992) 238–62.
2 Jacques Derrida, *The other heading: reflections on today's Europe*, tr. Pascale-Anne Brault and Michael R. Naas (Bloomington: Indiana University Press, 1992) 9.
3 Clifford Geertz, 'The uses of diversity', *Michigan Quarterly Review*, 25, 1 (1986) 105–23.
4 Thomas Hobbes, *Leviathan*, ed. Richard Tuck (Cambridge: Cambridge University Press, 1991) 88.
5 Robert Bringhurst and Ulli Steltzer, *The black canoe: Bill Reid and 'The spirit of Haida Gwaii'* (Vancouver: Douglas and McIntyre, 1991) 49–59.
6 Doris Shadbolt, *Bill Reid* (Vancouver: Douglas and McIntyre, 1986) 182.
7 Bill Reid, 'These shining islands', *Islands at the edge: preserving the Queen Charlotte Islands wilderness* (Vancouver: Douglas and McIntyre, n.d.) 24.
8 Luther Standing Bear, *Land of the spotted eagle* (Boston: Houghton Mifflin, 1933) viii.
9 Rita Joe, *Poems of Rita Joe* (Halifax: Abenaki Press, 1978) 4.

10 Bill Reid, *Gallant beasts and monsters* (Vancouver: Buschlen Mowatt, 1992) 15.
11 Carl Sandburg, 'Old timers', *Cornhuskers* (New York: Holt, Rinehart and Winston, 1918), cited in Bringhurst and Steltzer, *The black canoe*, 57–8.
12 Reid, *Gallant beasts*, 21.

2 DIVERSITY AND CONTEMPORARY CONSTITUTIONALISM

1 Michel Foucault, *L'usage des plaisirs* (Paris: Editions Gallimard, 1984) 14.
2 Reid, *Gallant beasts*, 25.
3 *Ibid.*, 25.
4 Edward W. Said, *Culture and imperialism* (New York: Knopf, 1993) 56, 50–1.
5 Ludwig Wittgenstein, *Philosophical investigations*, tr. G. E. M. Anscombe (Oxford: Basil Blackwell, 1967) s. 241.
6 Jacques Derrida, *Writing and difference*, tr. Alan Bass (Chicago: Chicago University Press, 1978) 282.
7 James Clifford, *The predicament of culture: twentieth-century ethnography, literature, and art* (Cambridge, Mass.: Harvard University Press, 1988) 95.
8 Peter Emberley, 'Globalism and localism: constitutionalism in a new world order', *Constitutional predicament: Canada after the referendum of 1992*, ed. Curtis Cook (Montreal: McGill-Queens University Press, 1994) 199–218, 202.
9 Adrienne Rich, 'Taking women students seriously', *Gendered subjects: the dynamics of feminist teaching*, ed. Margo Culley and Catherine Portuges (London: Routledge and Kegan Paul, 1985) 21–8, 28.
10 *Ibid.*, 24.
11 John Rawls, *Political liberalism* (New York: Columbia University Press, 1993).

3 THE HISTORICAL FORMATION OF MODERN CONSTITUTIONALISM: THE EMPIRE OF UNIFORMITY

1 Wittgenstein, *Philosophical investigations*, s. 115.
2 Henry St John, Viscount Bolingbroke, *A dissertation upon parties* (1733–4), *The works of Lord Bolingbroke*, 4 vols. (Philadelphia: 1841) vol. ii, 88, cited in Charles Howard McIlwain, *Constitutionalism:*

ancient and modern, revised edition (Ithaca: Cornell University Press, 1947) 3.

3 Cicero, *De re publica* (Cambridge, Mass.: Harvard University Press, 1963) bk. 1, s. 69.

4 Thomas Aquinas, *Summa theologiae*, 1–11, Q.97, AA.3, in S. Thomas Aquinas, *On law, morality and politics*, ed. William P. Baumgarth and Richard J. Regan (Indianapolis: Hackett Publishing Company, 1988) 79–81.

5 John Locke, *Two treatises of government*, ed. Peter Laslett (Cambridge: Cambridge University Press, 1991) second treatise, s. 30.

6 John Locke, *An essay concerning human understanding*, ed. Peter Nidditch (Oxford: Clarendon Press, 1975) 1.4.12, 92, discussed in Daniel Carey, *Travel narrative and the problem of human nature in Locke, Shaftesbury and Hutcheson* (doctoral thesis, 1993) chapter 3.

7 Edmund Burke, *The correspondence of Edmund Burke*, 4 vols., ed. George H. Guttridge (Cambridge: Cambridge University Press, 1961) vol. III, 350–1, cited as the motto in Peter James Marshall, *The great map of mankind: perceptions of new worlds in the age of enlightenment* (Cambridge, Mass.: Harvard University Press, 1982).

8 Locke, *Two treatises*, first treatise, s. 106.

9 Emmanuel Joseph Sieyès, *Qu'est-ce-que le tiers état?*, ed. Roberto Zapperi (Geneva: Groz, 1970).

10 Quentin Skinner, 'The state', *Political innovation and conceptual change*, ed. Terrence Ball, James Farr and Russell L. Hanson (Cambridge: Cambridge University Press, 1989) 90–132.

11 Thomas Paine, *The rights of man*, ed. Gregory Claeys (Indianapolis/Cambridge: Hackett Publishing Company, 1992) 43, cited in McIlwain, *Constitutionalism*, 2.

12 Locke, *Two treatises*, s. 25.

13 *Ibid.*, ss. 49, 108, 30.

14 *Ibid.*, s. 87.

15 *Ibid.*, ss. 28, 30, 27, 38, 30, 50.

16 *Ibid.*, first treatise, s. 130, second treatise, ss. 14, 37–8, 11.

17 *Ibid.*, s. 36.

18 *Ibid.*, ss. 42, 45, 32, John Cotton, 'John Cotton's answer to Roger Williams', *The complete writings of Roger Williams*, 7 vols. (New York: Russell and Russell, 1963) vol. II, 47.

19 Locke, *Two treatises*, s. 37.

20 *Ibid.*, s. 41.

21 Thomas Morton, *New English Canaan* (1632), The Publications of the Prince Society, ed. Charles F. Adams, XIV (Boston: 1883),

175–7; Pierre Biard, S.J., 'Relations', in *The Jesuit relations and allied documents 1610–1791*, 73 vols., tr. Reuben G. Thwaites (Cleveland: Burrows, 1896–1901) vol. III, 135.

22 Locke, *Two treatises*, ss. 107–8, 48–9.

23 *Ibid.*, s. 107.

24 *Ibid.*, ss. 108–24.

25 Roger Williams, 'The bloody tenant', in *Complete writings*, vol. III, 250.

26 Locke, *Two treatises*, s. 108.

27 Emeric de Vattel, *The law of nations or the principles of natural law*, tr. Charles G. Fenwick (Washington: Carnegie Institute, 1902), 1.8.81 (207–10).

28 Immanuel Kant, *Idea for a universal history with a cosmopolitan intent* and *Perpetual peace: a philosophical sketch*, in *Perpetual peace and other essays*, tr. Ted Humphrey (Indianapolis: Hackett Publishing Company, 1983) 29-40 and 107–44, 31–2, 124.

29 *Ibid.*, 111, 112 note, 123, 119, 125.

30 *Ibid.*, 118–19.

31 John Rawls, 'Justice as fairness: political not metaphysical', *Philosophy and Public Affairs*, 14 (1985) 223–52, 225, and see his development of this idea in *Political liberalism*, xxi–xxx, 8–11, 58–66, 140–50, 164–8, 220–7.

32 Samuel Pufendorf, *On the duty of man and citizen according to natural law*, ed. James Tully, tr. Michael Silverthorne (Cambridge: Cambridge University Press, 1991) 2.8.12, 144, 2.9.2, 146, and Severinus de Monzambano (Pufendorf), *De statu imperii Germanici (On the constitution of the German empire)* (Frankfurt: 1664).

33 Samuel Pufendorf, *On the law of nature and nations*, tr. C. H. and W. A. Oldfather (Oxford: Clarendon Press, 1934) 7.5.13, 1038–9; Locke, *Two treatises*, s. 212.

34 *Déclaration des droits de l'homme et du citoyen*, ed. J. Delène Création (Paris: Roger Rimbaud, 1989).

35 'Constitution', *Encyclopédie, ou dictionnaire universel et raisonné des conaissances humaine*, 58 vols., ed. Fortunato-Bartholomeo de Felice (Yverdon: 1770–80) vol. II, 189–91.

36 Emmanuel Joseph Sieyès, *Dire de l'Abbé Sieyès sur la question du veto Royal a la séance du 7 Septembre 1789* (Paris: 1789) 11, cited in Murray Forsyth, *Reason and revolution: the political thought of Abbé Sieyès* (Leicester: Leicester University Press, 1987) 138.

37 John Locke, *The educational writings of John Locke*, ed. James Axtell (Cambridge: Cambridge University Press, 1968) 325; Locke, *An essay concerning human understanding*, 2.33.6, 396.

38 Pierre Nicole, *Discourses on the being of a god, the immortality of the soul*,

the weakness of man and concerning the way of preserving peace with men,
tr. John Locke (London: 1712) 72–3, cited in Carey, *Travel narrative*,
chapter 3, 37.

39 John Locke, *A Report of the Board of Trade to the Lords Justices
respecting the relief and employment of the poor, 1697* (London: 1793)
10–11.

40 Hobbes, *Leviathan*, 239.

41 Alexander Hamilton, James Madison and John Jay, *The federalist
papers*, ed. Clinton Rossiter (New York: Mentor-Penguin, 1961)
38.

42 *Ibid.*, 42.

43 *Ibid.*, 61, 269, 161.

44 Dorothy V. Jones, *License for empire: colonialism by treaty in early
America* (Chicago: University of Chicago Press, 1982).

45 James Brown Scott, ed., *The Declaration of Independence, the Articles
of Confederation, the constitution of the United States* (New York:
Oxford University Press, 1917) 6.

46 Georgina C. Nammack, *Fraud, politics, and the dispossession of the
Indians* (Norman, Okla.: Oklahoma University Press, 1968).

47 William L. Stone, *Life of Joseph Brant-Thayendanegea, including the
border wars of the American revolution*, 2 vols. (New York: 1838) vol. II,
481–3.

48 Richard Rorty, 'On ethnocentrism: a reply to Clifford Geertz',
Objectivity, relativism, and truth (Cambridge: Cambridge University
Press, 1991) 203–10, 206.

49 Alasdair MacIntyre, *Whose justice? Which rationality?* (Notre Dame:
University of Notre Dame Press, 1988).

4 THE HISTORICAL FORMATION OF COMMON CONSTITUTIONALISM: THE REDISCOVERY OF CULTURAL DIVERSITY, PART I

1 Johann Nestroy, *Der Schützling* (*The protégé*), *Gesammelte Werke*,
7 vols. (Vienna: Verlag von Anton Schroll and Co., 1962) vol. IV,
603–715, 695. The quotation is the motto for this book and for
Wittgenstein's *Philosophical investigations*. For a discussion, see
Andrew W. Barker, 'Nestroy and Wittgenstein: some thoughts on
the motto to the *Philosophical investigations*', *German Life and Letters*,
39, 2 (1986), 161–7.

2 René Descartes, *Discourse on the method*, in *The Philosophical writings
of Descartes*, 2 vols., tr. John Cottingham, Robert Stoothoff and
Dugald Murdoch (Cambridge: Cambridge University Press,
1985) vol. I, 111–51, 116–18.

3 Wittgenstein, *Philosophical investigations*, s. 18.
4 *Ibid.*, s. 23.
5 *Ibid.*, ss. 122, 203.
6 Ludwig Wittgenstein, *The blue and brown books: preliminary studies for the 'Philosophical investigations'* (Oxford: Basil Blackwell, 1972) 17–20.
7 Wittgenstein, *Philosophical investigations*, s. 85.
8 *Ibid.*, ss. 198–201.
9 *Ibid.*, ss. 82, 84.
10 *Ibid.*, s. 75.
11 *Ibid.*, ss. 71, 144, Wittgenstein, 'Philosophy', *Philosophical occasions 1912–1951*, ed. James Klage and Alfred Nordmann (Indianapolis: Hackett Publishing Company, 1993) 160–99, 163, and G. E. Moore, 'Wittgenstein's lectures: 1930–33', *ibid.*, 46–114, 106.
12 Wittgenstein, *Philosophical investigations*, ss. 71, 127.
13 M. O'C. Drury, 'Some notes on conversations with Wittgenstein', *Recollections of Wittgenstein*, ed. Rush Rhees (Oxford: Oxford University Press, 1984) 97–171, 157:

> Wittgenstein: 'Hegel seems to me to be always wanting to say things which look different are really the same. Whereas my interest is in showing that things which look the same are really quite different. I was thinking of using as a motto for my book a quotation from *King Lear*, "I'll teach you differences" [*King Lear* i. iv.].'

14 Wittgenstein, *Philosophical investigations*, s. 131.
15 *Ibid.*, s. 67.
16 Wittgenstein, 'Remarks on Frazer's *Golden Bough*', *Philosophical occasions*, 119–55, 131–3.
17 Hobbes, *Leviathan*, 221, 106, 145.
18 Matthew Hale, *Reflections by the Lrd. Chiefe Justice Hale on Mr. Hobbes his dialogue of the lawe*, in W. S. Holdsworth, *A history of English law*, 7 vols. (Boston: Little Brown, 1924) vol. v, 500–18, 501–6.
19 Albert R. Jonsen and Stephen Toulmin, *The abuse of casuistry: a history of moral reasoning* (Berkeley: University of California Press, 1988) 293.
20 Quentin Skinner, *Reason and rhetoric in the philosophy of Hobbes* (Cambridge: Cambridge University Press, 1995) 15–16 of the typescript.
21 *Worcester v. the State of Georgia*, January term, 1832, 6 Peter's Reports, 515–97, reprinted in John Marshall, *The writings of Chief Justice Marshall on the federal constitution* (Boston: James Monroe and Company, 1839) 419–48, 426–7.

22 Sir William Johnson, 'To the Lords of Trade, November 13, 1763' and 'To the Lords of Trade, n.d.', *Documents relative to the colonial history of the State of New York*, 15 vols., ed. Edmund B. O'Callaghan (Albany, N.Y.: 1853–7) vol. VII, 572–81 and 661–6, 575, 665.

23 Alexander Henry, *Travels and adventures in Canada and the Indian territories between the years 1760 and 1776* (New York: I. Riley, 1809) 44.

24 Marshall, *Worcester*, 445, 435.

25 *Ibid.*, 427–30, 433, 427.

26 *Ibid.*, 441, 442, 431.

27 *Johnson and Graham's Lessee v. M'Intosh* (1823), *ibid.*, 262–86, 275.

28 Marshall, *Worcester*, 446.

29 'The Presentation by the Haudenosaunee confederation to the Canadian House of Commons Committee on Indian self-government, 1983', as explained by Grand Chief Michael Mitchell of Akwesasne, 'An unbroken assertion of sovereignty', *Drumbeat: anger and renewal in Indian country*, ed. Boyce Richardson (Toronto: The Assembly of First Nations, Summerhill Press, 1989) 105–36, 109–10.

30 David Maybury-Lewis, *Millennium: tribal wisdom and the modern world* (New York: Penguin, 1992) 260–1.

31 A. C. Parker, ed., *The constitution of the five nations or the Iroquois book of the Great Law* (Albany, N.Y.: The University of the State of New York, 1916, reprinted Ohsweken, Ont.: Iroqrafts, 1984) 53.

32 *Delgamuukw v. The Queen et al.*, 1991, 'Reasons for judgment of the Honourable Chief Justice Allen McEachern', in the Supreme Court of British Columbia, no. 0843, Smithers registry, 13. See Gisday Wa and Delgam Uukw, *The spirit in the land: statements of the Gitksan and Wet'suwet'en hereditary chiefs in the Supreme Court of British Columbia 1987–1990* (Gabriola, B.C.: Reflections, 1992), and Frank Cassidy, ed. *Delgamuukw v. the Queen: Aboriginal title in British Columbia* (Montreal: Institute for Research on Public Policy, 1992).

33 Seyla Benhabib, *Situating the self: gender, community, and post-modernism in contemporary ethics* (New York: Routledge, 1992) 54, cited in Iris Marion Young, 'Communication and the other: beyond deliberative democracy', *Democracy and difference*, ed. Seyla Benhabib (Princeton: Princeton University Press, forthcoming 1995) 28 of the typescript.

34 Iris Marion Young, 'Communication and the other', 28–9 of the typescript.

35 A. L. Getty and Antoine S. Lussier, ed., *As long as the sun shines and the waters flow* (Vancouver: University of British Columbia Press, 1983); Marshall, *Worcester*, 434.

36 Royal Commission on Aboriginal Peoples, *Partners in confederation: Aboriginal peoples, self-government and the constitution* (Ottawa: Minister of Supply and Services, 1993).

37 Edward W. Said, 'Representing the colonized: anthropology's interlocutors', *Critical Inquiry*, 15, 2 (1989) 205–25, 210.

38 Wittgenstein, *Philosophical investigations*, s. 67.

5 THE HISTORICAL FORMATION OF COMMON CONSTITUTIONALISM: THE REDISCOVERY OF CULTURAL DIVERSITY, PART II

1 Thomas-Jean-Jacques Loranger, *Lettres sur l'interprétation de la constitution fédérale, premiere lettre*, tr. as *Letters upon the interpretation of the federal constitution known as the British North America Act of 1867* (Quebec: Morning Chronicle, 1884) 14, 41–2.

2 *Ibid.*, 45.

3 *Ibid.*, 7, 45, 46.

4 *Ibid.*, 14–15.

5 Lord Watson, *Liquidators of the Maritime Bank v. Receiver General of New Brunswick*, the Privy Council, 1892, A.C. 437; I Olmstead 263, reprinted in *Federalism and the Charter: leading constitutional decisions*, new edition, ed. Peter H. Russell, Rainer Knopff and Ted Morton (Ottawa: Carleton University Press, 1990) 50–2, 52.

6 Loranger, *Letters*, 40–1.

7 Hobbes, *Leviathan*, 186.

8 William Knox, *The justice and policy of the late Act of Parliament for making more effective provision for the government of the province of Quebec* (London: 1774) 10–16. The following quotations run in sequence from pages 16 to 33.

9 Matthew Hale, *The history of the common law of England*, ed. Charles M. Gray (Chicago: University of Chicago Press, 1971) 48, 44, 53.

10 Locke, *Two treatises*, ss. 177, 179, 184, 192.

11 *Ibid.*, 192, 178.

12 Thomas Jefferson, *A summary view of the rights of British America*, ed. Thomas Perkins Abernathy (New York: Scholars' Facsimiles and Reprints, 1943) 6–7.

13 *Ibid.*, 21, 20, 8.

14 James Brown Scott, ed., *Declaration of Independence*, 3, 4, 5.

15 William Knox, *The justice*, 39–43.

16 Charles Howard McIlwain, 'The historical background of federal government', *Federalism as a democratic process*, ed. Roscoe Pound, Charles Howard McIlwain and Roy F. Nichols (New Brunswick: Rutgers University Press, 1942) 31–48.

17 James Madison, *The federalist papers*, 249, 248.

18 *Ibid.*, 249, 254–5, 250, 251.

19 *Ibid.*, 254, and Charles Beard, 'Selections from *An economic interpretation of the constitution*', in *The United States Constitution*, ed. Bertell Ollman and Jonathan Birnbaum (New York: New York University Press, 1990) 39–60, 54. Beard is citing John W. Burgess.

20 John George Lambton, Earl of Durham, *Lord Durham's report on the affairs of British North America*, 3 vols., ed. C. P. Lucas (Oxford: Clarendon Press, 1912) vol. II, 16, 22, 28, 28 note.

21 *Ibid.*, 16, 27, 28, 30.

22 *Ibid.*, 26, 35, 36, 37, 27, 46.

23 *Ibid.*, 46, 48.

24 *Ibid.*, 30–1, 63–4, 70.

25 *Ibid.*, 323, 324, 296.

26 Bhikhu Parekh, 'Superior people: the narrowness of liberalism from Mill to Rawls', *Times Literary Supplement* (25 February 1994) 11–13, 11.

27 Edward Said, *Culture and imperialism*, 262–81, 303–37.

28 Canada, *House of Commons Debates*, vol. IV, 1916, 3618, cited in Ramsey Cook, *Provincial autonomy, minority rights and the compact theory 1867–1921* (Ottawa: Information Canada, 1969) 61.

29 Lord Sankey, *Re The regulation and control of aeronautics in Canada*, 1932, Appeal cases 54, 70, cited in Royal Commission on Aboriginal Peoples, *Partners in confederation*, 22.

30 Avigail Eisenberg, 'The politics of individual and group difference in Canadian jurisprudence', *Canadian Journal of Political Science*, 27, 1 (1994) 3–21, 9.

31 *Québec v. Ford et al.*, 1988; *Federalism and the Charter*, ed. Russell, 557–81, 568, 574, 578.

32 *Ibid.*, 576.

33 *Regina v. Sparrow*, 1990, 3, *Canadian Native Law Reporter* (Supreme Court of Canada) 160–88.

34 Eisenberg, *The Politics*, 18.

35 Jürgen Habermas, 'Struggles for recognition in constitutional states', *Multiculturalism and the politics of recognition*, ed. Amy Gutmann (Princeton: Princeton University Press, 1994) 107–48, 108.

36 Wittgenstein, *Philosophical occasions*, ss. 181, 177.

37 Mary Wollstonecraft, *A vindication of the rights of woman*, ed. Miriam Brody (New York: Penguin, 1985) 87, 109, 88.

38 Wittgenstein, *Philosophical investigations*, ss. 173, 172.

39 *Ibid.*, s. 133.

6 CONSTITUTIONALISM IN AN AGE OF CULTURAL DIVERSITY

1 Clifford Geertz, 'The strange estrangement: Taylor and the natural sciences', *Philosophy in an age of pluralism: the philosophy of Charles Taylor in question*, ed. James Tully (Cambridge: Cambridge University Press, 1994) 83–95.

2 Octavio Paz, *The labyrinth of solitude* (London: Penguin, 1967), cited in Jamake Highwater, *The primal mind: vision and reality in Indian America* (New York: Meridian, 1981) motto and 9.

3 Bill Reid, verbal statement to the Wilderness Advisory Committee, Vancouver B.C., January 1986; Shadbolt, *Bill Reid*, 178.

4 Alain-G. Gagnon, Alain Noël, Guy Laforest *et al.*, *Groupe de recherche sur les institutions et la citoyenneté* (Montreal: 1993–), and 'The vision of a new relationship', *The Report of the Royal Commission on Aboriginal Peoples* (Ottawa: Minister of Supply and Services, forthcoming 1995).

5 Joseph A. Camilleri and Jim Falk, *The end of sovereignty? The politics of a shrinking and fragmenting world* (Aldershot: Edward Arnold, 1992).

6 Hobbes, *Leviathan*, 221.

7 Edward Said, *Culture and imperialism*, xxvi.

8 Wittgenstein, *Philosophical investigations*, ss. 215, 216.

9 John G. A. Pocock, *The ancient constitution and the feudal law: a study of English historical thought in the seventeenth century*, reissue (Cambridge: Cambridge University Press, 1987) 247–9.

10 Canada, Department of Indian Affairs and Northern Development, Statement of the Government of Canada on Indian policy (Ottawa: Indian Affairs, 1969), and Harold Cardinal, *The unjust society: the tragedy of Canada's Indians* (Edmonton: M. G. Hurtig, 1969) 78–9.

11 Carl Waldman, *Atlas of the North American Indian* (New York: Facts on File, 1985) 183–5.

12 Vaclav Havel, 'Needed: a new spirit for a new world', speech delivered in New Delhi and Bangkok, tr. Paul Wilson, *The Globe and Mail*, 28 February 1994, A 18.

Guide to further reading

This book is based on a larger study of European political thought from 1650 to 1750. The approach used is based on a monograph on Wittgenstein's philosophy and the humanities. Both these works will be published in due course. Almost all of the classic European texts I discuss are published in the series entitled Cambridge Texts in the History of Political Thought. Some of the best secondary scholarship on them, to which I am indebted, is in the Cambridge series Ideas in Context, edited by Quentin Skinner and Raymond Geuss. The best introduction to the early formation of modern constitutionalism is *The Cambridge history of political thought: 1450–1700*, edited by James Burns with the assistance of Mark Goldie.

In the book I give several reasons why I think it is unenlightening to study the politics of cultural recognition within the framework of the seven features of modern constitutionalism, especially the stages view of world history, identity and constitutionalism, in its variations derived from Locke, Smith, Kant, Hegel and Marx. This is analogous to studying the struggles for constitutional recognition of the seventeenth and eighteenth centuries in the terms of the sixteenth-century language of papal and Roman imperialism. Yet, alas, this is the way most political science and philosophy continues to be written.

As an alternative, I propose and practice a way of studying the politics of cultural recognition which involves four steps. These are: detailed historical and ethnographic descriptions of what the people engaged in the individual contests and debates say and do, including their languages, myths and histories; surveys of the ways in which the case under study interacts with other examples of the six forms of the politics of cultural recognition; redescriptions in the light of the three similarities and the three contrapuntal movements of imperialism and anti-imperialism canvassed in chapter 1; and critical discussions of the rival claims to recognition in accord with the three conventions of common constitutionalism.

Hence, the best introduction to the approach I recommend is this book and the case studies and works on method I cite in passing. For an introduction to the problems of method to which the book is a response, see Foucault, 'What is enlightenment?', Marcus and Fischer, *Anthropology as cultural critique*, Said, *Culture and imperialism*, Tully, 'Wittgenstein and political philosophy', and Tully, ed. *Meaning and context*, and *Philosophy in an age of pluralism*.

I have tried to mention sufficient works in the course of the book to provide an introduction to all the topics. In addition, for chapter 1, reference works on Aboriginal peoples are Dickason, *Canada's First Nations*; Sturtevant, *Handbook of North American Indians*; and Trigger and Washburn, *Cambridge History of the Native peoples of North America*. For an introduction to the global politics of recognition, see Dunn, *Crisis of the nation state?*. For eastern Europe, see Diuk and Karatnycky, *New nations rising*, and Falk, Johansen and Kim, *The constitutional foundations of world peace*, and Walker, *Inside/outside: international relations as political theory*, for the international dimension. My account of the aspectival character of cultural diversity is indebted to Wittgenstein, *Philosophical investigations*, 193–220, and Mulhall, *On being in the world*. For the Canadian Charter, see Beaudoin and Ratushny, *The Canadian Charter of Rights and Freedom*, and Hogg, *Constitutional Law of Canada*, for the constitution.

For chapter 2, Sanders, 'The current status of international indigenous issues affecting the Aboriginal peoples of Canada', discusses the claims of Aboriginal peoples for recognition at the United Nations. The Grand Council of the Cree, Status and Rights of the James Bay Cree, is one of the best examples of a claim for recognition.

For chapter 3, Morgan, *Inventing the people*, discusses the rise of popular sovereignty. Grotius' analysis of constitutional diversity of early modern constitutions is in *The laws of war and peace*, 1.3.8–13. A more detailed account of Locke on Aboriginal rights is given in Tully, *An approach to political philosophy*, 137–78, and to discipline, custom and reform on 179–280. For the constitutional debates in Paris in 1789, see Tully, 'Penser la Déclaration des droits de l'homme et du citoyen of 27 August, 1789'. Chimni, *The modern theory of natural law*, provides a survey of sociability in the theories of Grotius, Hobbes and Pufendorf, and Hundert, *The Enlightenment's fable*, discusses the pivotal role of Mandeville's psychology. The role of the constitution of the *Haudenosaunee* Confederation in the formation of the constitution of the United States is debated by Tooker, 'The United States constitution and the Iroquois league', and Johansen, 'Native America societies and the evolution of democracy'.

For chapter 4, Monk, *Ludwig Wittgenstein*, is a good introduction to Wittgenstein's life and thought. The three-volume study by Baker and Hacker is the best commentary on the *Philosophical investigations*. For the importance of section 122 and objects of comparison see Baker, '*Philosophical investigations* section 122'. Sharp, *Justice and the Maori*, for the Maori and the New Zealand constitution, Smith, *Appeals to the Privy Council*, for the Mohegan nation versus the colony of Connecticut, Vincent and Boers, *James Bay and Northern Québec*, for the James Bay and Northern Québec treaty, and Morse, *Aboriginal peoples and the law*. Tully, 'Aboriginal property and Western theory' provides more background to the Aboriginal and common-law system, and 'Placing the *Two treatises*' provides a fuller discussion of Aboriginal rights in eighteenth-century America.

For chapter 5, see Stevenson, *Ex uno plures*, and Vipond, *Liberty and community*, for the 1867 constitution, and Neatby, *The Quebec Act*, for 1774. Russell, *Constitutional odyssey*, is the best introduction to constitutional negotiations in Canada. For the Cherokee nation, Chief Justice Marshall and President Jackson at the end of chapter 6, see Burke, 'The Cherokee cases'; Rogin, *Fathers and children: Andrew Jackson and the subjugation of the American Indian*; Elhe, *Trail of tears*; and Krupart, *Ethnocentrism*, 163–73, for the memorials presented by the Cherokee.

Bibliography

Act for the Gradual Civilization of the Indian Tribes in the Canadas
1857, in *The historical development of the Indian Act*, second edition,
J. Leslie and R. Macquire (Ottawa: Indian Affairs and Northern
Development, 1983) 23–7.

Alcoff, Linda. 'Cultural feminism versus post-structuralism: the
identity crisis in feminist theory', *Signs*, 13–31 (1988) 405–36.

Alfred, Gerald A. *Heeding the voices of our ancestors: Kahnawake Mohawk
politics and the rise of Native nationalism in Canada* (Oxford University Press, forthcoming, 1995).

Allen, Paula Gunn. *The sacred hoop: recovering the feminine in
American Indian traditions*, revised edition (Boston: Beacon Press,
1992).

Allen, Theodore W. *The invention of the white race*. Vol. 1: *Racial
oppression and social control* (London: Verso, 1994).

Anderson, Benedict. *Imagined communities: reflections on the origin and
spread of nationalism*, revised edition (London: Verso, 1991).

Aquinas, Thomas. *On law, morality and politics*, ed. William P.
Baumgarth and Richard J. Regan (Indianapolis: Hackett
Publishing Company, 1988).

Ashcraft, Richard. *Revolutionary politics and Locke's 'Two treatises of
government'* (Princeton: Princeton University Press, 1986).

Axtell, James. *The invasion within: the contest of cultures in colonial North
America* (Oxford: Oxford University Press, 1986).

Ball, Milner S. 'Constitution, court, Indian tribes', *American Bar
Foundation Research Journal* 1 (1987) 3–139.

Baker, G. P. *'Philosophical investigations* section 122: neglected aspects',
Wittgenstein's 'Philosophical investigations': text and context, ed.
Robert L. Arrington and Hans-Johann Glock (London:
Routledge, 1991) 35–68.

Baker, G. P. and P. M. S. Hacker. *Wittgenstein: understanding and
meaning. An analytical commentary on the 'Philosophical investigations'*,
vol. 1 (Oxford: Basil Blackwell, 1980).

Wittgenstein: rules, grammar and necessity. An analytical commentary on the 'Philosophical investigations', vol. II (Oxford: Basil Blackwell, 1985).

Wittgenstein: meaning and mind. An analytical commentary on the 'Philosophical investigations', vol. III (Oxford: Basil Blackwell, 1990).

Barker, Andrew W. 'Nestroy and Wittgenstein: some thoughts on the motto to the *Philosophical investigations*', *German Life and Letters*, 39, 2 (1986) 161–7.

Barsh, Russell William. 'Aboriginal government in the United States: a qualitative political analysis', Paper submitted to the Royal Commission on Aboriginal Peoples (Ottawa: unpublished, 1993).

Beard, Charles. 'Selections from *An economic interpretation of the constitution*', in *The United States Constitution*, ed. Bertell Ollman and Jonathan Birnbaum (New York: New York University Press, 1990) 39–60.

Beaudoin, Gérald-A. and Ed Ratushny, eds. *The Canadian Charter of Rights and Freedoms*, second edition (Toronto: Carswell, 1989).

Benhabib, Seyla. 'Deliberative rationality and models of democratic legitimacy', *Constellations*, 1, 1 (1994) 26–52.

Situating the self: gender, community, and postmodernism in contemporary ethics (New York: Routledge, 1992).

'The generalized and the concrete other', *Ethics: a feminist reader*, ed. Elizabeth Frazer, Jennifer Hornsby and Sabina Lovibond (Oxford: Basil Blackwell, 1992) 267–302.

Berlin, Isaiah. 'Return of the *Volksgeist*', *New Perspectives Quarterly*, 8, 4 (1991) 4–10.

'The bent twig: on the rise of nationalism', *The crooked timber of humanity* (New York: Random House, 1992) 238–62.

Berman, Harold. *Law and revolution: the formation of the Western legal tradition* (Cambridge, Mass.: Harvard University Press, 1983).

Biard, Pierre, S. J. 'Relations', in *The Jesuit relations and allied documents 1610–1791*, 73 vols., tr. Reuben G. Thwaites (Cleveland: Burrough, 1896–1901) vol. III, 134–7.

Bock, Gisela and Susan James, ed. *Beyond equality and difference: citizenship, feminist politics, female subjectivity* (London: Routledge, 1992).

Bolingbroke, Viscount, Henry St John. *A dissertation upon parties* (1733–4), *The works of Lord Bolingbroke*, 4 vols. (Philadelphia: 1841).

Bowden, Peta. *Caring: an investigation into gender-sensitive ethics* (Doctoral thesis, McGill University, 1993).

Bringhurst, Robert and Ulli Steltzer. *The black canoe: Bill Reid and 'The spirit of Haida Gwaii'* (Vancouver: Douglas and McIntyre, 1991).

Buchanan, Allen. *Secession: the morality of political divorce from Fort Sumter to Lithuania and Quebec* (Boulder: Westview Press, 1991).

Bulkley, John. 'An inquiry into the right of the Aboriginal natives to the land in America', introductory essay to Roger Wolcott, *Poetical meditations* (New London: 1726) i–lvi.

Burger, Julian, Robert F. Kennedy Jr. and Rigoberta Menchü Tum, eds. *State of the peoples: a global human rights report on societies in danger* (Boston: Beacon Press, 1993).

Burger, Julian, ed. *First peoples: a future for the Indigenous world* (New York: Anchor Books, 1990).

Burgess, Michael and Alain-G. Gagnon, eds. *Comparative federalism and federation: competing traditions and future directions* (Toronto: University of Toronto Press, 1993).

Burke, Edmund. *The correspondence of Edmund Burke*, 4 vols., ed. George H. Guttridge (Cambridge: Cambridge University Press, 1961).

Burke, Joseph. 'The Cherokee cases: a study in law, politics, and morality', *Stanford Law Review*, 21 (1968–9) 500–30.

Burns, James H., ed., with the assistance of Mark Goldie. *The Cambridge History of Political Thought: 1450–1700* (Cambridge: Cambridge University Press, 1991).

Camilleri, Joseph A. and Jim Falk. *The end of sovereignty? The politics of a shrinking and fragmenting world* (Aldershot: Edward Arnold, 1992).

Canada, Department of Indian Affairs and Northern Development. Statement of the government of Canada on Indian policy (Ottawa: Indian Affairs, 1969).

Canadian Charter of Rights and Freedoms, the Constitution Act, 1982, R.S.C. 1985, Appendix II, no. 44, Schedule B. See Gérald A. Beaudoin and Ed Ratushny, eds., *The Canadian Charter of Rights and Freedoms*, second edition (Toronto: Carswell, 1989) 926–34.

Cardinal, Harold. *The unjust society: the tragedy of Canada's Indians* (Edmonton: M. G. Hurtig, 1969).

Carey, Daniel. *Travel narrative and the problem of human nature in Locke, Shaftesbury and Hutcheson* (Doctoral thesis, University of Oxford, 1993).

Carrithers, Michael. *Why humans have cultures: explaining anthropology and social history* (Oxford: Oxford University Press, 1992).

Cassidy, Frank, ed. *Delgamuukw v. the Queen: Aboriginal title in British Columbia* (Montreal: Institute for Research on Public Policy, 1992).

Chimni, Ravindar. *The modern theory of natural law: sociability in early modern European political thought* (Doctoral thesis, McGill University, 1995).

Cicero, *De re publica* (Cambridge, Mass.: Harvard University Press, 1963).

Clifford, James. *The predicament of culture: twentieth-century ethnography, literature, and art* (Cambridge, Mass.: Harvard University Press, 1988).

Clinton, Robert J. 'The proclamation of 1763: colonial prelude to two centuries of federal-state conflict over the management of Indian affairs', *Boston University Law Review* 69 (1989) 329–81.

Colden, Cadwallader. *The history of the five Indian nations of Canada which are dependent on the province of New York in America and the barrier between the English and French in that part of the world* (London: 1747).

Colley, Linda. *Britons: forging the nation 1707–1837* (London: Pimlico, 1992).

Constant, Benjamin, 'The liberty of the ancients compared with that of the moderns', *Political writings*, ed. Biancamaria Fontana (Cambridge: Cambridge University Press, 1988) 308–28.

Cook, Ramsey. *Provincial autonomy, minority rights and the compact theory 1867–1921* (Ottawa: Information Canada, 1969).

Cotton, John. 'John Cotton's answer to Roger Williams', *The complete writings of Roger Williams*, 7 vols. (New York: Russell and Russell, 1963) vol. II, 43–9.

Cronon, William. *Changes in the land: Indians, colonists, and the ecology of New England* (New York: Hill and Wang, 1983).

Crosby, Alfred. *Ecological imperialism: the biological expansion of Europe 900–1900* (New York: Cambridge University Press, 1986).

Déclaration des droits de l'homme et du citoyen, ed. J. Delène Création (Paris: Roger Rimbaud, 1989).

Declaration on the Rights of Indigenous Peoples (draft), as approved by the members of the working group on Indigenous populations and reported to the United Nations Subcommission on Prevention of discrimination and protection of minorities in August 1993.

Delgamuukw v. The Queen et al., 1991, the Supreme Court of British Columbia, no. 0843, Smithers registry.

Démeunier, Jean-Nicholas, ed. *Encyclopédie méthodique. Economie, politique et diplomatique*, 4 vols. (Paris: 1784–88).

Derrida, Jacques. *The other heading: reflections on today's Europe*, tr. Pascale-Anne Brault and Michael R. Naas (Bloomington: Indiana University Press, 1992).

Writing and difference, tr. Alan Bass (Chicago: Chicago University Press, 1978).

Descartes, René. *Discourse on the method*, in *The philosophical writings of Descartes*, 2 vols., tr. John Cottingham, Robert Stoothoff and Dugald Murdoch (Cambridge: Cambridge University Press, 1985) vol. I, 111–51.

Di Stefano, Christine. *Configurations of masculinity: a feminist perspective on modern political theory* (Ithaca: Cornell University Press, 1991).

Dickason, Olive Patricia. *Canada's First Nations: a history of founding peoples from earliest times* (Toronto: McClelland and Stewart, 1992).

Diuk, Nadia and Adrian Karatnycky. *New nations rising: the fall of the soviets and the challenge of independence* (New York: John Wiley, 1993).

Dockstator, Mark S. *Towards an understanding of Aboriginal self-government: a proposed theoretical model and illustrative factual analysis* (Doctoral thesis, York University, 1993).

Drury, M. O'C. 'Some notes on conversations with Wittgenstein', *Recollections of Wittgenstein*, ed. Rush Rhees (Oxford: Oxford University Press, 1984) 97–171.

Dunn, John, ed. *Crisis of the nation state?* (Oxford: Oxford University Press, 1995).

Democracy: the unfinished journey 508 BC to AD 1993 (Oxford: Oxford University Press, 1993).

Dunn, John. *Western political theory in the face of the future* (Cambridge: Cambridge University Press, 1993).

Durham, Earl of, John George Lambton. *Lord Durham's report on the affairs of British North America*, 3 vols., ed. C. P. Lucas (Oxford: Clarendon Press, 1912).

Eisenberg, Avigail. 'The politics of individual and group difference in Canadian jurisprudence', *Canadian Journal of Political Science*, 27, 1 (1994) 3–21.

Elhe, John. *Trail of tears: the rise and fall of the Cherokee nation* (New York: Doubleday, 1988).

Elshtain, Jean Bethke. 'The power and powerlessness of women', *Beyond equality and difference*, ed. Gisela Bock and Susan James (London: Routledge, 1992) 110–25.

Meditations on modern political thought: masculine feminine themes from Luther to Arendt (New York: Praeger, 1986).

Public man, private woman: women in social and political thought (Princeton: Princeton University Press, 1981).

Elster, Jon. *Local justice* (New York: Russell Sage Foundation, 1992).

Emberley, Peter, 'Globalism and localism: constitutionalism in a new world order', *Constitutional predicament: Canada after the referendum of 1992*, ed. Curtis Cook (Montreal: McGill-Queens University Press, 1994).

Escobar, Arturo. 'Discourse and power in development: Michel Foucault and the relevance of his work to the Third World', *Alternatives*, 10 (1984–5) 377–401.

Fabian, Johannes. *Time and the other: how anthropology makes its object* (New York: Columbia University Press, 1983).

Falk, Richard, Robert C. Johansen and Samuel S. Kim, eds. *The constitutional foundations of world peace* (Albany: State University of New York Press, 1993).

Felice, Fortunato-Bartholomeo de, ed. *Encyclopédié, ou dictionnaire universal et raisonné des connaissances humaine*, 58 vols. (Yverdon, 1770–80).

Fichte, Johann Gottlieb. *Addresses to the German nation*, tr. R. F. Jones and G. H. Turnbull (Chicago: Open Court, 1922).

Flax, Jane. 'Beyond equality: gender, justice and difference', *Beyond equality and difference*, ed. Gisela Bock and Susan James (London: Routledge, 1992) 193–210.

Fontana, Biancamaria, ed. *The invention of the modern republic* (Cambridge: Cambridge University Press, 1994).

Forsyth, Murray. *Reason and revolution: the political thought of the Abbé Sieyès* (Leicester: Leicester University Press, 1987).

Foucault, Michel. *L'usage des plaisirs* (Paris: Editions Gallimard, 1984).

'What is Enlightenment?', *The Foucault reader*, ed. Paul Rabinow (New York: Pantheon Books, 1984) 32–50.

Discipline and punish: the birth of the prison, tr. Alan Sheridan (New York: Pantheon Books, 1979).

Franklin, Benjamin. *Indian treaties published by Benjamin Franklin 1736–1762*, ed. Julian Boyd (Philadelphia: Historical Society of Pennsylvania, 1938).

Frazer, James George. *The golden bough: a study in magic and religion*, abridged (London: Macmillan, 1922).

Fuentes, Carlos. *The buried mirror: reflections on Spain and the new world* (New York: Houghton Mifflin, 1992).

Gagnon, Alain-G. and Guy Laforest. 'The future of federalism: lessons from Canada and Québec', *International Journal* 48, 3 (1993) 470–91.

Gagnon, Alain-G., Alain Noël, Guy Laforest et al. *Groupe de recherche sur les institutions et la citoyenneté* (Montreal: 1993–).

'Vers un nouveau pacte linguistique pour le Québec', *Groupe de recherche sur les institutions et la citoyenneté* (Montreal: 1993).

Geertz, Clifford, 'The strange estrangement: Taylor and the natural sciences', *Philosophy in an age of pluralism: the philosophy of Charles Taylor in question*, ed. James Tully (Cambridge: Cambridge University Press, 1994) 83–95.

Works and lives: the anthropologist as author (Stanford: Stanford University Press, 1988).

'The uses of diversity', *Michigan Quarterly Review*, 25, 1 (1986) 105–23.

'Local knowledge: fact and law in comparative perspective', *Local knowledge: further essays in interpretive anthropology* (New York: Basic Books, 1983) 167–234.

Gellner, Ernest. *Nations and nationalism* (Oxford: Basil Blackwell, 1983).

Getty, A. L. and Antoine S. Lussier, ed. *As long as the sun shines and the waters flow* (Vancouver: University of British Columbia Press, 1983).

Gilligan, Carol. 'Shifting paradigms: theorizing care and justice in political theory', ed. Monique Deveaux, *Hypatia* (forthcoming, 1995).

'Changing voices: the psychology and politics of difference', (Unpublished manuscript).

In a different voice: psychological theory and women's development (Cambridge, Mass.: Harvard University Press, 1982).

Goldie, Mark. 'The revolution of 1689 and the structure of political argument', *Bulletin of Research in the Humanities*, 83 (1980) 473–564.

Grand Council of the Cree of Quebec. Status and Rights of the James Bay Crees in the context of Quebec's secession from Canada (New York: United Nations Commission on Human Rights, 27 January–6 March 1992).

Griffiths, John. 'What is legal pluralism?', *Journal of Legal Pluralism and Unofficial Law* 24 (1986) 1–55.

Grotius, Hugo. *The laws of war and peace*, 4 vols., tr. F. W. Kelsey (Oxford: Clarendon Press, 1925).

Haakonssen, Knud. *Natural law and moral philosophy from Grotius to the Scottish Enlightenment* (Cambridge: Cambridge University Press, 1995).

Habermas, Jürgen. 'Struggles for recognition in constitutional states', *Multiculturalism and the politics of recognition*, ed. Amy Gutmann (Princeton: Princeton University Press, 1994) 107–48.

The theory of communicative action, 2 vols., tr. Thomas McCarthy (Boston: Beacon Press, 1984–7).

Hale, Matthew, *Reflections by the Lrd. Chiefe Justice Hale on Mr. Hobbes his Dialogue of the Lawe*, in W. S. Holdsworth, *A History of English Law*, 7 vols. (Boston: Little Brown, 1924) vol. v, 500–18.

The history of the common law of England, ed. Charles M. Gray (Chicago: University of Chicago Press, 1971).

Hamilton, Alexander, James Madison and John Jay. *The federalist papers*, ed. Clinton Rossiter (New York: Menton-Penguin, 1961).

Havel, Vaclav. 'Needed: a new spirit for a new world', speech delivered in New Delhi and Bangkok, tr. Paul Wilson, *The Globe and Mail*, 28 February 1994, A 18.

Hegel, G. W. F. *Philosophy of right*, tr. T. M. Knox (Oxford: Clarendon Press, 1952).

Henry, Alexander. *Travels and adventures in Canada and the Indian Territories between the years 1760 and 1776* (New York: I. Riley, 1809).

Herder, Johann Gottfried. *Outlines of a philosophy of the history of man*, tr. T. Churchill (London: 1800).

Highwater, Jamake. *The primal mind: vision and reality in Indian America* (New York: Meridian, 1981).

Hobbes, Thomas. *Leviathan*, ed. Richard Tuck (Cambridge: Cambridge University Press, 1991).

Hogg, Peter, *Constitutional law of Canada*, second edition (Toronto: Carswell, 1985).

hooks, bell. *Sisters of the yam: black women and self-recovery* (Toronto: Between the Lines, 1993).

Hume, David. *Essays Moral, political and literary*, ed. Eugene F. Miller (Indianapolis: Liberty Classics, 1985).

Hundert, Edward J. *The Enlightenment's Fable: Bernard Mandeville and the discovery of society* (Cambridge: Cambridge University Press, 1994).

Indian Act, 1990, ed. Donna Lea Hawley (Toronto: Carswell, 1990).

James, Susan. 'The good-enough citizen: citizenship and independence', *Beyond equality and difference*, ed. Gisela Bock and Susan James (London: Routledge, 1992) 48–68.

Jefferson, Thomas. *A summary view of the rights of British America*, ed. Thomas Perkins Abernathy (New York: Scholars' Facsimiles and Reprints, 1943).

Jennings, Francis. *The Invasion of America: Indians, colonialism, and the cant of conquest* (New York: W. W. Norton, 1975).

The ambiguous Iroquois empire (New York: W. W. Norton, 1984).

Empires of fortune: crowns, colonies and tribes in the Seven Years' War in America (New York: W. W. Norton, 1988).

Jennings, Francis, *et al.*, eds. *The history and culture of Iroquois diplomacy* (Syracuse: Syracuse University Press, 1985).

Joe, Rita. *Poems of Rita Joe* (Halifax: Abenaki Press, 1978).

Johansen, Bruce E. 'Native American societies and the evolution of democracy in America, 1600–1800', *Ethnohistory*, 37, 3 (1990) 279–97.

Jones, Dorothy V. *License for empire: colonialism by treaty in early America* (Chicago: University of Chicago Press, 1982).

Jonsen, Albert R. and Stephen Toulmin. *The abuse of casuistry: a history of moral reasoning* (Berkeley: University of California Press, 1988).

Kahane, David. *Shared understandings? Pluralism and challenges of political justification* (Doctoral thesis, University of Cambridge, 1994).

Kant, Immanuel. *Perpetual peace and other essays*, tr. Ted Humphrey (Indianapolis: Hackett Publishing Company, 1983).

Kelley, Donald. *The human measure: social thought in the Western legal tradition* (Cambridge, Mass.: Harvard University Press, 1990).

Kingston, Rebecca. *Montesquieu and the parlement of bordeaux* (Doctoral thesis, McGill University, 1994).

Knox, William. *The justice and policy of the late act of Parliament for making more effective provision for the government of the province of Quebec* (London: 1774).

Kristeva, Julia. 'Woman can never be defined', *New French feminism: an anthology*, ed. Elaine Marks and Isabelle de Coutivron (New York: Schocken Books, 1981) 137–41.

Krupat, Arnold. *Ethnocentrism: ethnography, history, literature* (Berkeley: University of California Press, 1992).

Kuper, Adam. *The invention of primitive society: transformations of an illusion* (London: Routledge, 1988).

Kymlicka, Will. *Recent work in citizenship theory* (Ottawa: Multiculturalism and Citizenship Canada, 1992).

Liberalism, community and culture (Oxford: Clarendon Press, 1989).

Lafitau, Joseph-Francois. *Moeurs des sauvages amériquains comparées aux moeurs de premiers temps* (Paris: 1724).

Customs of the American Indians compared with the customs of primitive times, 2 vols., ed. W. H. Fenton and E. L. Moore (Toronto: The Champlain Society, 1974–7).

Laforest, Guy. 'Philosophy and political judgement in a multinational federation', *Philosophy in an age of pluralism: the philosophy of Charles Taylor in question*, ed. James Tully (Cambridge: Cambridge University Press, 1994) 194–212.

De la prudence (Québec: Les éditions du Boréal, 1993).

Trudeau et la fin d'un rêve canadien (Sillery: Les éditions du Septentrion, 1992).

Laforest, Guy, Louis Balthazar and Vincent Lemieux, eds. *Le Québec et la restructuration du Canada 1980–1992* (Sillery, Québec: Les éditions de Septentrion, 1991).

Lahontan, Louis-Armand de Lom d'Arc, Baron de. *Dialogues curieux entre l'auteur et un savage de bon sens qui a voyagé*, ed. Gilbert Chinard (Baltimore, Paris, London: 1931).

Las Casas, Bartolomé. *In Defense of the Indians*, tr. Stafford Poole (De Kalb, Ill.: Northern Illinois University Press, 1992).

Leibniz, Gottfried Wilhelm. *Caesarinus Fürstenerius (De Suprematu Principum Germaniae)* (1677), *Political writings*, ed. Patrick Kelly (Cambridge: Cambridge University Press, 1988) 111–20.

Le Roy, Louis. *De la vicissitude ou variété de choses en l'univers* (Paris: Pierre l'Hullier, 1577).

Lloyd, Genevieve. *The man of reason: male and female in Western philosophy* (Minneapolis: University of Minnesota Press, 1984).

Locke, John. *Two treatises of government*, ed. Peter Laslett (Cambridge: Cambridge University Press, 1991).

An essay concerning human understanding, ed. Peter Nidditch (Oxford: Clarendon Press, 1975).

The educational writings of John Locke, ed. James Axtell (Cambridge: Cambridge University Press, 1968).

A Report of the Board of Trade to the Lords Justices Respecting the Relief and Employment of the Poor, 1697 (London: 1793).

Long, J. Anthony. 'Political revitalization in Canadian Native Indian Societies', *Canadian Journal of Political Science*, 23, 4 (1990) 751–74.

Loranger, Thomas-Jean-Jacques. *Lettres sur l'interprétation de la constitution fédérale, premiere lettre*, tr. as *Letters upon the interpretation of the federal constitution known as the British North America Act of 1867* (Quebec: Morning Chronicle, 1884).

Lugones, Maria C. and Elizabeth V. Spelman. 'Have we got a theory for you: feminist theory, cultural imperialism and the demand for "the woman's voice"', *Hypatia reborn: essays in feminist philosophy*, ed. Azizah Y. Al-Hibri and Margaret A. Simons (Bloomington: Indiana University Press, 1990) 18–31.

Lyons, Oren, John Mohawk, Vine Deloria, Jr. *et al.*, eds. *Exiled in the land of the free: democracy, Indian nations and the US Constitution* (Santa Fe: Clear Light Publishers, 1992).

MacDonald, Roderick A. 'Recognizing and legitimating Aboriginal justice: implications for a reconstruction of non-Aboriginal legal systems in Canada', *Aboriginal peoples and the justice system*, Royal Commission on Aboriginal Peoples (Ottawa: Minister of Supply and Services, 1993) 232–74.

MacIntyre, Alasdair. *Whose justice? Which rationality?* (Notre Dame: University of Notre Dame Press, 1988).

MacKinnon, Catharine A. *Towards a feminist theory of the state* (Cambridge, Mass.: Harvard University Press, 1991).

Macklem, Patrick. 'Distributing sovereignty: Indian nations and the equality of peoples', *Stanford Law Review*, 45, 5 (1993) 1312–67.

Maddox, Graham. 'Constitution', *Political innovation and conceptual change*, ed. Terence Ball, James Farr and Russell L. Hanson (Cambridge: Cambridge University Press, 1989) 50–68.

Malcolm, Noel. *Bosnia: a short history* (London: Macmillan, 1994).

Mandeville, Bernard. *The fable of the bees: or, private vices, publick benefits*, 2 vols., ed. F. B. Kaye (Oxford: Clarendon Press, 1924).

Marcus, George E. and Michael M. J. Fischer. *Anthropology as cultural critique: an experimental moment in the human sciences* (Chicago: University of Chicago Press, 1986).

Marshall, John. *The Writings of Chief Justice Marshall on the federal constitution* (Boston: James Monroe and Company, 1839).

Marshall, Peter James. *The great map of mankind: perceptions of new worlds in the age of enlightenment* (Cambridge, Mass.: Harvard University Press, 1982).

Martin, Calvin Luther. *In the spirit of the earth: rethinking history and time* (Baltimore: The Johns Hopkins University Press, 1992).

Martin, Jane Roland. *Reclaiming a conversation: the ideal of an educated woman* (New Haven: Yale University Press, 1985).

Massey, Calvin R. 'The locus of sovereignty: judicial review, legislative supremacy, and federalism in the constitutional traditions of Canada and the United States', *Duke Law Journal*, vol. 1990 (1990) 1229–310.

Maybury-Lewis, David. *Millennium: tribal wisdom and the modern world* (New York: Viking, 1992).

Maybury-Lewis, David, ed. *The prospects for plural societies* (Washington, D.C.: The American Ethnological Society, 1984).

McIlwain, Charles Howard. *Constitutionalism: ancient and modern*, revised edition (Ithaca: Cornell University Press, 1947).

'The historical background of federal government', *Federalism as a democratic process*, ed. Roscoe Pound, Charles McIlwain and Roy F. Nichols (New Brunswick: Rutgers University Press, 1942) 31–48.

McNeill, William. *Polyethnicity and national unity in world history* (Toronto: University of Toronto Press, 1986).

Meek, Ronald. *Social science and the ignoble savage* (Cambridge: Cambridge University Press, 1976).

Mendus, Susan. 'Losing the faith: feminism and democracy', *Democracy: the unfinished journey 508 BC to AD 1993*, ed. John Dunn (Oxford: Oxford University Press, 1993) 207–20.

Mendus, Susan and Ellen Kennedy, eds. *Women in Western political philosophy* (New York: St Martin's Press, 1987).

Merchant, Carolyn. *Ecological revolutions: nature, gender, and science in New England* (Chapel Hill: University of North Carolina Press, 1989).

Metzger, Charles H. *The Quebec Act: a primary cause of the American revolution* (New York: United States Catholic Historical Society, 1936).

Mill, John Stuart. *Three essays: on liberty, representative government, the subjugation of women*, ed. Richard Wollheim (Oxford: Oxford University Press, 1975).

Minow, Martha. *Making all the difference: inclusion, exclusion and American law* (Ithaca: Cornell University Press, 1990).

Mitchell, Michael. 'An unbroken assertion of sovereignty', *Drumbeat: anger and renewal in Indian country*, ed. Boyce Richardson (Toronto: The Assembly of First Nations, Summerhill Press, 1989) 105–36.

Monk, Ray. *Ludwig Wittgenstein: the duty of genius* (London: Jonathan Cape, 1990).

Molyneux, William. *The case of Ireland being bound by the acts of parliament in England* (London: 1698).

Montesquieu, Charles-Louis de Secondat. *The spirit of the laws*, tr. and ed. Anne M. Cohler, Basia Carolyn Miller and Harold Samuel Stone (Cambridge: Cambridge University Press, 1989).

Moore, Sally Falk. *Law as process: an anthropological approach* (London: Routledge and Kegan Paul, 1978).

Morgan, Edmund S. *Inventing the people: the rise of popular sovereignty in England and America* (New York: W. W. Norton, 1988).

Morse, Bradford W., ed. *Aboriginal peoples and the law: Indian, Métis and Inuit rights in Canada* (Ottawa: Carleton University Press, 1991).

Morton, Thomas. *New English Canaan* (1632), The Publications of the Prince Society, ed. Charles F. Adams, XIV (Boston: 1883).

Mudimbe, V. Y. *The invention of Africa: gnosis, philosophy and the order of knowledge* (Bloomington: Indiana University Press, 1988).

Mulhall, Stephen. *On being in the world: Wittgenstein and Heidegger on seeing aspects* (London: Routledge, 1993).

Nammack, Georgina C. *Fraud, politics, and the dispossession of the Indians* (Norman, Okla.: Oklahoma University Press, 1968).

Neatby, Hilda. *The Quebec Act: protest and policy* (Scarborough: Prentice-Hall, 1972).

Nestroy, Johann. *Der Schützling* (*The protégé*), *Gesammelte Werke*, 7 vols.

(Vienna: Verlag von Anton Schroll and Co., 1962) vol. IV, 603–715.

Nicole, Pierre. *Discourses on the being of a god, the immortality of the soul, the weakness of man and concerning the way of preserving peace with men*, tr. John Locke (London: 1712).

Norris, John. *The liberty and property of British subjects asserted in a letter from an assemblyman in Carolina to his friend in London* (London: 1726).

Nozick, Robert. *Anarchy, state, and utopia* (New York: Basic Books, 1974).

O'Callaghan, Edmund B., ed. *Documents relative to the colonial history of the State of New York*, 15 vols. (Albany, N.Y.: 1583–7).

Oestreich, Gerhard. *Neostoicism and the early modern state*, tr. David McLintock, ed. Brigitta Oestreich and H. G. Koenigsberger (Cambridge: Cambridge University Press, 1982).

Okin, Susan Moller. *Justice, gender, and the family* (New York: Basic Books, 1989).

Otis, James. *Rights of the British colonies asserted and proved* (Boston: 1764).

Pagden, Anthony. *Lords of all the world: ideologies of empire in Britain, France and Spain 1400–1800* (New Haven: Yale University Press, 1995).

European encounters with the new world (New Haven: Yale University Press, 1991).

Paine, Thomas. *The Rights of man*, ed. Gregory Claeys (Indianapolis/ Cambridge: Hackett Publishing Company, 1992).

Public good: being an examination into the claims of Virginia to the vacant Western Territory (first published 1780), in *The Complete writings of Thomas Paine*, ed. Philip S. Foner (New York: 1945) 303–33.

Common sense, ed. I. Kramnick (Harmondsworth: Penguin, 1976).

Parekh, Bhikhu. 'Superior people: the narrowness of liberalism from Mill to Rawls', *Times Literary Supplement* (25 February 1994) 11–13.

'The poverty of Indian political theory', *History of Political Thought*, 13, 3 (1992) 535–56.

'British citizenship and cultural difference', *Citizenship*, ed. Geoffrey Andrews (London: Lawrence and Wishart, 1991) 183–204.

Parker, A. C., ed. *The constitution of the five nations or the Iroquois book of the Great Law* (Albany, N.Y.: The University of the State of New York, 1916, reprinted Ohseweken, Ontario: Iroqrafts, 1984).

Patterson, Dennis. *Law and truth* (Oxford: Oxford University Press, forthcoming, 1995).

Paul, Daniel N. *We were not the savages: a Micmac perspective on the collision of European and Aboriginal civilization* (Halifax: Nimbus Publishing, 1994).

Pearce, Roy Harvey. *Savagism and civilization: a study of the Indian and the American mind* (Berkeley: University of California Press, 1967).

Pocock, John G. A. 'A discourse of sovereignty: observations on the work in progress', *Political discourse in early modern Britain*, ed. Nicholas Phillipson and Quentin Skinner (Cambridge: Cambridge University Press, 1993) 377–428.

  The ancient constitution and the feudal law: a study of English historical thought in the seventeenth century, reissue (Cambridge: Cambridge University Press, 1987).

  Virtue, commerce, and history (Cambridge: Cambridge University Press, 1985).

Pufendorf, Samuel. *On the duty of man and citizen according to natural law*, ed. James Tully, tr. Michael Silverthorne (Cambridge: Cambridge University Press, 1991).

  On the law of nature and nations, tr. C. H. and W. A. Oldfather (Oxford: Clarendon Press, 1934).

Pufendorf, Samuel, under the pseudonym Severinus de Monzambano. *De statu imperii Germanici* (*On the Constitution of the German empire*) (Frankfurt: 1664).

Rawls, John. 'The law of peoples', *On human rights: the Oxford Amnesty lectures 1993*, ed. Stephen Shute and Susan Hurley (New York: Harper Collins, 1993) 41–82.

  Political liberalism (New York: Columbia University Press, 1993).

  'Justice as fairness: political not metaphysical', *Philosophy and public affairs*, 14 (1985) 223–52.

  A theory of justice (Oxford: Oxford University Press, 1971).

Regina v. Sparrow, 1990, 3, *Canadian Native Law Reporter* (Supreme Court of Canada) 160–88.

Reid, Bill. *Gallant beasts and monsters* (Vancouver: Buschlen Mowatt, 1992).

Reid, Bill. 'These shining islands', *Islands at the edge: preserving the Queen Charlotte Islands wilderness* (Vancouver: Douglas and McIntyre, n.d.).

Reid, Bill and Robert Bringhurst. *The raven steals the light* (Vancouver: Douglas and McIntyre, 1984).

Rejali, Darius M. *Torture and modernity: self, society and state in modern Iran* (Boulder: Westview Press, 1994).

Resnick, Philip. *Thinking English Canada* (Toronto: Stoddart, 1994).

Rich, Adrienne. 'Taking women students seriously', *Gendered subjects: the dynamics of feminist teaching*, ed. Margo Culley and Catherine Portuges (London: Routledge and Kegan Paul, 1985).

Robertson, William. *The history of America*, ninth edition, 4 vols. (Edinburgh: 1800).

Rogin, Michael Paul. *Fathers and children: Andrew Jackson and the subjugation of the American Indian* (New York: Knopf, 1975).

Rorty, Richard. 'The priority of democracy to philosophy', *Objectivity, relativism, and truth* (Cambridge: Cambridge University Press, 1991) 175–96.

  'On ethnocentrism: a reply to Clifford Geertz', *Objectivity, relativism, and truth* (Cambridge: Cambridge University Press, 1991) 203–10.

Rousseau, Jean-Jacques. *On the social contract*, tr. Judith R. Masters (New York: St Martin's Press, 1978).

  Discourse on the origin and foundations of inequality among men: the first and second discourses, tr. Roger D. and Judith R. Masters (New York: St Martin's Press, 1964) 77–228.

Royal Commission on Aboriginal Peoples. *Partners in confederation: Aboriginal peoples, self-government, and the constitution* (Ottawa: Minister of Supply and Services, 1993).

  The Report of the Royal Commission on Aboriginal Peoples (Ottawa: Minister of Supply and Services, forthcoming, 1995).

Royal Proclamation of 7 October, 1763. *Native rights in Canada*, ed. Peter A. Cumming and Neil H. Mickenberg, second edition (Toronto: General Publishing Company, 1972) 291–2.

Russell, Peter H. *Constitutional odyssey: can Canadians be a sovereign people?* (Toronto: University of Toronto Press, 1992).

Russell, Peter H., Rainer Knopff and Ted Morton, ed. *Federalism and the Charter: leading constitutional decisions*, new edition (Ottawa: Carleton University Press, 1990).

Said, Edward W. *The politics of dispossession: the struggle for Palestinian self-determination 1969–1994* (New York: Pantheon Books, 1994).

  Culture and imperialism (New York: Knopf, 1993).

  'Representing the colonized: anthropology's interlocutors', *Critical Inquiry*, 15, 2 (1989) 205–25.

Sandel, Michael. *Liberalism and the limits of justice* (Cambridge: Cambridge University Press, 1982).

Sanders, Douglas. 'The current status of international Indigenous issues affecting the Aboriginal peoples of Canada', Report to the Royal Commission on Aboriginal Peoples (Ottawa: unpublished, 1993).

Schlesinger, Arthur M. Jr. *The disuniting of America: reflections on a multicultural society* (New York: Whittle Communications, 1991).

Scott, James Brown, ed. *The Declaration of Independence, the Articles of*

Confederation, the constitution of the United States (New York: Oxford University Press, 1917).

Seeley, John Robert. *The expansion of England* (Chicago: University of Chicago Press, 1971).

Seyssel, Claude de. *La monarchie de France*, ed. J. Poujol (Paris: Librairie d'Argence, 1961).

Shadbolt, Doris. *Bill Reid* (Vancouver: Douglas and McIntyre, 1986).

Shakespeare, William. *King Lear* (New York: Signet Classics, 1963).

Sharpe, Andrew. *Justice and the Maori: Maori claims in New Zealand political argument in the 1980s* (Auckland: Oxford University Press, 1990).

Shelley, Mary. *Frankenstein or the modern Prometheus* (London: Lackington *et al.*, 1918).

Sieyès, Emmanuel Joseph. *Dire de l'Abbé Sieyès sur la question du veto Royal à la séance du 7 Septembre 1789* (Paris: 1789).

Qu'est-ce-que le tiers état?, ed. Roberto Zapperi (Geneva: Groz, 1970).

Singer, Joseph William. 'Sovereignty and property', *Northwestern University Law Review*, 86, 1 (1991) 1–55.

Six Nations. *The redman's appeal for justice: the position of the six nations that they constitute an independent state* (Brantford, Ontario: 1924).

Skinner, Quentin. *Reason and rhetoric in the philosophy of Hobbes* (Cambridge: Cambridge University Press, 1995).

'The state', *Political innovation and conceptual change*, ed. Terrence Ball, James Farr and Russell L. Hanson (Cambridge: Cambridge University Press, 1989) 90–131.

Slattery, Brian. 'First Nations and the constitution: a matter of trust', *Canadian Bar Review* 71 (1992) 261–93.

Slotkin, Richard. *Regeneration through violence: the mythology of the American frontier 1600–1860* (Middleton: Wesleyan University Press, 1973).

Smith, Adam. *An inquiry into the nature and causes of the wealth of nations*, 2 vols., ed. R. H. Campbell and A. S. Skinner (Oxford: Clarendon Press, 1976).

The theory of moral sentiments, ed. D. D. Raphael and A. L. Macfie (Oxford: Clarendon Press, 1979).

Smith, Anthony D. *National identity* (London: Penguin, 1991).

Smith, Jennifer. 'Canadian confederation and the influence of American federalism', *Canadian Journal of Political Science*, 21, 3 (1988) 443–63.

Smith, J. H., ed. *Appeals to the Privy Council from the American plantations* (New York: 1950) 417–42.

Sophocles. *The three Theban plays: 'Antigone', 'Oedipus the King', 'Oedipus at Colonus'*, tr. Robert Fagles (Harmondsworth, Middlesex: Penguin, 1984).

Spelman, Elizabeth V. *Inessential woman: problems of exclusion in feminist thought* (Boston: Beacon Press, 1988).

Standing Bear, Luther. *Land of the spotted eagle* (Boston: Houghton Mifflin, 1933).

Stannard, David E. *American holocaust: Columbus and the conquest of the new world* (Oxford: Oxford University Press, 1992).

Stevenson, Garth. *Ex uno plures: federal–provincial relations in Canada 1867–1896* (Montreal: McGill-Queens University Press, 1993).

Stone, William L. *Life of Joseph Brant-Thayendanegea, including the border wars of the American revolution*, 2 vols. (New York: 1838).

Sturtevant, William C., ed. *Handbook of North American Indians*, 20 vols. (Washington, D.C.: Smithsonian Institute, 1980–).

Takaki, Ronald. *A different mirror: a history of multicultural America* (Boston: Little Brown, 1993).

Tamir, Yael. *Liberal nationalism* (Princeton: Princeton University Press, 1993).

Taylor, Charles. 'Charles Taylor replies', *Philosophy in an age of pluralism: the philosophy of Charles Taylor in question*, ed. James Tully (Cambridge: Cambridge University Press, 1994) 213–58.

'The politics of recognition', *Multiculturalism and the politics of recognition*, ed. Amy Gutmann (Princeton: Princeton University Press, 1994) 25–74.

Reconciling the solitudes: essays on Canadian federalism and nationalism, ed. Guy Laforest (Montreal: McGill-Queens University Press, 1993).

'To follow a rule', *Rules and conventions: literature, philosophy, social theory*, ed. Mette Hjort (Baltimore: The Johns Hopkins University Press, 1992) 167–85.

Sources of the self: the making of the modern identity (Cambridge, Mass.: Harvard University Press, 1989).

Tobias, John L. 'Canada's subjugation of the Plains Cree, 1879–1885', *Sweet promises: a reader on Indian–white relations in Canada*, ed. J. R. Miller (Toronto: University of Toronto Press, 1991) 212–42.

Tooker, Elisabeth. 'The United States constitution and the Iroquois League', *Ethnohistory*, 35, 4 (1988) 305–36.

Trigger, Bruce. *Natives and newcomers: Canada's 'Heroic Age' reconsidered* (Montreal: McGill-Queens University Press, 1985).

Trigger, Bruce and Wilcomb Washburn, eds. *Cambridge history of the Native peoples of America* (Cambridge: Cambridge University Press, 1995).

Trigger, Bruce and Wilcomb Washburn. 'Native peoples in Euro-

American historiography', *Cambridge history of the Native peoples of America* (Cambridge: Cambridge University Press, 1995).

Trouillot, Michel-Rolph. 'Anthropology and the savage slot: the poetics and politics of otherness', *Recapturing anthropology: working in the present*, ed. Richard G. Fox (Santa Fe: School of American Research Press, 1991) 17–44.

Tuck, Richard. *International order and political thought from Grotius to Kant* (Oxford: Oxford University Press, forthcoming, 1995).

Philosophy and government 1572–1651 (Cambridge: Cambridge University Press, 1993).

Tully, James. 'Diversity's gambit declined', *Constitutional predicament: Canada after the Referendum of 1992*, ed. Curtis Cook (Montreal: McGill-Queens University Press, 1994) 149–98.

'Aboriginal property and Western theory: recovering a middle ground', *Property rights*, ed. Ellen Frankel Paul, Fred D. Miller, Jr. and Jeffrey Paul (Cambridge: Cambridge University Press, 1994) 153–80.

'Placing the *Two treatises*', in *Political discourse in early modern Britain*, ed. Nicholas Phillipson and Quentin Skinner (Cambridge: Cambridge University Press, 1993) 253–82.

An approach to political philosophy: Locke in contexts (Cambridge: Cambridge University Press, 1993).

'Wittgenstein and political philosophy', *Political Theory*, 17, 2 (1989) 172–204.

'Penser la Déclaration des droits de l'homme et du citoyen of 27 August, 1789', *Proceedings of the Canadian Political Science Association annual meeting, 1989* (Ottawa: University of Ottawa, 1989).

Tully, James, ed. *Meaning and context: Quentin Skinner and his critics* (Princeton: Princeton University Press, 1988).

Philosophy in an age of pluralism: the philosophy of Charles Taylor in question (Cambridge: Cambridge University Press, 1994).

Turpel, Mary Ellen. 'On the question of adapting the Canadian criminal justice system for Aboriginal peoples: don't fence me in', *Aboriginal peoples and the justice system*, Royal Commission on Aboriginal Peoples (Ottawa: Minister of Supply and Services, 1993) 161–83.

Turpel, Mary Ellen. 'Indigenous peoples' rights of political participation and self-determination: recent international legal developments and the continuing struggle for recognition', *Cornell International Law Journal* 25, 3 (1992) 579–602.

Turpel, Mary Ellen and Ovide Mercredi, *In the rapids: navigating the future of First Nations* (Toronto: Viking, 1993).

Van Alstyne, Richard W. *The rising American empire* (New York: W. W. Norton, 1974).

Van Dyke, Vernon. 'Justice as fairness – for groups', *American Political Science Review*, 69 (1975) 607–14.

Vattel, Emeric de. *The law of nations or the principles of natural law*, tr. Charles G. Fenwick (Washington: Carnegie Institute, 1902).

Vincent, Sylvie and Garry Bowers, ed. *James Bay and Northern Québec: ten years after* (Montreal: Recherches Amérindiennes au Québec, 1988).

Vipond, Robert C. *Liberty and community: Canadian federalism and the failure of the constitution* (Albany: State University of New York Press, 1991).

Wa, Gisday and Delgam Uukw. *The spirit of the land: statements of the Gitksan and Wet'suwet'en hereditary chiefs in the Supreme Court of British Columbia 1987–1990* (Gabriola, B.C.: Reflections, 1992).

Waldman, Carl. *Atlas of the North American Indian* (New York: Facts on File, 1985).

Walker, R. B. J. *Inside/outside: international relations as political theory* (Cambridge: Cambridge University Press, 1993).

Walzer, Michael. *Spheres of justice: a defense of pluralism and equality* (New York: Basic Books, 1983).

Weber, Max. *Economy and Society*, 2 vols., ed. Guenther Roth and Claus Winch (Berkeley: University of California Press, 1978).

Webber, Jeremy. *Reimagining Canada: language, culture, community, and the Canadian constitution* (Montreal: McGill-Queens University Press, 1994).

Weinstock, Daniel. 'The political theory of strong evaluation', *Philosophy in an age of pluralism: the philosophy of Charles Taylor in question*, ed. James Tully (Cambridge: Cambridge University Press, 1994) 171–93.

Wharton, Samuel. *Plain facts: being an examination into the rights of the Indian nations of America to their respective territories* (Philadelphia: 1781).

White, Richard. *The middle ground: Indians, empires, and republics in the Great Lakes region, 1650–1815* (Cambridge: Cambridge University Press, 1991).

Williams, Robert A. *The American Indian in Western legal thought: the discourses of conquest* (Oxford: Oxford University Press, 1990).

Williams, Roger. *The complete writings of Roger Williams*, 7 vols. (New York: Russell and Russell, 1963).

Winch, Peter. *The idea of a social science* (London: Routledge and Kegan Paul, 1958).

Wittgenstein, Ludwig. *Philosophical occasions 1912–1951*, ed. James

Klage and Alfred Nordmann (Indianapolis: Hackett Publishing Company, 1993).

Culture and value, tr. Peter Winch (Oxford: Basil Blackwell, 1980).

The blue and brown books: preliminary studies for the 'Philosophical investigations' (Oxford: Basil Blackwell, 1972).

Philosophical investigations, tr. G. E. M. Anscombe (Oxford: Basil Blackwell, 1967).

Wolf, Eric R. *Europe and the people without history* (Berkeley: University of California Press, 1982).

Wolin, Sheldon S. 'Democracy, difference, and re-cognition', *Political Theory* 21, 3 (1993) 464–83.

Wollstonecraft, Mary. *A vindication of the rights of woman*, ed. Miriam Brody (New York: Penguin, 1985).

Maria, or the wrongs of woman (New York: W. W. Norton, 1975).

Young, Iris Marion. 'Communication and the other: beyond deliberative democracy', *Democracy and difference*, ed. Seyla Benhabib (Princeton: Princeton University Press, forthcoming, 1995).

Justice and the politics of difference (Princeton: Princeton University Press, 1990).

Index